Book Five
The Sexual Laws

Second Edition

By K Kobayashi

The author expounds in this book how to solve the sexual problem for average single people – focused on men – and presents the solution getting help from the doctrine developed by the Buddha.

Strictly Literary™,
PO Box 242,
Scarborough, Queensland, Australia, 4020.
www.strictlyliterary.com
Phone: 0413 004 138
First published by Strictly Literary, Australia, in 2016

First Published 2016

Second Edition 2020

ISBN: 978-0-9923297-9-2

The author K Kobayashi is issuing the following series of books:

Book One *Idealism and Materialism*
Book Two *Religion*
Book Three *Communism*
Book Four *The Third Prophecy*
Book Five *The Sexual Laws*

Though the series is a coherent unit with the unified purpose, each book is designed to be read independently from the others. The first three books are preparing for the proposal and the last book is augmenting the proposal. His core proposition is in Book Four *The Third Prophecy*; in fact it can be expressed in one simple sentence 'To love a child is not to make one'.

He proposes the love which is the most beautiful and the strongest the humans will ever know; and unless this love is stronger than the love between the sexes the proposal does not make any sense. People imbued with this love gladly discard everything else including their sweethearts. As the concession to an idealised state of being single the sweethearts, unmarried, may remain friends to have sex with precaution against pregnancy. Buddhists and Christians have always taught their adherents to be single all their life. The author firmly believes that marriage has been the greatest curse of the human race. Men and women suffered tremendously through marriage all these millenniums still they could not work out the way out. Only the love of the Third Prophecy leads the ordinary people to stay out of marriage with the unwavering conviction.

This love when adopted by an individual will fulfil what the first (idealism; and religion as crystallisation of idealism) and second (materialism; and communism as an extreme form of materialism) prophecies promised but did not deliver in full to the humans and human societies. This love when adopted by a society as a whole will fulfil not only the first and second prophecies to the full but also will solve many serious problems the humans have had all these millenniums as well as the humans may have in the future. The acceptance of this new way of life by the bulk of the population will result in hugely reduced population with the predominantly beneficial results to the humans. This leaves one serious problem for the ordinary men and women, that is, how to solve their sexual problem. The author proposes the solution of this problem mainly addressed to single men in Book Five *The Sexual Laws*. He expounds the solution getting the idea from 'mind only' developed by the Buddha; the mind only concept is explained in Book Two *Religion*.

The author wants to prove beyond reasonable doubt that the arrival of the societies dominated by this new way of life is inevitable in the future provided the humans act according to the survival instinct as they have done all these millenniums. Since his message is contrary to the people's way of thinking in the past and present, he thinks that the ordinary people at present do not comprehend the message of the Third Prophecy, and it will take one century for the general public to fully appreciate its teaching and live according to its creed.

Contents

Introduction

I am a confirmed bachelor. Book Four *The Third Prophecy* explains how I have come to this conviction to such a degree that I even deserted a woman I dearly loved. The central theme of the prophecy is love of children and contains nothing else. Being single brought me many practical benefits, among them happiness and moderate wealth may be the main. However, I have had a sexual problem which was the only major drawback to this state. Since my proposition encourages men to be single all their life, I have the obligation to address the sexual problem arising from being single, apart from my practical necessity to confront the difficulty in my personal life. The rich, the famous and the powerful men would not have any problem in finding sexual partners outside marriage; many women would submit being flattered by the advances of these people. However, this series of books is addressed to the ordinary people, and we expect the average single men, myself included, would have a considerable difficulty. Even I were married, I would still have some sexual problems though they may be somewhat modified. The essence of the Third Prophecy is love and sex is not its part. Buddhism and Christianity teach the earnest adherents to be single all their life, not telling them how to cope with the sexual problem. The sexual problem is a challenge to this new life style and this book on the sexual laws is my response.

If many (undefined) people do not marry in the future as I propose in The Third Prophecy, people will behave sexually and otherwise differently, resulting in men's getting sex easier than in the past and at present. However, this book proceeds on the assumption that women will not give in easily to men's sexual advances in the predicted future.

I refer to the situation in Section 5, Chapter 3 Manifestations of Third Prophecy, Book Four that in the future when the Third Prophecy becomes widespread in a society resulting in a huge number of people (men and women) remaining single. At that time a large number of blocks of units, some blocks catering for unisex and some mixed, will be built accommodating only single people with the various facilities for convenience, and I made a brief note that legitimate sexual service for men and women should be provided. The business catering for sex will be legitimate and respectable, and the society will not look down this kind of service as prostitution or escort service as it does today. The people (men and women) engaged in this service will be proud of solving people's sexual problem, of making money and of paying tax, and many daughters and sons of good families will openly discuss their experiences in the course of their trade.

I often related at work my habits of visiting brothels, masturbating and going after a married woman. Nobody derided me on these revelations. A few people commented that many people do those things in the hiding but do not admit openly. One man warned me that the companies do not promote the people who tell these matters in the open and I have to tell lies. I do not see admitting these activities as sinful in itself but certainly what I did was definitely against religious teachings. People must have felt uneasy when I said I was a religious man and at the same time I engaged in these unreligious conducts.

All living things, of course including humans, have the overriding principle of survival of the individuals and the preservation of the species. This strong instinct manifests as acquisition of necessities of life, sex, religion, idealism, materialism, racism, nationalism, sexism and arts among other survival techniques. This series of books begins with the topics of idealism and materialism, and ends with the topic of sex. It also has the books on religion, communism and The Third Prophecy, but does not deal with any other of the above subjects as the major topic.

I had to develop certain lines of thoughts to combat the sexual difficulty. Unfortunately to us, the literati by tradition have treated sex as a taboo subject until recently, and the decent people tended not to discuss the matter openly, though sexual urge has been a serious problem to many people--majority of men and some women--through the centuries, rather, through the millenniums. Men have spent a lot of time thinking about sex and also enormous amount of money in an effort to alleviate constant and desperate sexual drive and further sex has been a source of anxiety and strife, yet surprisingly men have known very little about the nature of the urge and how to cope with it.

Since puberty I was prurient and failed badly in dealing with my sexual desire towards women. I have no doubt that I committed more sins of ethical nature, though not of criminal character, in my sex life than all my other sins put together. It is a fair comment that majority of men make mistakes in the matter of sex, especially during adolescence when the sexual awakening takes place and they have a chapter on sex they would rather forget and do not want to discuss with other people.

It is generally true that men of the various ages go mad on sexual heat and do all kinds of crazy things. It seems that Harold Holt, the Australian prime minister, drowned in the sea in 1967, was showing off to the ladies present that he was a good swimmer. Holt is the man who cautiously introduced the policy overriding the White Australia policy. If he had known what the immigration policy of Australia would be at the early 21st century, he most likely would not have proposed his policy in the first place. Also Adolf Hitler, when he was Fuhrer, was delighted with and showed himself off in the present of the ladies. Even I take into account the above observations, what I went through sexually were shameful to the extreme and haunt me at the onset of my old age. This book does not disclose my shameful acts as far as they are irrelevant to the discussions.

Since I am a religious man, I often wondered why I had not died as a punishment for all my sexual misconducts. The reflection suggested to me that the sexual sins may be different in nature from other sins. I try to get to know the reasoning behind in Section 1, Chapter 2 Judaism-Christianity-Islam, Book Two *Religion*. I feel at times that if I had had a little knowledge about the subject, I would not have fared as badly as I did. I also feel at times that in the overwhelming tide of my sexual drive the small knowledge may not have made any difference to my sexual improprieties.

Many popular novels and movies deal with love and sex between men and women; the authors and movie makers see correctly that the general public want to see love and sex in the various settings. This book deals with only the matter of sex and does not include the love of the ordinary use.

We must go deeper than the sexual phenomena to have the right understanding. Sex as many other manifestations of life has covered-up motives; humans make many decisions subconsciously and they are not even aware why they behave in certain ways. Noting the symptoms is not interesting in itself and besides does not explain why they take place.

Science and engineering normally separate the following two components:

- careful and systematic observations and measurements
- development of theories to confirm, interpret and formulate the above data

(McTaggart, Findley & Parkin 1992, p. 17)

The general approach adopted in this book is induction: from particular to general. However, this approach has a critical flaw in the assumption that the general public have always correct understanding of sex. I have found that some sexual notions of people are wrong and as a result these erroneous ideas are causing problems. In this sense, the sexual observations are different from the observations in such disciplines as nature, science and engineering: in the latter all observations are correct and valid as long as the observers do not make mistakes. In the case of sex, as in any other human behaviours unlike nature, science and engineering, in addition to mistakes in the observations and analyses, there is some possibility that people behave on misconceptions. The doers think they are right but in fact they are acting on the wrong premises.

For example, a bachelor may think that he can solve all his sex problems after marrying his sweetheart. However, for the majority of men the wishful thinking turns out to be false. In fact he cannot behave otherwise and the reason becomes obvious as the argument of this book proceeds. After wedding he may find his sexual desire to the other women is just as strong as before marriage and as a result he may think something went wrong: he may be at fault or the cohabitation is not working as it should. This puts the pressure on marriage. The humans are remarkably adaptable animals, and a man would put aside the other marital problems if his wife gives the unconditional sexual satisfaction. If I used only induction technique, I would not be able to locate where the problem lies in this context. I present a few more examples of this kind and one of them is so incredible that its acceptance puts all the concepts on sex upside down, as readers will find in the text to follow.

To try to overcome the above difficulty I analyse some observations using Buddhist doctrine 'mind only (or emptiness)' which I expound in a crude form in Section 2 Mind Only (or Emptiness): Haecceity of Buddhism, Chapter 3, Book Two *Religion*. We assume that the Mind Only (or Emptiness) concept is correct and hence the analyses thereof are deductions: from general to particular. I adopted this contradictory approach in an effort to get to the bottom of the sexual thinking of men and in a lesser degree of women.

Possibly by observing a large number of sexual phenomena among men and women, we should be able to induce the Mind Only (or Emptiness) theory, provided we can judge which phenomena are true or false as the cases may be. In the foregoing example, the bachelor's belief that after marriage he, assuming he is normal, would lose an interest in the other women is false, and the reality is that he would have sexual urge to all beautiful and young women before and after marriage. I will try to explain in the text why this is so getting help from the above doctrine the Buddha preached.

In the Christian Bible the authors start the argument with the premise that God is the alpha and omega (Isaiah 44:6), that is, God is everything, and its spirit runs through the Bible. Buddhism starts on the premise that everything is an illusion. Mind Only (or Emptiness), the essence of Buddhism as I understand, has a lot wider scope of applications than I present in this book, and I can use it to explain people's attachment to wealth, dominance, honour, fame, or whatever people crave in this world. The notion that women as sex objects are illusions applies to any other desired objects. Consequently it is not hard to construct similar laws like the sexual laws in any of the attachments. Some of the laws are applications of the abstract concept of Mind Only (or Emptiness) in the similar way we find applications in the real life of the scientific truism.

Readers will notice immediately that I used a double standard in applying Mind Only (or Emptiness) in the analyses. The doctrine teaches us that life and everything in the world are an illusion, urging us to quit all pleasures including sexual orgasm. The strict adherence to the Buddhist theory would force us to stop all sex activities rather than to live with them. However, with all my efforts over the years I could not give up sex. Accordingly sex, to me, is not an illusion but a reality and I had to devise a way to handle it. The Mind Only (or Emptiness) concept is used to look at the sexual objects, not the sexual urge, as illusions and encourage readers to deem sex drive in an entirely different--and correct light. This book takes the middle path, acceptable to the average men. Sexually women are illusions; in other words, to think women as sex objects is wrong. However, the sexual desires and pleasures are not esteemed as illusions. I am going to build a half-way house, practical if not idealised, which most men are content to live in. I do not adopt the binary system of right or wrong in explaining the theories but rather argue that the various evidence supports a certain view.

I present the observations and analyses in Chapter 1, and in Chapter 2 the sexual laws which I judge to be important in understanding men's sexuality. They all should not contradict readers' correct understanding of sexual experiences.

All people, men and women, must go through the problem of sexual tensions in their life. Nizer wrote: The greatest single cause for family unit breakdown and divorce is a fundamental sexual inadequacy within the marital unit (Masters and Johnson 1966, pp. vi, vii). Dr William Masters, the great pioneer of modern sex therapy in the United States, wrote, 'As many as 50 per cent of all Americans--single or married--have developed or will develop sexual difficulties at some point in their lives' (Westheimer 1994, p. 242).

I have written this book primarily for single men to help cope with the sexual urge: that constant drive to have sexual intercourse with every good-looking woman. This book is not sex manuals or how to make love or techniques of lovemaking, which are widely available in the book market. Also this book does not rely heavily on the statistical presentations of the sex life of the respondents. It relies primarily on my personal experience and observations and a few books on sexuality to correctly interpret the observations in order to get to the bottom of sexual conducts of men. The sexual laws in this book seek the universal laws applicable for the average men in any era and place. Since it is about the ordinary men and also addressed to the ordinary readers, it considerably retreats from the ideals the religious teachers preach on the sexual matter.

Rene Descartes, however hard he tried, could not deny one fundamental thinking, 'I think, therefore I am'. He made this thinking the basis of Cartesian (his) philosophy. I, on my part, however hard I tried, could not remove one perennial thinking, 'I want to make love to a good-looking woman'. I make this thinking the basis of the sexual laws. This desire is expressed from the viewpoint of heterosexual men and the thrust of the argument in this book proceeds on this basis. The above desire leads to the practice that men cannot stop having sex with or without women. Also average men do not rape or murder women for sexual gratification. This book does not deal with these extremes. Statistically speaking, the homosexual men, are hardly exceptions to the general rules and this book makes some reference to the homosexuals whom I include in the average men. I met many homosexuals who behaved in a perfectly normal manner non-sexually.

Buddhism insists on abstinence from all sexual activities. The Christian Bible urges the followers to have sex only within the sanctity of marriage and strictly prohibits any abnormal sexual practices. I did my best to behave properly in the sexual matters. However, I was unable to suppress my sexual urge no matter how hard I tried. If I had abandoned all sexual thoughts and acts, I would not have written this book and would be teaching sexual abstention instead. After so many years of failed attempts, I have arrived at the notion that sexual desire is a natural phenomenon for healthy men; moreover sex is a part of human existence. I now hold the view that it is better to accommodate sex in a correct manner rather than try to fight against it without success. Since the majority of men cannot stop having sex whether with or without women, this book proceeds on that premise.

In this book I am dealing with only sexual desire and act, excluding such notions as looking at women as status symbol or socialising media. I would say that the other objects take the place of women in the latter sense. Cars, houses, jewels or professions and the like can be status symbols; social clubs, schools or workplaces and the like can be socialising media. However, sex stands on its own and anything else cannot substitute it. Sex is its own purpose and is not the means to achieve something else as far as pleasure goes, though it is true that sex is often used to obtain a job or a favour.

Readers who have sexual difficulties, not of clinical nature, are well advised to go through the propositions with open mind. Ten per cent of Australian men suffer from sexual impotence and this book simply does not refer to the problem of this kind. The sexual problems some people are having may come from their fundamental flaws in assessing the nature of their sex drive and this book may help correct the views, hopefully lessening the difficulties. Masters and Johnson discovered through their sexual treatments over the years that attitudes and ignorance rather than any mental or physical illness are responsible for most sexual problems. A lack of sexual desire, equally divided between men and women, is the most frequent complaints in regard to sexual dysfunction. (p. 163)

Many Americans, men and women, are not satisfied with their sex life. According to the Journal of the American Association:

- 25% of women are unable to achieve orgasm,
- 30% lack interest in sex,
- 30% of men suffer from premature ejaculation or other sexual dysfunction.

(Bader 2002, p. 142)

The premise of this book goes counter to the above dysfunction and centres in the effort to overcome the strong sexual desire of single men. This book deals with the oversexed problem of single men, whereas the sex therapists mostly deal with the sexual underperformance of men and women.

It is often said that an effort to overcome difficulties or contradictions has made possible progress in any field. I do not see the sex problem as an exception to the above general rule. The sexual laws are worth knowing for men since they spend enormous time, money and effort to try to alleviate the sexual longings. I am hoping I have made some contribution to the general readers in this regard.

People tend to think that sexual desire is impulsive and beyond reason. The ancient to classical sages believed that learning about wisdom made people wiser. In a similar logic I base this book on the belief that learning about sex makes people behave sexually wiser. This book centres on male sexuality and the argument proceeds on the sexual drive of men. I have come to believe that the females would behave in a similar manner, given similar financial and social settings as for the males; however, I also discuss some inherent differences between the sexes in Section 14, Chapter 1.

Readers may readily agree with some conclusions I have reached after analyses because the propositions match with their experience or their notions about sex. Some laws seem quite different from what they are led to believe through the course of their life. As readers will see I conceived these propositions in a careful study, and only when they match with the convincing argument and in some cases the clinical study I present them as laws.

My curiosity about the gap between what the average men behave sexually in the course of daily life and what men really want in their sexual fantasy led me to study further. I present my research on this point in Section 2 Sexual Restraints, Chapter 1.

Sex had been a taboo subject before the 20th century in the overt culture of the Western world and possibly of any civilised communities of the world with the notable exceptions of the Greek and Roman worlds. Montaigne, who lived in France in the latter part of the 16th century, related that in his society it was not permissible for decent people to discuss about sex. He further wrote, however, boys spread about the pictures of naked women in passages and staircases of palaces. (Montaigne 1965, p. 654) Schopenhauer wrote in the early part of the 19th century that sex was ever present in our minds but the convention stated that we should not discuss about it (Janaway 1994, p. 49). As a matter of fact the writers of legitimate books in the pre-modern era did not have enough knowledge to argue about the subject intelligently. Besides, many of these male writers might have had some sexual difficulties as we can easily conjecture from the male sexual behaviours of today. For example, some male writers might have involved in illicit sexual relations with women or even with men; masturbated regularly; felt sexual urge towards their daughters or the other people's wives. The writers with these problems might have had conscience to dictate them not to talk or write about sex.

We may get the impression that the human evolutionary progress whose driving force was survival was made gradually over the millenniums; however, it seems to be more accurate to say that leaps and jumps characterise the human evolution. In fact this is also the case with the advancement of sexual studies.

In the fields of science and engineering a large numbers of people have contributed to the advancement; however, if we focus our attention to the particular discipline of an era, only a few people made a significant contribution. As a matter of fact this is the case with sex. A handful of people significantly expanded the sexual knowledge; we can trace the significant advancement of sexual studies from Freud to Kinsey to Masters and Johnson.

The academics researched and freely discussed sex only after World War Two. Prior to WW II, Sigmund Freud (1856-1936) made the psychological aspects of sex, centring on: infant sexuality, libido, erogenous zones and Oedipus complex. Though his initial writings on sexuality were ignored or ridiculed at first, his theories eventually won over the scientific community. Freud was aware that his speculation on sexual matters lacked physiologic supporting data.

AC Kinsey (1894-1956), doctor in zoology, and his helpers compiled the reports on human sexual practices obtained by techniques of direct questions. They made the sociologic investigations but the data were not designed to interpret physiologic or psychologic response to sexual stimulation. *The Kinsey Reports* (published in 1948 and 1953) became the best sellers, not so much by the contents but the sensations they created (Wright 1977, p. 248). Possibly the underlying reason for becoming the best seller is that there was the public hunger for sexual knowledge in the atmosphere of a lack of information about the virtually taboo subject (Westheimer 1994, p. 161).

Dr WH Masters (1915-) and VE Johnson (1925-) carried on the works of Dr Kinsey who was also aware that his researches were deficient in direct scientific observations (Wright 1977, pp. 250-1). Dr Kinsey wrote, 'The materials are still scant and additional physiologic studies will be needed'. He had a plan to carry out the tests needed at the time of his death. (Brecher 1967, p. 36)

Masters and Johnson tackled the problem of sex from the physiologic aspects, conducting many experiments to answer their queries. They carried out the tests in Saint Louis laboratory spanning 11 years. Whether they got the clue of physiologic experiments from Freud or Kinsey is possibly irrelevant to the development of sexual understanding. In fact Van de Velde (1873-1937), a gynaecologist, was the first man who had investigated sexual physiology (Masters & Johnson 1966, p. vii). He summarised his findings in *Ideal Marriage* (c. 1926).

Masters, a physician, and Johnson, a psychologist and his research associate, pioneered in the scientific sexual arousal and the treatment of sexual problems. They married in 1971 and divorced in 1993. They wrote their findings in *Human Sexual Response* (1966). This book became a best seller. It is the comprehensive study of the human sexual activity focusing on the physiology and anatomy. Many sex therapists today use the techniques Masters and Johnson developed in the 1960s. The couple focused their attention on non-organic problems such as exhibited in premature ejaculation and impotence.

There are three traditions running in the sphere of the sexual deviations. The deviations refer to not only the sexual perversions such as sadism, masochism, zoophilia, urolagnia, fetishism, nymphomania, satyriasis, homosexuality, voyeurism and exhibitionism but also what we feel normal such as masturbation and nocturnal emissions.

Kraft-Ebing (1840-1902) published *Psychopathia Sexualis* (1886) and utterly condemned all the sexual deviations as the diseases leading to criminal activities. Sigmund Freud followed the suit but sought to cure the deviations. Henry Havelock Ellis (1859-1939) presented quite tolerant attitudes towards the deviations in *Studies in the Psychology of Sex* (1896-1928). He also argued for sexual education, equal rights for women, and decriminalisation of the consenting homosexual activities in private among other issues. (Sadock, Kaplan & Freedman 1976, pp. 71-8)

Explaining why I present men's sexuality in the form of laws in this book may be in order here.

The ancients, particularly before the Neolithic Revolution, did not see any regularities or laws in most of which surrounds them. As time went on they looked into their surroundings closely and they realised that they had certain laws. For example, they had to know the right time for sowing and hence the laws of the seasons. Natural laws may refer to the laws of nature or any laws that seem to be natural in any discipline. For example, the sexual urge is natural if men want women but it is thought to be unnatural if men want men.

In any field of human activities we find the governing principles pertaining to the subject. There are bodily, mental, occupational, familial, moral, scientific, economic, linguistic and social principles to mention only a few. We all know that our body is under certain laws, and to promote its health we have to eat the right amount of correct foods and also to do the right amount of correct exercises. Many people seem not to understand that our mind, job and family have certain laws and we have to look after them with the right knowledge. If we don't, we reap a curse as the Bible—though it centres on our mind activities—says, and we end up in such a state as having a personal tragedy, losing job and breaking down of family. The Bible addresses to not only an individual but a nation as a whole in terms of faith to the Almighty. When we look at the two main worldly passions, wealth and sex, obviously people did not see any regularity for many millenniums in their hot pursuits in spite of the fact that human minds have natural tendency to look for the regularities or the laws.

Adam Smith discovered that the capitalist economy had laws peculiar to it and was the first individual to formulate these laws (Roll 1961, p. 140) in his celebrated book *Inquiry into the Nature and Causes of the Wealth of Nations* (1776). Though mercantilism and physiocracy both of which he was acquainted with had been proposed as economic theories in Europe, these doctrines were hardly social sciences in the modern sense of the terms. These theories were immature and confined in specific aspects of the economy, though the physiocrats conceived economy as a whole in the 1750s and 1760s but it is said that their theories contained many flaws.

Adam Smith attacked the mercantile system vigorously and also wrote that the physiocratic system was defective and cannot be the policy basis of the national government. He enunciated the benefits of division of labour in the manufacturing environments but in fact Plato had earlier proposed the concept in his book *Republic*. *The Wealth of Nations* also received criticism that it contained no original thoughts and it was not wholly scientific. However, nobody can deny that the book inspired almost all schools of thoughts, that is, classical, Marxian and nationalist. (Robbins 1998, p. 129)

Adam Smith witnessed the surging of the Industrial Revolution (1760-1840) in Britain. Economically this phase is industrial capitalism, and commercial capitalism had been in force for three centuries prior in Western Europe. Human greed for wealth was prominent not only in the phase of capitalism bur for millenniums, probably since people had enough to satisfy the basic human needs of food, clothes and shelter. I find it convenient to class desire for wealth as a part of materialism in this series of books, though that may not necessarily be correct. The workers as well as the capitalists have strong desire for wealth, but the central focus of capitalism is capital and its society is geared around money for industry and commerce and in a lesser degree for farming. The success or failure of a business venture is measured by the percentage profit of the capital laid out, though there are divergent theories as to why and how the profit is generated in the venture. He showed that there was regularity in the economic activities and advocated some measures to take for the welfares of the nations, and many nations adopted his theories as the basis of their economic policies. The laissez faire economic system he advocated was advantageous to the most competitive nations: Britain during its Industrial Revolution and US just before the Depression of 1930s. (Kennedy 1987, p. 360) Economics today is a well-established social science taught all over the world even in some former communist nations and he is regarded as the founder of economics. Before the presentation of these models, people thought that the economy they were under was a jumble of possessive desires and activities without any discerning pattern, as most people of today think so about their sexual desires and activities.

The economic theories were developed to understand the economic activities and to make rational decisions; in the similar fashion the sexual laws are developed to understand the sexual activities and to make rational decisions. It has been shown that the strong desire for profit, though its motive is greed, is not entirely honourable among the various survival techniques, belittles the various production and trading problems in the capitalist countries. The real problems are in the competition and the share of the market among the producers, as well as the recessions and depressions which the consumers and producers bring about. In the similar fashion the strong desire for women belittles the various problems in cohabiting with women. The problems are in the competition for the share of the females. I present this book from the viewpoint of heterosexual men and the thrust of the discussions proceeds on this basis, though I present some references from the female or homosexual viewpoint. I believe the inclusions of the latter give deeper insight into the sexual matters.

Since resistance characterises women, they can be classed as material. I class wealth as a part of materialism in this series of books. Men's desire to acquire as many women as possible may be the same desire to acquire as much wealth as possible.

The cosmos is the world or the universe considered as the well-ordered system and can mean in itself harmony or order. When people extract the orders from the cosmos, they become laws. The Bible may be said to be the God's law or the law in the Kingdom of Heaven. According to the Bible God's law always leads to truth and justice. The Buddha's teachings are sometimes referred to as Dharma or the Law. The laws of Christianity and Buddhism are those of the minds, and not those of science such as the origin of the world, nor those of human body, nor those of economic wellbeing.

Economics deals with the laws of the society rather than those of the individuals, whereas the sexual laws delve into the individual activities rather than the society as a whole. The main focus of attention of economics is the trade, the industry and the nation, though it also refers to individuals as well as international activities. Also the economic theories are more abstract than concrete; whereas the sexual laws are more concrete than abstract. The thought experiments, definitely not the laboratory experiments, helped form the economic laws; whereas the thought as well as laboratory experiments, the sexual laws. For these reasons majority of people do not have the opportunity to use the results of economics whereas majority of people can find many opportunities to use the results of the sexual laws in their daily life. The usefulness and scholarship have more to do with the scope of theoretical development and the applicability and not on the inherent natures of the subjects. That is to say, we cannot make a general statement that economics or the sexual laws as a subject is more scholarly or useful than the other.

One of the benefits in acquainting with the laws in general is that we can predict the responses of certain stimuli. Therefore in our examples we can predict the economic and sexual responses to some extent, thus we can control to some degree the economic and sexual behaviours. For example, we all know that if the sellers lower the price of the commodities, they can sell more (quantitative response only) in a set period; however, the economists can predict reliably how many more they can sell to the graded lowered prices (price-quantitative response) after the market analyses. Thus the data give the manager the necessary basis to maximise the overall profit in a set period which is the aim of the capitalist production and trade.

The theoretical pricings of the economists can be wrong if the researchers are incompetent or do not do the research correctly. The managers price their commodities with the experience; however, this pricing can be wrong too if they don't take into account the natures of the complicated market, the status of economy or the whimsicality of the buyers. One way of setting the prices may be to fix the profit of the commodities first. Since they know the production costs, transport costs etc., they can calculate the selling prices by adding the profits to these costs.

There is some confusion as to where the regularity comes from. Adam Smith believed that Invisible Hand regulated the economic system and the humans did not have anything to be worried about, that is, by following the individual profit motives the net result for the society was good. He was overly optimistic in the light of the economic history and it turned out that his theories could not cope with many economic problems of the later societies. In contradistinction to his view, many people expressed the belief that the moral laws, thus any other laws by implication, are a part of nature, nothing to do with the will of God. They insist that rewards and punishments for our thoughts and conducts not come from God but be simply the law of nature: If we do not follow the ethical laws of nature, we are caught up with bad consequences, in the same way if we do not look after our body, naturally we become sick in due course. As long as people make correct observations and decisions, it is immaterial whether they come from God or nature. People institute the same policy and get the same result.

The desires for wealth and sex originate in the survival instincts as the fundamental reason. Since they give high degree of pleasure in the prosecution they have been prominent features of the human activities for the individuals and the society as a whole. They are not parts of God (Truth) unlike justice and love for the fellow human beings, though certainly love for wealth and sex is intense. 'Introduction to Series' in Book One *Idealism and Materialism* delves into the matter from this angle with some specific reasons why and how these desires exist.

The starting point of capitalism is the desire for profit for the laid out capital, that is, quantity of money, ignoring the qualities of different currencies that circulated occasionally in a community through human history. The starting point of the sexual laws is men's desire for good-looking women, that is to say, quality and quantity of women. Through the history of mankind, cupidity (desire for money) and concupiscence (desire for sex) dominated the minds of the majority of men, each of them at times being independent, at times assisting the other and often sacrificing the other. To acquire women, men normally have to show their wealth and to spend a large amount of money to keep them. These desires are assumed in the daily life of the general public and in the process the moral codes are often ignored in the intense quests. However, the religious or ethical persons tend to deny the above desires for them and the laws governing in economics and sex do not apply in their life, at least in the overt cultures. The number of these people are small compared with the majority hence their existence does not affect these laws appreciably.

The desire for profits led to the creation of the multitude of industrial and commercial firms and capitalist farms in the private sector, which Karl Marx clearly indicated (Marx 1971, p. 360). The government industries did not go after the profits, standing on the entirely different premises. Marx ignored the plight of the government industries, which were in any case not prominent in his contemporary society, as well as the plight of small proprietary shops (manufacturing and retail) and farms which were in fact the dominant business forms of his contemporary society.

As a matter of fact I never worked out the reasons why some government institutions of today such as of productions and services, not of defence, welfares and education, were not interested in profit seeking. I raised this question many times with the managers for whom I worked. They answered that the profits in the government factories did not mean anything, though the taxation department is keen to get as much tax they can get hold of. If the government institutions are sold on the stock market, the private institutions thus created seek profits eagerly. Hence it looks that the non-seeking of profits in the government enterprises are more to do with the government policies rather than the natures of products and services. I would say that if the managers' salaries and their prospects of promotions are tied with the profits their government firms make they would be interested in profits. However, this notion also faces a challenge in that the managers may simply raise the charges of the public utility to attain the desired result, or withdraw the unprofitable products or services to the detriments for some sections of the community.

Is it an exaggeration to say that the sexual desire led to the creation of families? Section 5 Marriage as Institution, Chapter 1, Book Four *The Third Prophecy* looks into the reasons for the establishment of families as we know. There is no question that the religious establishments are built on a single ground of faith. For example, the Christian churches are built on the faith in Jesus Christ. The governments of the various nations are built on the composite grounds which are hard even to enumerate, though there is no doubt that they are built for the survival of the people as a whole within the nation. Similarly families are built on composite reasons which are hard to assess. Singleness is definitely advantageous financially for males or even for females though they miss out on sex. According to some researchers the families are set up for sexual reason. Some say they are set up for economic reason in bringing up the children. If people say marriage is for sex, all marriages should break down when there are no sexual unions between husbands and wives. If people say that marriage is for finance to support the children, all marriages should break down when there are no children involved. Still it is definitely the fact that some marriages survive without the benefits of sex and children. However, this book refers to the behaviour of average or ordinary men hence the small number of the exceptions to the general statements should be permissible.

It is reasonable to say that when the couples are to be united in marriage, affection and sex play the major role, and when they have children the economy plays the major role. The male sexual desire gives the impetus for marriage if not for the maintenance. There are certainly more than the two desires to maintain this social institution. It seems that the urge to live together as husband and wife is deeply ingrained in people's psyche. Here again, a fair number of men and women have lived on their own, and this premise is not valid for these people. There are a huge number of researches carried out in the fields of firms, and governmental and religious establishments but there are little researches made in the working of the families. The reason may be that the majority of people are familiar with the family life and they don't see any laws governing them, though I have come to believe that the complicated laws govern the families.

I got to know through fishing for perch that many of them are in a group but a small number of them live outside the group. If we speculate that the grouping is for survival, we have to offer the explanations why some perch do not belong to a group. Similarly if we speculate that marriage is for survival, we have to offer the explanations why a small number of men and women have opted, the number being increasing, to stay single.

The human desire for profits is such a strong feeling as for the use of the products and services that the existence of the private firms seems to be assured provided the government correct the deficiencies of the society. Also the sexual desire of men is such a strong feeling until men are advanced in age compared with the affection to women which can evaporate with minor incidents, the existence of the families seems to be assured, too. It looks that the private firms and families will not collapse until people find better ways of satisfying these desires.

Communism could not replace the capitalist firms because its theories were not only incorrect when viewed as a working system, and it did not replace the desire for profit of the capitalist economy with something just as strong to keep the production going with so many problems. Communism collapsed at the early 1990s in the European context and has been in wholesale retreat ever since as theory and practice, but there is no indication at the early 21st century that capitalism will collapse in the foreseeable future. For the theorisation of communism, refer to Book Three *Communism*. The high divorce rate of the recent years suggests that marriage as institution may collapse though people at present are just as eager to marry as in the past. I wrote in Book Four *The Third Prophecy* that many people will not want to marry and the families as institution will collapse upon the introduction of the new philosophy because the prophecy introduces love stronger than the love between men and women, though certainly it does not eliminate the sexual drive which is akin to eating and drinking. The Third Prophecy does not try to wreck the family institution as the communists did with capitalism, but following the prophecy leads to the 'withering away' of the families as Marx said with regard to the states; it is a by-product (one of minor) of the prophecy.

Though capitalism has a connotation of complex supporting theories, it stands on one foundation of profit. Subsistence economy such as the peasant farming could not consider the profit under the strain of sheer survival, which existed both before capitalism came into being and after the bulk of the economic activities in the nation became capitalistic. The desire for making money built the various firms in the capitalist countries, and the sexual desire is the single greatest, if not the only, reason for establishing the families. These desires don't have to be taught and thought to be inherent in humans. Communism was built on planning, disregarding the profit motive of the entrepreneurs though the communists still recognised the consumer desires. The communists tried to eliminate the private firms to be replaced by the government firms.

The elaborate theories by Karl Marx could not replace capitalism which has lasted only half a millennium in Europe. Among a large number of the nations of the world at present, only a small number of them are said to have the fully capitalist economy. Families were in the human societies the world over as long as the sociologists can trace back the human societies for thousands of millenniums, in other words, families were universal phenomena beyond the time and place frames. I present the excerpts from Friedrich Engels' work on the evolution of families in Section 1, Chapter 1 of this book, under the heading of 'Marriage and Sex'. As far as I can work out it did not enter into Karl Marx's mind that the family institution might collapse in the future, though he stated that the state would disappear just after the introduction of communist society. The state he meant was the government and not the nation as a whole. Some Russian communists in the heat of the revolution prophesised withering away of the family. It is on record that just after the October Revolution in Russia some utopian Bolshevik leaders talked about the disappearance of families; however, the opposite happened and the record number of men and women married craving personal security (Kenez 2006, pp. 71, 116). Also we have to take into account that capitalism stands on one ground of profit motive, whereas families stand on the complex grounds. Private firms normally collapse when they stop making money. Families also stand on a shaky ground when the husbands lose a sexual interest in their wives, though there are other bonds to unite the families.

We should not think that capitalism might have collapsed having inherent defects, but rather we should think that communism was not strong enough to bring about the collapse of capitalism. Capitalism whose foundation is money was strong enough to bring about the collapse of feudalism whose bond was the loyalty of masters and subordinates at the various sections of the community apart from money. The statement that capitalism will not collapse because of strong human greed is not correct. It is right to say that nobody has ever devised a better social system to satisfy the innate human greed. People will change to the better social system in the similar fashion most married men will change their wives if they can find better women. Also the statement that the family will not collapse because of strong men's sexual desire is not right. It is more correct to say that the family will collapse if somebody devises the better means of solving male sexual drive, or better life views as I present in Book Four.

One interesting aspect about the laws in general is that we often don't know the causes behind them, though we are sure they are at work. To cite an example, gravitational force is a fundamental law in science and engineering, but nobody knows why this force exists in the first place. Isaac Newton formulated a law of gravitation and supported the gravitational theory with detailed and convincing mathematical proofs of its existence in *Mathematical Principles of Natural Philosophy* (1687), widely known as *Principia*, but did not explain why the force existed in the first place (Mercer 1996, p. 587). This book is considered as one of the greatest contributions in science, and was the last major intellectual work in England written in Latin. The second and third edition appeared in 1713 and 1726. This universal force between the two bodies with masses, however small or large, does not depend on our brain activity, has existed since the universe was born and will be working even when humans die out from the earth though without recognising brains nothing makes sense at all. This universal gravitational pull is proportional to the product of two masses and inversely proportional to the square of the distance between them, and can be measured experimentally. It is an attractive force and its magnitude does not depend on the kind of the matters but depends solely on the mass. The gravitational acceleration is the fundamental force in nature which puts the solar system in the regular motion and the very reason why the humans exist. The moral laws are, in contrast, dependent on our thinking faculty but here again we don't know why some of these laws are deemed to be universal truth. I have a sneaky suspicion that since the inquiring minds of the ancient world could not come up with the valid reasons for the various laws, however hard they tried, they eventually attributed the phenomena to the work of God that is beyond human reasons and does not admit any scrutiny: in popular parlance all the bucks stop at God.

Another interesting aspect of the laws generally is that new laws often invalidate the existing laws. The theories Adam Smith developed were valid when the pure competition predominated in the economy as was the case when he published his book in Britain in the latter part of the 18th century, and cannot deal with the various problems such as of recessions and depressions originating in the excessive production by the machines, which did not eventuate in his life time.

John Dalton (1766-1844) established that atoms were indestructible and immutable (Williams 1987, p. 306). This proposition lasted nearly a century, but was invalidated when the nuclear physics was developed. If the scientists religiously had adhered to the Dalton's theory, they could not have developed the nuclear physics and atomic bombs. Also Einstein established that mass and energy were interchangeable according to a fixed scale (p. 30), which no earlier scientists imagined possible. Further, Newton proposed that gravity is an interacting attractive force existing between two masses, ignoring the speeds of the masses and time. Einstein insisted that gravity is a curved or warped field in space-time, that is, space and time are curved or warped wherever matter or energy is present, and of objects interacting with space itself (Mercer 1996, p. 958). He was subsequently proved right by monitoring: British astronomers observed starlight being bent around the sun during an eclipse. If there is a mass (or energy) at any one spot, space and time would curve around it, the curvature being proportional to the amount of the mass: the curvature is the reciprocal of the radius of curvature. When another mass (or energy) moves into this space the attractive force is generated between the two masses. The gravitational theory published in *Principia* by Newton dominated since; however, it was known that this theory could not explain several phenomena. In the early 20th century Albert Einstein proposed his gravitational theory (a part of general theory) of relativity and satisfied the scientists who had experienced the difficulties with Newton's theory. Einstein's theory is conceptually different from Newton's; however, the former does not negate the latter which is of sufficient accuracy for all but the most precise applications. Einstein's field equation reduces to Newton's law of gravitation for slow speeds and weak fields.

The Epicureans in the classical Greece postulated that the atoms, which were bodies having some weight and a natural movement downward, have built the world (Montaigne 1965, p. 407). This statement does not contradict the Newton's theory of gravitational force but only the speculation and we can hardly call it a law.

The sexual laws developed in this book are meant to be the universal laws, applicable beyond time, the national boundaries and even men's ages. However, seeing that even the scientific laws are subject to change, readers must accept that the sexual laws can change. I am to cite a few examples. The perceptions of female body beauty are quite different among the individual men of the same community: also the various cultures of the past presented the perceptions of quite different kinds. However, they are all unanimous that women must be young and beautiful for men's sexual usefulness. As a matter of fact, the female beauty is what men desire as their ideal shape in their offspring, which explains the divergence of preferences individually and socially. The female youthfulness contributes to the survival and wellbeing of the mother and the baby. The laws presented help comprehend the individual differences in the same community, the different presentations of the different cultures and the uniformity of female youth and beauty. In point of fact I put out a proposal concerning masturbation in Section 13, Chapter 1, though the general public, I am sure, do not accept it as valid at present.

I have crystallised the sexual observations and analyses as best I could and presented the findings in the form of laws. Since these principles are synoptic, they tend to be theoretical and general rather than particular. They have proved to be correct in my experience to my satisfaction. Some laws may sound ludicrous at first to some readers since they are contrary to popular beliefs. I beg readers to pass the judgement only after careful perusal of the text in view of their sex life. Readers must feel that the propositions are correct and valid in the light of their experience before they can be of any use for them. The laws of this nature apply only in general terms, and readers will find the exceptions to the rules as are expected as for the models of many other disciplines. The exceptions may take the form of a small number of deviations in a large number of observations, or a small number of cases where the laws are not valid at all.

In presenting my investigations readers will notice that I raised rather strange questions in an effort to unravel fundamental nature of sex. For example, to start an argument, I asked myself why men are eager to make love with young and beautiful women. This kind of question is not normally asked in the daily life because people take familiar happenings in life for granted. In order to convince readers that this approach is not as stupid as it may appear at first reading, I am to present my defence next.

'Socrates is always asking questions and stirring up discussion, never concluding, never satisfying; and says he has no other knowledge than that of opposing. Homer, though he was probably blind, laid the foundations equally for all schools of philosophy, to show how indifferent he was about which way we went.' (p. 377)

Plato wrote that wonder is the feeling of a philosopher, and philosophy begins in wonder (Harbottle 1897, p. 411).

Thomas Alva Edison (1847-1931), the great inventor, used to ask, as a boy, questions which other people took as a matter of course. His father thought his son was stupid. He often said, 'I cannot make anything of him. He's always asking foolish questions'. Thomas tried to satisfy his insatiable inquisitiveness by carrying out his own experiment for each query. He prepared himself for his numerous inventions by experimentation since he did not have theoretical background. (Rowland-Entwistle 1988, pp. 4-11) He entered the educational school in 1854; however, because of a serious hearing problem developed at an early age he was bored and labelled as a misfit, and quit school, after attending the school sporadically for five years. His mother, former teacher, guided his education. Edison, perhaps the most prolific inventor in history, is credited with as many as 1300 inventions (Mercer 1996, p. 983), and singly or jointly he held 1093 patents. Some people regard his development of the research laboratories as his greatest achievement. He built a laboratory in Menlo Park in 1876 and began research works with his assistants. Next in 1886 he built another laboratory, in fact 10 times larger than the one in Menlo Park, in West Orange. However, he had the quality of being a poor manager and organiser. His genius lay in his in-born inquisitiveness and his untiring efforts to solve the problems with the methods he himself could not explain.

It took a genius of Sir Isaac Newton to discover the law of gravity by observing a falling apple though everybody knew that a weighty object, unsupported, fell to the ground.

It seems that the inquisitiveness of the toddlers is a fertile ground of inventions. A man who made a research into the nature of inventiveness concluded that the inventive persons have some childishness in their way of thinking. The inventors also have unreasonableness of toddlers who try to find the solution to the contradictions of their surroundings rather than try to adjust themselves to the situation they are in, which is usual for the adults. A kindergarten female teacher said that she learned more from her cares than she taught them. These remarks appeared in separate television documentaries. The reason behind this phenomenon may be that the adults go through a set thinking with some preconceived concept; whereas the toddlers are free from the restraints and express the ideas freely, though these ideas may be poor and even ridiculous at times. We need the intelligence of the adults to make the good ideas of the toddlers work.

Gabriele Lusser Rico wrote the following passage in conjunction with a natural way of writing:

> Children have few conceived notions about what the world ought to be like, about how they should feel, about what they must do according to prescribed formula. The world is sheer possibility and a child's characteristic stance towards it is wonder. (Rico 1983, p. 55)

Wonder and storytelling are the fundamental characteristics of the children and the creative persons. And they in turn generate the playfulness, the willingness to take risks and the spontaneity. (p. 50)

During infancy and before the acquisition of language the right brain is dominant. Though this statement is only a hypothesis, it is generally believed that the right hemisphere of the brain is mainly responsible for the generation of new ideas. (p. 73)

It is known that logical thinking hampers creativity. Engineering is based on logic. Arts are based on imagination and creativity. However, I noticed through years of engineering works that imagination and creativity often resulted in an interesting and crucial development. I have no doubt that through the course of scientific and technical developments of human endeavours, imaginations played vital roles. In other words, without imaginations we do not have present state of high achievements in science and technology and will not be able to develop further however hard people wish. It is also true that engineering expertise is required to implement the new ideas and I was not allowed to do the higher duty until I acquired the necessary skills.

I have come to the conclusion that most of the sexual behaviours of men and women originate in the desire for survival as the text discloses. Humans have behaved through the history based on survival instincts though there were some exceptions in regard to people and behaviours: some people at times and even persistently behaved according to pleasure and not according to survival. Animals and plants act according to the survival instinct though plants do not have any conscious self. What are common to both are the cells, the basic building block of their structures. All living things are made up of cells--humans, animals, plants, insects, bacteria and viruses--they all have survival instinct as their fundamental drive of life. Cells want to keep living as self and species for whatever reasons we may ascribe, whether the bodies (the aggregates of cells) have conscious self as for humans, or not as for plants. We still ask ourselves a question why some humans commit suicide if they are guided only by the survival and pleasure principles.

Similarly do the laws of the universe originate in the survival of the universe?, though the universe is not a living thing. Without the gravitational acceleration the universe does not exist at least as we know it. Do we have to have space and time for the existence of the universe? Do we have to rely on the concept of God to justify the laws in the universe? Did the universe make an evolution based on its survival and it adopted only the laws favourable such as a law of gravitation and discarded others? Will we find in the future a universe where the law of gravitation does not exist or where all the living cells are configured so differently that they do not strive for survival? These questions are too speculative and philosophical for the book of the sexual laws and hence fortunately for me I do not have to answer them in this book. The answers in any way do not change the sexual laws presented in this book, which seeks the laws in our world.

Chapter 1 Sexual Observations and Analyses Thereof

Section 1 Sexual Desire

The opposite sex intrigues the boys before puberty, though they cannot work out why the females are different yet so fascinating. I still remember a conversation I had with my classmate sitting next to me in the primary school. Both of us discovered one day in the class room that both had wanted to make our pretty female teacher naked and whip her to our delight. I did not know at the time and possibly still do not know today why the fancy of that nature gave me pleasure. However, at puberty sex takes on a new dimension and gives a concrete expression to the above fanciful imagination.

The following incident took place at the same primary school a few years later. During a lunch break, it so happened that the charming and popular girl was left with several boys and me in the classroom. I cannot recall what triggered the boys--I am sure they did not plan--they decided to take her underpants off in order to satisfy the curiosity about the female anatomy. They did not intend to rape: I do not think any of them knew what the rape was and much less they carried it out. I did not join them in the attack though I was a willing observer. She squatted on the floor, holding her underpants tightly with her both hands, crying loud continually. A couple of pupils blocked the exit of the classroom. Now and again one of the boys dashed forward and grabbed her undies to forcefully undo but each time met with the girl's determined and desperate resistance and even louder cry. The struggle lasted for quite some time, when suddenly our male teacher came through the door and all the boys quickly dispersed as if nothing had happened.

The boys acted as they pleased without any regard to the girl and would have had little emotional impact from the incident. These boys were rough in their behaviour and resorted to fist fights often to try to settle the differences. However, I now believe that the incident left a deep scar on the victim: she must be having its flashback all through her life.

Strange thing about this incident was that none of the boys, myself included, for all I knew, received any reprimand or any lecture from the school authority or the parents. To think back now, either the teacher kept the disturbance to himself or the head master thought it wise not to make a case. Nobody would have known how to deal with the sexual behaviour of this kind from the boys who were many years before puberty.

I recall another incident. One day I caught a large frog in the garden of my home and tried to burn it alive inside the fireplace connected to the bathtub. My family, seeing what I was trying to do, scolded me harshly; I stopped it only after a couple of rebukes. Later in my recollection I always associated this attempt with a way of releasing sexual desire which I had not known anything about at the time. Sexual awakening was then taking place within me but I did not know what it was or how to let it go. Until boys have sexual orgasm, they don't know what sex is all about how many times they hear about it. I still believe that sexual feeling, though immature, gave me an urge to burn a frog.

On our way home from the secondary school, we often witnessed the young male teachers go into the brothel. To think back, it was better for them not to hide the brothel visits from the school children. The school authority could not have acted in any way since the prostitution at that time was legal in Japan.

Psychological Stages of Development by Freud

Sigmund Freud formulated the following psychosexual stages of development (Westheimer 1994, pp. 222-5).

The first of Freud's psychosexual stages is the oral phase. He saw in this oral phase a generalised sexual state, not sexual in the reproductive sense of intercourse, but in the sense that it creates excitation, a building up of tension and a release in intense pleasure. (p. 223) The baby since birth sucks its mother's breasts, not only to receive nourishment but to derive an enormous gratification. The adult receives the similar gratification from kissing and oral sex. The oral stage exhibits personality traits such as dependency, selfishness and aggression.

Around the second year of life, the baby learns to control bodily functions especially toilet training and feels it has become independent. Orderliness, meanness and stubbornness characterise this anal stage.

Between the third and fifth years the children are curious about genitals and this phase is called the phallic stage. Male and female children's interest centres in phallus. The phallic stage has the personality traits such as conceit and self-assurance. During the phallic stage, the boys are sexually attracted to their mothers (Oedipus complex) and the girls to their fathers (Electra complex). By the age of six most children move onto the latency stage, after realising that they cannot have their parents of the opposite sex.

Around the age of seven, the children enter into sexual quiescence and pay attention to the discovery of ego, the education and team sports (the latency stage). Residues of the oral, anal and phallic (with Oedipal and Electra complexes) stages all find new outlets in the formation of adolescent sexuality and identity (puberty). During puberty the boys and girls direct their sexual attention to the peers of the opposite sex and this phase is called the genital phase. The genital (of both sexes) stage is a mental stage in which an affectionate relationship with the opposite sex is established.

Physiology of Men's Sexuality

The hypothalamus is, in mammals, the most ancient part of the brain in evolutionary terms. The hypothalamus is a sexual control centre at the base of brain, also regulating body temperature, hunger, thirst and pituitary gland. (Dulbecco 1987, p. 151) The hypothalamus secrets a hormone which stimulates to activate the pituitary gland. A short stalk connects the pituitary to the hypothalamus. In humans, the sex hormones are continually produced at a low level after birth until puberty, when their production increases and becomes pulsating (p. 186).

Puberty is the time of life when a boy starts to become sexually mature. His reproduction organs develop, and his testes start producing sperms. Puberty is triggered by a hormone released by the pituitary gland, the size of a pea, at the base of the brain. This stimulates the testes to release the male sex hormone, testosterone, which controls the changes happening to his body. (Fenwick & Walker 1994, p. 22) Most boys attain puberty between 13 and 15.

These two hormones are working as communicators which carry out distant communication by spreading through the blood. The ductless glands secrete hormones which are discharged directly into the blood stream. Most chemical substance, of course including the hormones, produced by the human body is regularly absorbed into the blood as they circulate through the body. (Velde 1965, p. 12)

The sequential chains of hormone govern the reproductive system of the male and female. The hypothalamus secrets the hormone (GnRH) which reaches the anterior pituitary. The pituitary in turn in response to GnRH secretes the hormones (FSH & LH). These hormones stimulate the gonads to produce the gametes (sperm or ova) as well as the sex hormones. The sex hormones and a gonadal hormone Inhibin exert feedback effects on the amount, more or less, of GnRH, FSH and LH. (Arthur, Sherman & Luciano 1986, p. 552) The GnRH-secreting cells in the hypothalamus receive synaptic input from other neurons, some excitatory and some inhibitory (p. 563).

The seminiferous tubules in the testes produce the sperm, and testosterone is created by the endocrine interstitial cells lying in the small connective spaces between the seminiferous tubules (p. 553).

Puberty is a part of adolescence. Adolescence is the period of growing up and embraces the whole change from childhood to adulthood. Puberty signals the competency and maturity in the sexual term. (Smith 1968, p. 297) Male puberty starts with an enlargement of the testes at 10 to 12; however, mature sperm are not produced until the age of 14 to 16. Even after the sexual maturity, the boys, as for the girls, keep growing physically and physiologically. (p. 299)

The first menstruation of the girls does not signify that they are capable of having babies but they can carry babies in a year or so (p. 298).

Both the puberty and growth spurt occur earlier for girls than boys. Consequently the girls of 12 to 15 are often both taller and heavier than the boys of the same age. The boys not only have their growth spurt later, but carry on growing for a longer period. The girls stop growing at 20 or 21 but the boys keep growing until 23-25. (p. 298)

Both sexes have the following three hormones in the varying proportions. At puberty the sexual glands in testicles and ovaries start producing these hormones, mostly built of proteins, in a large quantity:

- Androgens, steroid hormone, give the male secondary sexual characteristics like a deep voice, facial hair and muscular physique. Testosterone, a hormone of libido, is one of the androgens. The androgen hormones circulate in the male body and give rise to the male's ability to produce and secrete semen as well as to function sexually. Androgens and especially testosterone are sometimes called the male sex hormone. A man normally produces 6-8 mg of testosterone daily; more than 95% in the testes and the remainder in the adrenal glands. A woman produces 0.5 mg of testosterone daily in the ovaries and the adrenals. (Masters, Johnson & Kolodny 1985, p. 78)
- Oestrogens (a family of female sex hormones) promote development of the female secondary sexual characteristics and one of its main tasks is to organise the sexual monthly cycle. Oestrogens are produced not only by the ovaries but by the placenta though in a small quantity. (Arthur, Sherman & Luciano 1986, p. 231)
- Progesterone specialises in the mechanism of pregnancy.

Male hormones, or androgens, are made in the testes by cells between the sperm-producing tubules. Female hormones, or oestrogen and progesterone, are made in the ovaries by cells. The ovaries first make androgen and then convert it to oestrogen. In the testes, too, a proportion of the androgen produced is converted to oestrogen. (Dulbecco 1987, pp. 183-4) The cortex of adrenal glands in both men and women also secretes some sex hormones, especially androgens. At the stage of embryo the potential testes is exactly the same as the potential ovaries, that is, at embryo there is no distinction of the sexual organ of males and females.

Androgens give the maleness or the male secondary sexual characteristics to both men and women. Androgen steroids, when given to women, induce the development of a beard, a big penis like clitoris, deep voice, enlargement of muscles and a high sexual appetite. (p. 216)

A man's testes begin to manufacture sperm at the time of puberty and produce an order of 50 000 sperm per minute, every minute of every hour, well into old age. It takes about 70 days for a sperm to be produced.

Contrary to our expectation, sperm production is a steady process and unrelated to the repetition of ejaculation. If the ejaculation does not take place through abstinence or inability, the sperm stored in the epididymis die, and are removed by the process used to get rid of all foreign matters in the human body. With the repeated ejaculation the number of spermatozoa in an ejaculate decreases rapidly. (*Encyclopedia of Love & Sex* 1972, p. 63)

Sperm is only 0.05 millimetre long. A sperm cell is about 0.0025 mm in diameter at its head. Ninety per cent of semen is in fact water. Each ejaculation gives between two and seven millilitres of semen. The spermatozoa moves about like a tadpole and swims 1-4 mm a minute. The sperm have a short life. They live perhaps one hour in the vagina and up to 40 hours within the uterus or cervix.

A man ejaculates 80-300 million, normally 200 million, sperm through an orgasm, though sperm is only a small portion of semen and the bulk of the semen is the fluid that nourishes sperm.

Using the above figures, that is, 50 000 sperm are produced every minute and an ejaculate contains 80-300 million sperm, we can calculate how many times of sex a man should have in one week on the postulate that when a man uses up all the sperm produced in a week he is on the optimum. A man should have sex once every 1.11-4.17 days. This figure can be converted to indicate that a man should have sex 1.68-6.31 times per week.

Men's urge to expel the semen in the body is the sexual desire. Majority of men after puberty cannot resist the expulsion process and look for suitable females for sexual outlets. If they cannot find any, they normally masturbate. Excess semen is either ejected from the body by wet dreams or reabsorbed into the body. Biological process only partially explains men's sex drive patterns. Upbringing has a great deal to do with men's sexual behaviours. (Wright 1977, p. 7)

Sperm are created in the testes until men die. Often men are frightened not to be able to pass water with the depletion of sperm, not knowing what is happening and go to see a doctor. Repeated sex or repeated masturbation causes the depletion of sperm. A doctor cures the problem with one injection.

Semen consists of
3-5% sperm
65% secretions from seminal vesicles
30% secretions from prostate
(Westheimer 1994, pp. 258-9)

As I recall, the urge to have orgasm was ashamedly strong throughout my youth and I cannot pin point at what age the desire was strongest. As I aged I learned to control the drive to some extent. However, according to research, it seems that the sexual desire peaks around 19 years of age for the bulk of males. The amount of secretive hormone also supports the proposition. The secretion of the male hormone which largely regulates the sexual drive reaches the highest level at about the age of 19 and gradually declines for the rest of men's lives. Most of Kinsey's male respondents said that they had begun masturbating between the age of 13 and 15, but many of the women surveyed said they had begun after the age of 25. Studies indicate that nearly all boys have masturbated to orgasm by 18 years of age. (pp. 30, 175)

Surveys show that by their late teens, about 90 per cent of boys masturbate regularly. The number for girls varies from as low as 60 per cent to as high as 80 per cent. (Fenwick & Walker 1994, p. 26)

One American survey showed that over 90% of men still had erectile potency at the age of 50, over 80% at the age of 60, over 70% at 70 and even 25% at 80. These figures do not necessarily indicate the ability to achieve orgasm. AC Kinsey reported that the American male of 50 was still having about two orgasms on average a week, and of 70 about once a week. (Smith 1968, pp. 60-1)

Kinsey reports that the American couples make love:

4 times a week when aged 15-20,
3 times a week by the age of 30,
twice a week at forty,
once a week at sixty.

(p. 69)

Masters and Johnson showed, in spite of the above universally observed phenomena, that the age is not a crucial factor in sexual response for both men and women. With proper interest and approach people can enjoy sex well into their 80s. (Wright 1977, p. 253)

Men after puberty always have sexual desire at the back of their minds. Sexual urge for men, triggered by the continual secretion of semen like a spring of water, wells up continually. When men see women of their fancy, men want to be close to them, to touch them, to make them naked, and can never be satisfied until the final act of sexual intercourse and ejaculation. Though the urge to have sex is all the time in men in varying intensity, men are in reality constrained to act their wishful thinking by morals or by various possibilities such as rejection, fighting and priority at hand. Many men approach and pay to the prostitutes, the desperate feeling belittling the possibility of contracting various diseases such as venereal diseases and HIV. Many opt for masturbating.

When men are engaged in some mental or physical activity, sex tends not to come into their conscious minds because of the way minds operate. The human minds are peculiar in that they can think only one thing at a time and cannot stop thinking while awake and possibly while asleep. Hence, when men are thinking of something men simply push aside lewdness (pleasurable), in the same way men temporarily forget other strong emotions such as mental or physical pains (unpleasant) and flashbacks (pleasurable or unpleasant). It is men's daily experience that photographs of naked girls and sighting of beautiful women whether in real life or on films triggers back the sexual urge.

The sexual urge is vague and hard to put down for the pre-puberty boy until he finds the way to let the strong feeling release physiologically. The modes of expressions which result from the uncertainty of the minor's sexual drive are hard to predict because they depend on many factors: his in-born trait, availability and environment. Eventually they may take the forms of heterosexuality, homosexuality, bisexuality, bestiality, and masturbation using palms or any other preferred methods.

Though the sexual objects can vary among boys, it seems that once they settle in the preferred mode they do not deviate from it a great deal in their life time. We can see the similar trait in our food selection: once the preferred food is set we do not deviate from it a great deal in our life time. Hence this observation sets the pattern that people from every nationality think that the food they prepare and eat are the best in the world. The above general rule concerning the sex and food preferences seems to be broken unexpectedly for a small number of people from unknown reasons.

It strikes me quite strange that the sexual preference is not only fixed for a man through his life, but the way he performs his sexual activity is mostly fixed. Both of these requirements come, undoubtedly, from his wish to maximise sexual pleasure under the given circumstances and become the habit of life time.

A prostitute on my second meeting told me how I made love to her on the first visit. She further said that every man performed his sexual act differently in his preferred way.

I wanted to know from another prostitute in bed with me what day of the week the brothel was busy. I wanted to visit the brothel when it was not busy to receive good attention. She replied, 'There is no such thing. One day of a week can be very busy but I cannot tell if that is the case in the following week or the next'.

Among the hundreds of prostitutes I came contact with, some displayed peculiar antics in lovemaking. I was anxious to fondle the breasts of a prostitute. She mistook it as a means to excite her sexually and said, 'Business! Business!' She soon realised that she made a mistake and I was genuinely interested in her breasts. She must have been rather surprised with my antic and said pointing her lower jaw towards her private part, 'They all go for that'. And she placed a pillow under her bottom, wanting to see my penile thrust into her vagina. One girl, while I was making penile penetration, held her toes with her hands--her right toe with her right hand and similarly with the left side. She must have raised the sexual sensitivity with this rather peculiar posture. One girl told me she masturbated regularly: it was quite strange to me seeing she was young and pretty. One girl dozed off while I was making love to her. When a girl told me she was bisexual, I was so much intrigued how they made love. I asked her how they made love without penile penetration. She said that the other girl used her fingers. Some girls said that they were married and a few among them said that their husbands knew they worked as prostitutes. Quite a few of the girls said they worked as prostitutes because they liked it. One prostitute screamed as she climbed down the bed after I had had sex with her, 'How lucky I am. I am getting paid for doing what I like to do!'

A man has certain modus operandi in how to make love to a woman and more generally in trying to calm his sexual longing. The sexual mode of men is similar to that of criminal conducts. Every criminal has its own modus operandi in carrying out a crime, which often gives the police the useful clues in the course of investigation. The fixed pattern of the criminal activities by the same criminal must come from the innate character as well as the acquired knowledge; certainly the criminals as for men in their sexual habits modify their mode after acquiring new knowledge. A man has a characteristic way of maximising the pleasure of crime and the pleasure of lovemaking under the given conditions. Rather the pleasure of crime and the pleasure of sex may be the same in the deep psychological workings. Criminals cannot stop committing crime and also men cannot stop having sex, in both cases because of the excitement in performing. Virtually all men succumb to the sexual pleasure; however, only a small number of men succumb to the pleasure coming from committing crimes. The above observed phenomena suggest that the criminal and sexual wonts are, as any other human activities, not arbitrary as we might expect at the first glance but determined by the deep rooted psychological process, hence merit careful study for this reason alone.

When a man does not have a woman friend or wife who is prepared to go to bed with him, his longing for women is strong and universal but genuine. Once he has found a woman sexually available to him, his desire towards other women is just as strong, losing genuineness and sharply focusing on the comparison with the other women. This specific thinking is inferior to the previous general longing, which he is possibly aware. The similar reasoning applies vis-a-vis the acquisition of wealth, honour, authority, fame, or whatever men generally covet. Once men get what they want, they want more or better with lax mind. Hence, Jesus Christ said, 'Blessed are the poor'. I might say with the equal conviction, 'Blessed are the men who do not have their own women'.

Men try to derive maximum pleasure from sexual activity and the physiological process of sexual orgasm in its conclusion, which leads to divergence of sexual preferences. They probably do not know why a sense of pleasure is important for the seemingly simple act of semen discharge. I know that good quality orgasm--whether it comes from making love with woman, from masturbation or from wet dream--reduces the tension, and hence brings temporary satisfaction. I also found that semen discharge without adequate gratification left me with mental disturbance. Strangely the wet dreams, though we do not stimulate our body, bring mental relief: probably this is the way nature ordains our mind and body.

As for acquiring money which is the sphere of economics, men go to an extraordinary length to acquire women for sexual purpose. Both are really strong inclination of men; however, men are prepared to sacrifice wealth to obtain women in marriage or outside marriage.

After acquiring wealth and women men can feel happy. Though they are quite different objects, these two sets of happiness are really the same sort or on the same level in terms of survival.

When we are hungry, thirsty, cold, hot, horny, or we have to pass water or defecate, we feel the urge to satisfy the need. When it is satisfied, we feel happy in a physiological sense. This happiness is on a different level from the happiness we normally use. Nature tells us by means of unhappy feeling to satisfy our physiological requirements. Consequently, many people are not happy because they are overweight; still they keep eating too much food in order to satisfy their hunger and thirst. We can also see this phenomenon in men's quest for women: men may sacrifice many other things in their life to satisfy their sexual need. Thus we have to differentiate happiness or unhappiness of between a physiological sense and an ordinary psychological sense.

There is another level of happiness coming from the worldly affairs such as drinking, gambling and taking drugs. As for the happiness arising from satisfying the physiological needs, the worldly happiness is independent of the happiness of psychological sense.

There is another happiness coming from the practice of idealism, among others. This higher mode of happiness is also independent of happiness coming from satisfying the physiological needs or the worldly affairs.

There are divergent desires in men but there is one desire that needs special attention in conjunction with sex, that is, the desire to be happy in the psychological sense. Virtually all men want to be happy and to have sex and they strive for happiness and good quality sex. For men under normal circumstances sex and happiness are the purpose and ultimate end rather than means. However, the sexual desire is probably independent of the inclination to be happy. Both of these strong feelings exist in men's mind side by side and come out into their conscious mind from time to time, affecting the decisions. These two inclinations sometimes interfere, one pushes away the other at times, and they cooperate under some circumstances. The premise that happiness and sex are almost independent inclinations in men seems to me to give important clues in understanding men's sexuality and hence to explain the various manifestations of sexual conducts. I am to present several expansions of the idea in the next few paragraphs.

We can say that men's sexual desire is so strong that it overrides another human need to be happy; however, it is more in accord with the reality to think that sex is independent of another basic human requirement to be happy. Sex is the physiological urge to discharge semen from men's body, and happiness is another urge, almost universal and possibly biological, to be content. Independence of the various desires possibly stems in the fact that the different parts of the brain regulate these drives. Hunger and thirst are independent of each other, therefore hunger may be satisfied but men can still feel thirsty. Hunger and thirst are satisfied by eating and drinking respectively through the mouth; however, the body recognises the independence, and the anus discharges the solids and the penis the liquids. Also the penis discharges the semen.

To be healthy is one human requirement; however, sexual drive depends on the health: if men feel sick they don't want to have sex. Men want sex only after they satisfy the basic human requirements such as hunger, thirst, body temperature and health, hence sex is dependent on them being satisfied. These requirements are essential to the human survival and more important than the other requirements such as sex, happiness, and wealth acquisition. Men instinctively grade the importance according to the survival requirements. Men make decisions consciously or subconsciously depending on how important the fulfilments are for their survival. Hunger, thirst, being cold or hot, being unhealthy: to correct these deficiencies are fundamental for the survival hence they have absolute priority. Next comes the need to satisfy biological and physiological desire of sex. I have come to the conclusion that to better understand the nature of sex we have to separate sex in the above sense and sexual longing for women. Next come the desires for women, wealth and happiness. Men need to satisfy the sexual longing as much as the desires of wealth acquisition and happiness. Interestingly the similarity extends further. When men do not have any of them satisfied, they are desperate to obtain it: however, once satisfied, they do not appreciate it.

Drugs, alcohol, gambling, power, sex, wealth, fame, honour, and any other common human pursuits, if taken to the extreme, become independent of happiness for the doers. Some men want these things no matter what and it seems that happiness is no longer their prime concern. Moderation in sexual matter is an absolute virtue as for moderation in satisfying the basic human needs such as eating and drinking, as well as the human pursuits above mentioned. Excess in any one of them brings unhappiness to the doers in due course without fail. We also have to explain why people engage in pleasure seeking such as taking addicted drugs, drinking alcohol, gambling, eating good foods, wearing fine clothes and living in luxurious houses, which do not seem to contribute to survival on the surface at least. In the deeper psychological analyses, it may turn out that they are important for the survival of the humans as long as they are taken in moderation.

Catherine Howard, Henry VIII's fifth wife, continued her sexual promiscuity even after marrying him. She must have known that she would be beheaded if she was caught of adultery since she knew that Anne Boleyn, his second wife, had been executed for alleged marital infidelity. Catherine was caught of adultery and executed.

The males of both the mantes and the black widow spiders even risk their lives, to approach and mate their larger female species: if the former cannot make a quick escape after mating, they can be eaten by the latter (Dulbecco 1987, p. 196). The males of redback spiders always get eaten by the females at the end of the copulation. In these cases the dominant feeling of the males may be the desire to produce their offspring rather than the sexual urge.

The parents' concern over their son in regard to his association, for friendship or marriage, with an undesirable girl often meets with his strong resistance. The parents' main interest is his happiness, whereas his main interest is friendship and sex. Under the above premise, it is expected that these interests often do not go together. Sex and happiness are two different kettles of fish, hence objection to marriage on the ground of happiness of the people concerned does not have a persuasive force whether it be against the institution of marriage or against particular partners.

Men after intellectual reasoning may come to a conclusion that 'We will be happier if we keep away from women' in the domestic context. The conclusion may be true and be worth more than all the teachings on how to be happy but is virtually impossible to practise for average men, since happiness and sex drive belong to separate spheres of human feeling. There are no causal relationships between happiness and sex activity. Men can feel happy or unhappy about their sex activities but only by chance. The true position is that they must have sex whether they are happy or not. The same logic applies to any other addictions, such as alcohol, drugs and gambling, if the addictions are extreme. People, observing the desperate addicts, may comment that they must be happier if they keep away from the addicting stuff. However, this feeling is misguided since sex corresponds to the extreme form of the addictions and these people themselves are addicted to sex. When drunk or under the influence of drugs or under the compulsion to gamble, men do not have full control of their minds. In the similar manner, men under the strong urge for women don't have full control and tend to behave in an irrational fashion.

The fact that the ordinary men could not live without women up to the present does not mean they are not capable of it in the future. If readers peruse Book Four *The Third Prophecy*, they should be able to understand that the average men can do just that. However, it is obvious that men cannot go on without occasional sexual orgasms, whether without women, or with partners of women or men. I present this book on sex to guide men for better handling of sexual desire.

If sex were dependent on happiness, that is, if men would seek sex only to the extent they feel happy, human race would have entirely different society and history. Many men would have remained single, thinking they would lead better life without women. That would have resulted in no scramble to obtain women, hugely depleted population, no war and no wide spread starvation.

Suppose a young man goes out with a girlfriend for a night: his intent is, beyond reasonable doubt, to have sex with her. If he is asked on the following day if the date was really worth the money and time, he, more often than not, says he does not know the answer. All he felt was he wanted to make love to her, and he got what he wanted or missed out. The night out can be assessed as happy or unhappy. The success or failure can be judged only on the sexual plane. Here again we can see happiness and sex act on two different planes.

Virgins do not know if a sexual intercourse is pleasurable or not since they have never had sex with men. Some men in their eagerness to sleep with them may argue that it is illogical for the virgins to detest the offer of intercourse. These men may wonder why many girls are keen to protect their virginity: their experiences indicate majority of women enjoy sex. However, homosexuals may approach these men for anal intercourse and these men, being non-homosexuals, would be horrified with the thought. The homosexuals may argue in a similar fashion that since the non-homosexuals do not have the experience of anal sex there is no reason to detest it, and they want to have a go. If the homosexual men do not get what they want, they are left wondering why.

The sexual matters in this book deal with only the general rules, and the exceptions to the rules are naturally expected as in any other rules of life. I have met an insignificant number of men who were rather unconcerned with their sex life: either non-existent or not important. These people can ignore their sexual drive, not by their belief but by their nature as far as I can work out. There are some men who claim they don’t feel any stirring of the sexual drive. They may have a severe hormone deficiency or mental problem or strong willpower blocking the urging of the desire. (Masters, Johnson & Kolodny 1994, p. 45) The above situation is similar to the small number of moralists who believe that happiness is not and should not be the object of their life. These people are also the exceptions to the general rule of society, in this case through their belief and not by their natural inclination.

Sex for men originates in biological process of semen production in their bodies. Its cycle ends in the semen ejaculation. A series of physiological events takes place between sexual arousal and orgasm. We naturally assume adequate secretion of relevant hormones and the proper function of the central nervous system together with the other necessary bodily and mental functions for the execution. The semen discharge through urethra is a form of physiology like eating, drinking, urinating and excreting: we have to eat, drink, urinate and excrete, in health and unhealth as well as in happiness and unhappiness. However, the urge to have sex intercourse during the cycle is very much psychological and comes like the unending waves of the ocean, though sexual urges are irregular unlike regular waves. It is also social in the sense that men are submerged or constrained in the social setting. As a matter of fact the influences affecting the sexual desires, though they all end in mind, are numerous and tend to amplify or inhibit the interest (Swanson 1974, p. 94). It grips men suddenly in their conscious mind: strangely enough, not conforming to the above cycle proposition, and sometimes not subsided by the subsequent semen discharge. I also noticed that the sexual intensity changed like roughness or mildness of the waves. Men are beset with stronger sexual urge for some time and comparatively weak drive for the subsequent period from unknown reasons. Psychological nature of sex drive manifests in the divergence of sexual preferences, in irregularity of arousal, and also in sudden loss of interest due to trifle matters.

The ejaculation of semen at orgasm follows a definite sequence. The prostate, vas deferens and seminal vesicles contract as a result of sympathetic stimulation, emptying the semen into the urethra. The semen is then expelled from the urethra by a series of rapid contractions of the urethral smooth muscles as well as the skeletal muscles at the base of the penis. (Arthur, Sherman & Luciano 1986, p. 50)

The testes of most, though not all, mammals are held outside the body cavity in a scrotal sac which is one or two degrees cooler than the body temperature. The maintenance of this difference in temperature appears to be essential for the testes to function properly and indeed for them even to retain their structure intact. When artificially heated, the tubules which produce the sperm rapidly degenerate. This situation can be easily brought about by fixing testes artificially with a ligature onto the abdomen. (Wood 1974, p. 116)

Food, clothes and shelter are often cited as basic human needs. One fundamental reason why humans must have adequate covers for the body (immediate cover as well as cover with some space from body) is that they have to keep their body temperature within certain range for comfort and survival, though there are other reasons such as social courtesy and personal vanity. In fact this basic requirement to be warm goes deeper than just being superficial and can be observed before a sperm cell and an egg cell are united for reproduction. The eggs are kept inside the female bodies to be at the same temperature as the body. Sperm cannot develop at normal body temperature, so the testes hang outside the body, in the cooler scrotum. (Fenwick & Walker 1994, p. 24) Tight jeans can raise the temperature of the scrotum, preventing sperm from developing properly (p. 25). When the surrounding atmosphere is cold, the balls retract to the body thus warming the testes. They stretch away from the body in the hot environment. We can observe this change before and after having a shower. The skin of the scrotum is thin and brown, devoid of fatty tissues. Below the skin is a layer of involuntary muscles, which alter the appearance of the scrotum as the ambient temperature changes.

Confucius made the following remark possibly in a jocular mode: 'I have yet to see the man who loves virtue as much as he loves feminine beauty' (Chien 1979, p. 11). We cannot compare meaningfully two different things such as cheese and chalk or virtue and female body. It is nonsensical to say I like cheese better than chalk or I like virtue better than woman.

It is fashionable for men to have good quality food, drink and sex. Men take in food and drinks through gullets, and discharge semen through urethras. Without doubt one source of pleasure in these activities comes from tactile sensation by the moving food, drink and semen within the body canals. These pleasurable sensations are not altogether different from: when dogs are stroked by the owners; when babies are cuddled by the parents; when men are gently caressed by their lovers. However, this mechanical explanation of pleasure source is far short of accounting for men's deep attachments to food, drink and sex. Besides it does not give us satisfactory answer to such questions as: why many young men are keener to have good sex than good food and drink; why there are so many personal variations in the preferences of these pleasures of life; why average men seek eagerly these pleasures in the first place instead of satisfying themselves with what is available easily as the religions teach them. Most men perhaps can live without good quality food and drink but most say that life is not worth living without sex with or without women.

Sex gives men a tremendous pleasure. In an effort to experience this pleasure, men put out a great effort to acquire women and in the subsequent lovemaking process. In fact men put out the best performance in these matters. It may be possible to direct this good performance to something else for the good of themselves and society. If men direct this enthusiasm to learning and working, they themselves will be surprised to see what a tremendous achievement they would make.

The Bible deals with many subjects which concern our everyday life. However, I noticed that the sexual references in the Testaments are appreciably smaller in proportion to the people spend in thinking about sex. They deal the subject in general terms except in the Deuteronomic laws. The laws prescribe death to anybody who transgresses the moral sexual practices; that is what the author thought proper. Sexual intercourse with an animal, homosexuality and illicit sex are all punishable by death, though I doubt if these laws were enforced in the biblical times to the letters except in cases where the transgressions were referred to the authority. The Qur'an (Koran) prescribes the practical punishment for adultery: The woman and man guilty of adultery or fornication flog each of them with a hundred stripes (Qur'an 24.2). I am sure that the people in the Jewish community and Arabic community spent as much time thinking about sex since the primitive era onwards as the modern people do. I also believe that a small number of references spared on sex in the Bible are not so much to teach people to spare small portion of their thought but the authors had the sexual difficulties of their own and did not know how to deal with them.

I have come to believe that it is better to learn to live with sex rather than to ignore its existence or to try to suppress without success. Men have to manage the sex drive for virtually all adult life. Most men, during active sex life, and even both before puberty and after change of life, are interested in women. At some periods of my life I suppressed sex in the hope that I might forget the sense of pleasure coming from orgasm, but I realised it was a false hope after weeks or months of sexual abstinence. Possibly I would have overcome the problems of drinking, gambling or drug taking by the strong will capable of restraining sex drive for such a long period. Seemingly, these pleasures are all in the same boat, but through my experience I learned that sex was different from the other addictions and more fundamental to human existence. This proposition also matches with the observation that virtually all adolescent and adult men succumb to sexual pleasure or addiction but not necessarily to the other addictions. Addictions are the extreme form of pleasure seeking and do not refer to the moderate intake of the pleasure.

If it had been successful for me to give up sex by following the religious teachings, I would be teaching just that and would not have written this book. If we ignore someone or something (sex in our discussion), it takes offence and would retaliate if it can, though an inanimate object has no feeling but we get the same effect. By ignoring the existence of sex life, we do not gain anything. We had better acknowledge the problem and learn to cope with it. That is why I have presented this book.

Men often talk about money in the overt culture and are money-crazed. In the covert culture the different things are happening: the average men cannot shake off Eros (a Greek god of love) and Nemesis (a Greek god of vengeance) from their minds. Lewdness and a sense of revenge always obsess men but somewhere in their minds they think that is wrong and try to hide these feelings from the public scrutiny, though at times they reveal these inner thoughts to a limited audience. I got the foregoing notion talking to many men and I myself cannot shake off the desires for women and revenge. The religions teach them with little success to remove these undesirable inclinations from their consciousness and place good thought, primarily love, in their stead. Even a baby takes revenge by biting its mother, though the mother may not realise it is revenge. According to Freud, the baby's suckling of the mother's breasts is a sexual manifestation in conjunction with receiving the nourishment. This may explain the fact that breast feeding arouses most mothers sexually.

Sex and Five Senses

I stated in the earlier part of this section that men's strong sexual desire stems from the survival instinct of the human species. The testes of healthy men continually secrete a large number of sperm and it is more natural for men to discharge them out of the urethra rather than to suppress the urge to let the sperm die and eject from the body. The average men opt to have orgasms with or without women. Ejaculation of the semen brings to men not only intense pleasure but also physical and mental relief. Men, though not all of them, have a natural tendency to have pleasure and to avoid pains. Apart from and in conjunction with the above three fundamental reasons--survival, biology and pleasure--five senses are involved in the sexual conducts, increasing the pleasurable feeling of sex. Without any doubt one of the reasons why men cannot extricate themselves from sex is that there are five senses participating in the sexual pleasure.

Men are endowed with five senses, all of which participate in lovemaking. The stages of the psychological development by Freud earlier mentioned are the fixation of the child on the body organ in the phases of the development; however, it is interesting to note that the adults in the process of lovemaking return to these phases, showing particular interest in some of the phases:

- Appearance of female body fascinates men (seeing). Women spend a lot of money and care on their appearance to enhance their sexual desirability.
- Men's tongue goes through woman's body with delight (taste). Babies of both sexes have a habit of putting everything into their mouths, to enjoy its taste and probably to see if it can be eaten. In the same way men in lovemaking are repeating what they did as babies.
- Men are obsessed with the desire to touch bodies of females (tactile). Freud contends that all tactile stimulation and response are sexual in origin, as we witness in the mammalian behaviours (Kinsey, Pomeroy & Martin 1948, p. 163). He probably means all bodily contact including oral contact by tactile stimulation. It seems that touching not only between the lovers but also between the family members is an important way of communicating. Shaking hands, hugging and kissing can effect stimulation.
- Female voices are pleasant to men (hearing).
- Though men are not overtly conscious of smell of female body (olfactory) during love-making session, I am sure it plays some part, seeing the mammalian origin of the human species. Women are well aware of this fact and pay utmost care for their sexual partners not to smell bad odours emanating from their bodies. We do not have to resort to the poem by Plautus: A woman smells good when she does not smell (Montaigne 1965, p. 228). They spend a large amount of money to buy perfumes for this purpose. Men are so stupid that they are not capable of distinguishing the perfume from the female body smell. In fact, nature designed the smell and taste of the sexual organs of the opposite sex to be sexually arousing (Brewer 1997, p. 62). Women are also careful that their men don't suffer from the smell emanating from their fart and defecation.

Getting sexual pleasures from the five senses is not the end but merely increases the sexual desire. Only the sexual orgasm puts an end to the cycle of sexual activities.

The other forms of sense pleasure are limited to the particular senses. Music is the hearing pleasure. Painting, sculpture and scenery appeal only to the eyes. Eating good food is for smell and taste. Certainly these sense pleasures give the additional mental satisfaction, apart from the fact that they satisfy the senses.

I do not know any other objects which may give men such high degree of fascination to all sense organs and at the same time such high degree of relief in semen ejaculation as in sex. It is not too hard for men to give up other human pursuits such as wealth, fame and power. It is virtually impossible for men to give up sex. One reason must lie in the fact that only sex and no other pursuits engage all five senses in their fulfilments. Many men, single or married, are prepared to sacrifice a big part of their wealth and time in an effort to obtain good-looking women for sexual purpose.

Buddhism teaches that all perceptions through five senses are illusions and unsubstantial, and exhorts the followers to stop all worldly and sexual activities. However, denying all perceptions is contrary to the common belief. Accordingly the general public would misunderstand the adherents who follow the precept to the letter. I have never met a man who does not appreciate his five senses in the worldly objects, such as food, clothes, houses and the female bodies.

Marriage and Sex

The pair bonding such as we see in today's marriage is not confined to the human species and is widely observed in some animals and birds. For instance, albatrosses and ducks are said to mate with the same partners for life. People with the common sense know that the friends in the true sense are hard to come by, the marriage partners are hard to find, and good marriages are rare.

Monogamy:

Men's monogamous relationship with women which is observed in civilised marriage and de facto is a compromise in terms of finance and population ratio of men and women. Men want a large number of women for sexual enjoyment but financially average men can keep barely one woman. It also seems fair to say that a man is united with only one woman in terms of the equality of the sexes and the population ratio.

This form of marriage which is predominant in the civilised society today in fact contains many seeds of problems:

- The average men cannot be satisfied with one wife. They have to suppress this feeling or at times they grab an opportunity of infidelity.
- If the enmity develops between the couple, the situation becomes unbearable.
- Traditionally men got sex from their wife in exchange for the financial support; wives had to put up with the dominance of husbands because the former could not get well-payed jobs. In recent times, the females have become financially independent and they do not need the husbands to support them. I believe this is one underlying reason for divorce. There is a recognisable trend developing in recent times that monogamy is collapsing as the high rate of divorce indicates.

Group Marriage:

A group (several or a larger number) of men are married with a group (several or a larger number) of women. Sexually men have several or a larger number of choices for the night. Economically men have to support on average only one woman: some men and some women work and the household chores are left to non-working men and women. If the enmity develops between two members, they simply avoid meeting or talking. There is always an option that a member of the group leaves seeking for another group but its impact is kept to a minimum. The benefits of the group marriage are greater sexual availability with reasonable financial burden and in addition the expulsion or defection of one member does not affect greatly the rest of the member, sexually, financially and even emotionally. When a baby was born to a female member, in the past they did not know and did not care who the father was. However today DNA technique can ascertain it.

No Western experiment in group marriage has managed to survive more than a few years; because the pair bonding is such a strong force that the group marriage after a while collapses. The conclusion is that for today's civilised thinking monogamy is natural but the group marriage is not, and that monogamy is the basic rule for the humans but the polygyny and polyandry are opportunistic alternatives when a man or a woman has wealth or power. (Fisher 1992, p. 72)

The Origin of the Family, Private Property and the State offers an interesting insight into the transition from the group marriage to monogamy. Friedrich Engels wrote that Karl Marx started on the above book building on the research Lewis H Morgan made, and Engels took over the task after Marx' death. The thesis emphasises, as the following paragraphs brief, the economic aspects of the marriage institutions rather than love between the sexes. I do not necessarily agree with the oversimplification and the overemphasis on economic aspect in the following account of the families. Also some terms in the following paragraphs are not in accord with our everyday use.

Group marriage was characteristic of savagery; pairing family, barbarism; monogamy, civilisation. Engels used the terms group marriage and pairing family, not the way we normally understand today. Group marriage, as Engels uses, was essentially hetaerism, that is, men commonly shared women. However, since the father of the children thus born could not be attributed to a particular father, matrilineality had to develop. This system was favourable for the females and created mother right. It seems that in-breeding, such as between parents and children and between sisters and brothers, were prohibited in group marriage. However, Engels does not deny the possibility that in the early part of group marriage, the indiscriminate sexual activities were carried out.

Men reduced the number of women to only one, thus creating pairing family making clear who the father was when children were born, though men sacrificed greater availability of women. Pairing of loosely united couple took place for longer or shorter periods and the children thus born belonged solely to the mother. This system carried both the remnant of hetaerism and the harbinger of patrilineality. Men passed their property only to their sons. This was the transition to monogamy.

Out of paring family developed monogamous family as we understand today with the far greater rigidity of the tie which could not be dissolved easily. It produced children of undisputed paternity thus establishing patrilineality and passage of property to the sons, and attaining the dominance of men. (Marx & Engels 1970, pp. 191-334)

This book on the sexual laws deals with primarily sexual matters and does not try to assess the merits and demerits of married life from broader perspectives. Bertrand Russell wrote that the good sexual relationship has a great deal to contribute to good marriage. The loss of sexual interest by the husbands in their wives can lead to other strifes in the marriage. The humans are incredibly adaptable animals and if somebody or something is important for them, they swallow so many inconveniences to accommodate them in some way or another. Obviously to place too much or too little importance on sex among married couples is wrong: people must assess the degree of its importance and learn how to deal with it.

It is generally true that nothing is more interesting for men than women, and nothing is more interesting for women than men. When men cohabit with women, all kinds of situation will arise; men may like or dislike women, do things together or fight with women. Sexually, men invariably lose an interest in women after repeated sexual acts. Men have to understand that traditionally women were esteemed as sex objects and child bearing and nothing else by nature. Hence men who look for something else in women would be disappointed.

Section 5 Marriage as Institution, Chapter 1, Book Four expounds marriage as I see.

When a man loves a woman, he believes that that status will last for good. It is not a human nature that he refrains from marriage, thinking that he would soon lose an interest in his sweetheart or she would become old and ugly after so many years. He marries her and discovers what nature or God, as the religions teach, ordained for him that the love between the sexes is an illusion and the people must direct their minds on something more subliminal. There are many considerations in marriage apart from sex, such as finance, up-bringing of children, compatibilities among the family members, and dominance and decision-making processes within the family. The possibility that sex is not the only bonding force between the married couple can be seen when there are no longer sexual activities between the spouses still many families live together. For example, after men become impotent such as because of old age many marriages still survive. At divorce non-sexual considerations such as money, children and emotions come to the fore. Many people are so traumatised at this time that they cannot carry on with their usual duties in the society. However, just before men and women get united in matrimony, these considerations are not likely their prime concerns and they are submerged in a blissful thinking of affection and sex. When a couple fall in love and want to share their lives together, they feel they have no alternatives but to marry.

Ultimately we can explain effectively most human activities if we consider what are useful or important or pleasurable for us, that is, our survival and selfish needs. I have also found that we grade these actions according to what we consider to be useful or important or pleasurable for us. For example, the jobs are important for us because they provide us with what we want--money, security, satisfaction and prestige; the children are important for their parents because they give them joy of life; ethics is important to some people because it justifies their moral existence.

The institution of marriage does not offer any reasons to be an exception to the above general rule and hence we can best interpret it in terms of need bases. Accordingly we can surmise that men want wives for both sexual and non-sexual needs. Non-sexual elements must be diverse and complex since every man would put forward good reasons. Among the factors men feel they must have wives when we take out the sexual element, I am sure that psychological and social considerations are prominent. It is hard to answer whether average men would still marry women of their choice without involvement of sex, that is, only for non-sexual considerations. The question is possibly nonsensical because we cannot take out sex on its own from the other reasons for marrying.

When we look at marriage from the selfish viewpoint--as we are trying here--being married has merits when it suits the purposes and demerits when it does not suit the purposes for the married people. So we can expect a lot of problems from cohabitation (married or de facto) since there are many expectations crisscrossing from two sides. Certainly single men would have some problems of their own, but not of complicated matching. Men standing on one side of the fence tend to look the other side with envy, which naturally results from the selfish causes. The single and married men tend to look at the other side with some envy.

The popular movies can show people what the successful marriages are like and they hope before marriage that theirs would be similar. Many men plunge into matrimony with the women of their desire and adoration, not knowing their feeling would soon evaporate under the normal course of events. When men get to know what is happening around the anus of their female sexual partners, still they adore them sexually they are not normal. Women, on their part sensing that once men have enough of them men invariably lose interest in them, would not let their boyfriends make love to them easily. Women do their best to hide their true identity, mental and physical, before marriage. After marriage they relax their attitude and their true shape come to the fore to the disappointment of their husbands.

In marriage, people accept what they have and tend to get bored--bored with their mates, bored with the sexual relationship, bored with rather limited social contacts and bored with the humdrum of routine daily life (Wright 1977, p. 81).

Adultery is a symptom that there is something wrong in the marriage (p. 85). Often the first sign of marital problem shows up as the decline of sexual activity between the couple. The major deterrent of sexual adventures after marriage is fear. Fear of getting caught, of throwing away everything and of hurting innocent family members. (p. 82) Also unattached women are reluctant to associate with married men because the latter would have limited time and finance apart from a worry of detection and its consequences.

Marriage gives some security to men in that men secure women for sexual purpose as well as some assurance that the children thus born are theirs and nobody else's. Unless they are married, other men are free to approach and can go to bed with them, though this prohibition is only the accepted social convention.

The recent research of Liverpool, an international seaport, Britain, by Robin Baker and Mark Bellis shows that around 10 per cent of children born are not fathered by the ostensible fathers but sired by someone else (Taylor 1996, p. 77).

Erasmus sarcastically threw a rhetorical question, 'Who would marry if they rationally anticipated the pains and problems?' in *Praise of Folly* (1511). He further commented that a little folly made the world go round more smoothly (Mercer 1996, p. 396).

There are many poems denigrating women and marriage in the ancient to classical Greece. Here are some of them:

Euripides wrote, 'Instead of fire, another fire more fierce, more hard to quell flamed forth--a woman' (Harbottle 1897, p. 329). 'He who would wed is marching toward repentance' was read by Philemon (p. 342). 'Better to bury a woman than to marry her' was by Chaeremon (p. 347). Democritus wrote, 'Some who are masters of many men are yet slaves to women' (p. 371). Whoso has trusted women, eke has trusted thieves [Hesiod] (p. 443). A bridegroom already is by his bride enslaved [Euripides] (p. 456). How faithless women's nature! [Menander] (p. 466)

The good man I knew well for many years used to tell me he was like in a prison having a family, though I also knew his wife who was as good as a woman could be.

An economist concluded that the females were inferior to the males because the former had smaller heads than the latter (Robbins 1998, p. 225).

It is unreasonable for men to marry for the sole purpose of sexual enjoyment, since their wives would not stay young and pretty for long. Assuming a girl marries at 20 years of age and one of the spouses dies when she is at 80; her average age during marriage is 50. Most men would not agree to wed 50 year old women, yet that is what is expected from the successful marriage. Besides, we have to make further allowance: at the time of wedding men's sexual desire is the strongest and women are the most beautiful during the span of marriage.

If men know precisely what they are getting into, most would not marry. The problem is that they don't know what the marriage is like until they marry. There are happiness and pleasure in marriage in the same way in crimes and drug takings. All these human activities have another thing in common, that is, people who engage in these have to suffer in the long run to negate their happiness and pleasure.

It is often quoted that a house is the most expensive item in our life. I have reckoned that a wife with children is more money consuming than a house for an average man. Certainly this reckoning is wrong if the wife works carrying a small family. Even if she does not work outside the family, it is hard to put monetary figures to her sexual and domestic services.

A man who stays single can have a young and pretty prostitute at any time he wants, even he becomes advanced in age. Admittedly this notion has a serious flaw in that the man may contract various diseases such as VD and AIDS. However, a man who sleeps with non-prostitute is taking some risks, too.

Men, in their desperation to solve their sex problem, do all kinds of crazy things and possibly marriage is one of them. Men under the influence of alcohol and drugs tend to err in judgement and similarly men under the strong sexual desire tend to make mistakes in their dealings.

Certainly solving men's sexual problem seems to be the prime factor in deciding to get married. Marginal utility for food and sex is similar in their applicability. When men are hungry, they feel intense need for food and prepared to do almost anything to obtain something to eat. Similarly, when men are under strong sexual urge, they are prepared to do many things to acquire women. This may be the primary reason why men decide to go ahead with marriage though there are lots more in marriage than sex. For majority of married men sex from their wives means little because men can have it easily: Marginal utility of sex from their wives is small. If we express more easily, one measure of value of anything is that it is hard for men to have it. Anything that can be had easily such as the sexual service from their wives means little to most men.

The following propositions appear in the economic book referring to the commodities of the economic sense, but the crux of the ideas equally applies to women:

> According to Senior, our desires do not aim so much at quantity but at diversity; not only are there limits to the pleasure which commodities of any given class can afford, but the pleasure diminishes in a rapidly increasing ratio long before these limits are reached. Gossen begins by stating that the aim of all human conduct is to maximise enjoyment. (Roll 1961, pp. 343, 374)

The above idea is also well expressed in the popular saying: Variety is the spice of life.

Anyhow a majority of men opt for marriage. Over 90% of all American men and women marry. However, the successful and happy marriages are rare. Most men before marrying are aware of this fact and normally have ample opportunity to learn what women and married life are like. The social convention requires that married people do not tell their marital problems to the other people and also pretend that their marriage is working well even when it is not. It is a logical statement from the everyday observations that most men would be happier if they remain single. Yet, they have a compulsion to live with women they like. Many of the married men cannot stand the strain of cohabitation. They may divorce their wives, desert the families, and in some cases tragically kill their family members and even themselves. These same people who went through the pains and suffering of living together and survived want to marry after some cooling off period. Why can this be so?

An ancient Greek poet read a poem: War and woman are necessary undying evils. The poet was referring to women in the domestic situation and not to the professional competency of women. In the pre-modern times, not only in the Greek world but the world over, men successfully excluded women from the professional jobs. Apart from the common feelings on the two subjects, the poet contrasted wars which eliminated people with women which propagated people. Probably the poet's highest intelligence is revealed in the observation that war was necessary, which was beyond his personal experience. The Greeks with all their wisdoms were fated to live with the two evils. Modern men also are no better: They have not learned to live without women in spite of the availabilities of great teachings of the world over as well as the enormous varieties of entertainments. People today would express the feeling in the following manner: We cannot live with women yet cannot live without them. Male chauvinist pigs or men habitually abuse women don't tell the whole story in that they cannot live without women. Men through the millenniums accumulated a vast amount of knowledge in the myriads of fields yet have not learned to live without women. Also there are a lot of wars in today's world. How can it be so?

The boys before puberty may wonder why the adults cannot live without the two evils. However, in growing up process, they realise that they must have women for sexual outlet and wars because of human defects.

I wondered many times why the ruler of a nation wanted a piece of land which did not rightfully belong to him and often made war sacrificing so much money and so many people. This desire of the ruler for the good territories may be compared to a man's desire for good women. Both ever want more of a good sort.

The average men most likely cannot live without cohabiting with women, even they can get sex freely from their girlfriends or prostitutes. It may be wrong to assess marriage as for life in the binary system: happy or unhappy; successful or unsuccessful, since marriage as for life is a mix of complicated emotions, real or pretentious. People have to wait for the arrival of the new philosophy which I expound in Book Four *The Third Prophecy* to get to know the satisfactory answers to the foregoing questions. This book teaches that love as I define, not wisdom or knowledge of any persuasions, prompts average men to live without women in the domestic context.

Pleasures

Solon, one of the seven sages in the ancient Greece, taught, 'Flee pleasure, for it brings sorrow in its train' (Harbottle 1897, p. 389). Anaxandrides read a poem, 'Never make thyself a slave of pleasure; that befits a wanton woman, not a man' (p. 420). Euripides wrote, 'Short is the joy that guilt pleasure brings' (p. 341). Pythagoras wrote, 'None can be free who is a slave to, and ruled by, his passions' (p. 367). Bias wrote, 'Take wisdom as your provision for the journey from youth to old age, for it is the most stable of all possessions' (p. 379). Control thy passions, lest they take vengeance on thee [Epictetus] (p. 405). Whatever's too sweet, brings in its train a bitter ending [Pinder] (p. 509). When thou fair women seest, marvel not; great beauty's oft to countless faults allied [Menander] (p. 401). These poems seem to be true today as they must have been to the Greeks of antiquity, which is precisely the reason why the ancient and classical Greek philosophers are held in high esteem even today.

There are many more poems concerning pleasure from Latin source. If ye would conquer love, he must be fought at his first onslaught; sprinkle but a drop of water, the new-kindled flame expires [Ovid] (p. 52). Beauty is a fragile gift [Ovid] (p. 72). Short life is theirs who know not self-restraint; pray not to love too much the things you love [Martial] (p. 96). In love are all these ills; suspicions, quarrels, wrongs, reconcilement, war, and peace again [Terence] (p. 98). Toil and pleasure, so dissimilar in nature, are nevertheless united by a certain natural bond of union [Livy] (p. 119). All the greatest virtues must lie dormant where pleasure holds sway [Cicero] (p. 131). No pleasure's free from pain; in all our joys something of trouble ever comes between [Ovid] (p. 132). Immoderate indulgence must produce some terrible misfortune in the end [Terence] (p. 164). Look far and wide, how many flourishing cities luxuries overthrown. Not the anger of the gods, nor armed enemies are so to be dreaded as thou, O Pleasure, once thou hast crept into the hearts of men. [Silius Italicus] (p. 6) The love of money grows with growing wealth [Juvenal] (p. 20). Worthless indeed are wine and love, if with impunity the drunkard and the lover work their will [Plautus] (p. 165). In everything we do, all our keenest pleasure end in satiety [Cicero] (p. 199). There is no pleasure the constant enjoyment of which does not breed satiety [Pliny the Elder] (p. 199). Afflicted by lover's madness all are blind [Propertius] (p. 260). Make light of pleasure: pleasure bought with pain yields little profit, but much more of bane [Horace] (p. 273). 'Tis easier far to shun the snares of love than, being caught, to break through Venus' bonds, and from her nets escape [Lucretius] (p. 305). Yet what delight can rank and honour bestow, since every joy is balanced by its woe! [Juvenal] (p. 223) There abides in us a holy spirit, our guardian, who matches overall that comes to us of good and evil [Seneca] (p. 255).

Montaigne wrote. That is what an old Greek verse says, in this sense: The gods sell us all the good things they give us. That is to say, they give us none pure and perfect, none we do not pay at the price of some evil. Socrates says that some god tried to lump together and confuse pain and pleasure, but that, not being able to come out successfully, he decided to couple them, at least by the tail. Metrodorus used to say that in sadness there is some alloy of pleasure. (Montaigne 1965, p. 510) There is no evil without its compensation (p. 511). That is to say, there is no misfortune that cannot be compensated in the future.

The Qur'an (Koran) gives out the following verse: Then, shall ye be questioned that day about the joy ye indulged in (Qur'an 102.8). *The Arabian Nights' Entertainment* (*The Thousand and One Nights*) reads:

> A female has overthrown a thousand forts of steel and stone calling 'My own!' Her eyes are black decoys, her hairs are hunting nets for boys; but she names them joys. (Mathers 1953, p. 4)

Today we express the dilemma in this way: Many men would keep company with women, in the hope of having sex with them, not seeing any other reason and often disliking them. The sense of pleasures arising from sex, tobacco smoking, gambling, drinking alcohol and taking drugs are all different yet they all give temporary comfort. I made a brief acquaintance with a man who could not stop annoying and picking up people because of his intense pleasures which are hard to understand by the other people. He ended up in a mess of his own making. Nobody knows why the sufferings of corresponding intensities follow the pleasures, though we are certain of the correspondence.

Tobacco gives people pleasures but it has harmful effects. Many smokers, addicted to nicotine, want to quit smoking because of the sense of pleasure and relief followed by its consequent withdrawal symptoms, apart from money burned and a high probability of getting cancer.

How can we prove the proposition that we have to pay for all the pleasures, though my life experiences strongly approve it. The Bible says, 'Everyone who looks at a woman with lust has already committed adultery with her in his heart' (Matthew 5:27), though it does not say in what way he would be punished. Do we really pay for this thought? We are not sure because of its minor nature and a multitude of happenings in our life. We grant them their pleasure for a little while: in the end shall we drive them to a chastisement unrelenting (Qur'an 31.24). This verse derives from the careful observations of our daily life and many philosophers the world over noted this phenomenon since antiquity. I believe that these philosophers, true to the foregoing verses, avoided pleasures as much as humanly possible. However, I also believe they could not suppress one pleasure of sex. Sex has had universal attraction for all people, men and women, and especially men could not live without occasional orgasms with or without women. It is unrealistic to try to live without sex by mere philosophising about pleasure and consequent suffering. The literati must have carried on the sex life discreetly, opting not to talk about it. In the process of acquiring women, men have to go through so much strife with the women as well as with the other men eyeing for the same women.

Book 2 *Religion* details a concept that we can equate God with Truth and also another concept that God punishes or rewards us by the distance or closeness to God. Section 1, Chapter 2 Judaism-Christianity-Islam refers. When we are engaged in a pleasurable activity we are away from God (Truth). When we are under suffering we are close to God (Truth). Possibly pleasure and suffering are not the only means of alienating or approaching God (Truth); however, it seems that their repetitions make it the permanent stay. Thus we can see the truth more clearly if we are subjected to sufferings of long duration than if we are under pleasures of long duration.

The sages in a few places of the world at the early classical era lectured that any thinking and any conduct, however minute or large, have good or bad consequences of corresponding magnitude, as I explain in B Reward and Punishment for Thought and Conduct, Section 3, Chapter 7, Book One. Any conduct comes from the thought to do and is carried out by thinking and their focus was really on thinking. In the biblical tradition, God makes sure of the correspondence. In Buddhism the eternal and immutable laws look after the correspondence. The sages did not prove the above assertion but drew the conclusion from both the traditional culture and their own experience. The gravitational acceleration is unalterable truth applicable to any two masses, however small or large; however, Newton did not prove the law as to its cause when he proposed it. Do we have to prove the assertion concerning the pleasures and the consequent sufferings? When the pleasure is intense such as coming from drug taking or parenting, the above assertion seems obvious to us. Can we prove that every pleasure, however small or large, brings some suffering corresponding to its strength? Is it an immutable law which nobody can escape? Are we punished by every sexual thought and conduct?, though many people may not realise it. When a man and a woman fall in love, is the pleasure coming from it negated by suffering at the same time or occurring in the future as many people testify?

Confucius said, 'Women and small men are hard to live with'. Thus he effectively admitted that mastering his teachings did not make men impregnable from women and the unethical men.

The Bible teaches moderation in some pleasures. Moderate drinking, sex within the legal sanction and in fact moderate enjoyments of some kinds are permitted. For example, the Bible gives out the following passages:

> Wine is very life to human beings if taken in moderation. What is life to one who is without wine? It has been created to make people happy. (Sirach 31:27)

However, it places a strict prohibition on all pleasures on Sabbath because, it states, the Sabbath days belong to God and not to the followers. God did all the works creating the world for six days and rested on the seventh. He blessed the seventh day and made it holy. (Genesis 2:2-3) In another context the Bible says that men should not approach women under menstruation for sexual purpose. Under the biblical instructions, men are allowed to have sex with their wives only for six days a week provided the women are not having menstruation. (Leviticus 15:20-30; 18:19)

Is this the truth: Moderate sex, as for moderate physical exercise and moderate drinking, promotes health; if these are taken excessively, they go against health? How about the proposition that we all pay for all pleasures? Does the health in the foregoing statement refer only to the physical health? And do we still suffer mentally? It is well established that drinking alcohol can damage the kidneys and impair the judgements as at driving a car.

We know from our observations that the adults, male or female, have remorse from their wild sexual adventures in their youths.

We do not have to have recourse to religions to infer that pleasure and mental pains are two sides of the same coin: high ecstasy is followed by acute suffering; mild pleasure, by mild suffering, in the future of which we cannot be sure as to the time and the mode for most cases. The ecstasy and consequent sufferings of the heavy drug takers are obvious to us because we can see them clearly. We have to pay for pleasure of any kind; physical, mental or sexual. The currency we use to buy pleasure is the pains of some form. I believe that giving up women for average men would be equivalent to giving up the drug for average addicts. If successful, in both cases they feel happy with some sense of loss which diminishes as time goes by. However, as far as the sex drive is concerned, it does not diminish after a long period of abstention.

In fact the above observation is a part of larger scheme of life. We know from our experience that unhappiness follows happiness and happiness, unhappiness. When we feel happy, we are sowing the seeds of suffering. When we feel miserable, the happy moment is around the corner. Intense sexual pleasure is punished in some way or another, though we cannot ascertain easily in what manner the punishment is meted out among the myriads of good and bad happenings of the daily life. I am certain that this punishment is the reason behind the sexual prohibition especially outside marriage in the traditional ethics.

It is generally true that unhappy and degenerate individuals seek self-indulgences of all sorts. This observation is true even to the whole generation. When a nation is divided and at each other's throat, people naturally try to escape from the pains. Many people find consolation in pleasures. A small number of people cultivate and elevate them to higher level of wisdom: This has been the way the humans made advancements through the course of the history.

There are obvious defects with pleasure seeking. Pleasure seeking is inferior and less courageous than trying to solve the various problems of life, not only the philosophical difficulties of life but the irritations and conflicts of daily occurrence. The Buddha taught that if there is a problem, look into it intently instead of skirting it. Pleasures are deflections from the harsh reality of life. When people have problems, which is the usual state for the average people, they seek consolations in sex, drinking alcohol, gambling, eating good food and the like. In the long course, the habit of pleasure seeking hinders the habit of problem solving: pleasures only put aside the problems at hand. The various religions teach people to avoid pleasures so as to obtain the real insight into their life, one of whose results may be happiness.

Pleasure seeking is an avoidance and escape from the reality of life and gives only temporal relief while the pleasure is in force. It does not solve the various problems at all for any length of time. Anybody, men and women, unintelligent, morally inferior, uneducated, rich or poor, can engage in pleasures, whereas only the brave seek to solve the problem.

Sex and Sexism

In the course of evolution, human species, men and women, have developed brain power or cunningness as a survival means and dominated over the other living things. They developed the various survival techniques in turn using the thinking faculty as I mention in 'Introduction to Series', Book One *Idealism and Materialism*. In the similar logic, womenfolk have used sex as a surviving means within the human society. Women have been often abused that they were good only for one thing and nothing else. The abuse did not take into account the fact that men had not learned to live without women, hence in this sense women could abuse men that men were no better than women. Women got, traditionally, what they wanted--food, clothes, shelter, wealth, fame, honour and so on--indirectly through men. This was another reason why men have abused women. These abusive men have not understood that the strong sex drive of men was the other side of the coin that women were useless for anything else but for sex: Women have lived by the men's sexual urge, hence did not have to be good at anything else. Sex and sexism are in fact the other side of the same coin: men's strong sexual drive has generated the inferior mental and physical status of women.

People, men and women, under normal circumstances try to get most out of what they have. For example, people normally do their best to get the highest price for a commodity they want to dispose. Also people try to get the most out of the professional skills they have. Hence, we can hardly blame women for trying to get most out of their sexual worth. Men have been even more abusive towards women because of the females' small physiques. Women, about half of the human population, have been in constant fear of being raped because of men's sexual and physical strengths. The researches have shown that the reason for rape is not so much to try to solve the rapists' sexual urge but for the men who are unsuccessful in the society in many ways to try to dominate the physically weaker women.

Men in the past made a serious mistake by excluding women from the professional occupations. Men could live without women in the professional fields but could not live without women domestically because of the strong sexual desire. Hence the net result was that men had to financially support women who were untrained occupationally and kept in ignorance politically. This sorry situation is being rectified today in all economically advanced countries of the world. People have to realise that the position of women has been set through a long evolutional process and hence it takes a long time to correct the mistake.

Not giving the job opportunity to women and minority races means the rest of the community must pay for it in some way; disturbances in the community, unhappiness of these people, and the rest of the community must financially support these people. In most of the advanced countries of the world today, the equal opportunity is an important political plank to remedy this unfortunate situation.

It is well established that women voters do not necessarily support female candidates at an election. Women vote for a woman candidate only when they convincingly agree with her views. This phenomenon appears in many other fields, such as firm and family. In this sense women are not united and show strong tendency not to cooperate among them. They cooperate willingly when competent males lead them. This situation is considerably different for so-called minority races. The minority people tend to support their candidates willingly as if they support their friends, especially if the candidates are capable.

I have come to believe that the propositions that men are inherently superior to women and men are intrinsically stronger in sexual terms than women are without foundations. The relative position between men and women at present is only the outcome of the evolutionary process. When we train physically and mentally, it is assured that we develop our physiques and brains, which can be said to be the evolutionary process within our life span. Women, traditionally, relied solely on sexual attraction for survival. As a consequence women did not have to develop any other faculties except for their beauty and mannerism. The pretence that women did not enjoy sex suited both men and women. That affectation was natural since money flowed from men to women in some form or another in exchange for sexual favour, besides that false display inflamed men's sexual appetite. As sexual equality is stressed today and women develop their professional capabilities, women do not have to pretend any longer that they are receiving end of men's sexuality. Since the evolution takes time for its fruition we are talking centuries before the true equality between men and women, professionally and sexually, as for the different races, can be achieved.

The Buddha was married and had a son; however, he left the family in order to seek the relief from the unbearable mental agony. Socrates and Confucius were married and had children. It seems that no amount of learning decreases men's constant yearning for women.

Probably we can say that the wise men are no better than dogs and cats sexually. However as far as my understanding goes, the Buddha after enlightenment and Jesus Christ during his ministry did not have any sex life. The New Testament does not say if Christ is married or not; however, Dr Barbara Thiering, who is an expert on the Dead Sea Scrolls, concluded after research Christ was in fact married. A few other people reached the same conclusion, and one of them said that Christ addressed his son just before he died citing a sentence in the New Testament (John 19:26).

We all know that sexual desire is strong for men and even for women. We also know well that we must keep the desire in secret and curb the execution of the desire in many situations. The next section deals with this restraining aspect of the sexual desire.

Section 2 Sexual Restraints

The very denying or sublimating of sex reflects its importance (Lloyd 1964, p. 442).

The universe has not only a characteristic of order--good for humans--but also that of disorder--bad for humans. For example, the farmers desperately seek the sunshine and moderate rains at the right season, and the humans detest the storms anywhere in the world. Interestingly, the fish of every size very much enjoy the heavy rains and moderate storms, which supply nutrients to the coastal water for the small fish and at the same time their predators come close to the shore. Only when the storms are extremely severe under the specific environment, the fish seem to suffer from them. The two qualities of order and disorder are sometimes side by side on equal strength, sometimes one dominates the other, and sometimes one succeeds the other, but the two always exist in nature. This phenomenon in nature has corresponding influence on the human nature and society: after all people are parts of the universe. Both the universe and the humans are bipolar or dichotomous. People have been both builders and destroyers of civilisations. Peace and war have alternated the history of virtually every human society. The Book One of this series deals with idealism and materialism which are irreconcilable in their essence, though they are the two major ideological bases of the historical development. All the people have enemies and friends. Religions were born out of the interactions between the good and the evil: If everything in the world had been good people would not have felt a yearning for religions. Dialectic focuses on the two contradictions, which is to result in the exalted state.

If we turn our attention to the topic of this book, that is, sex, we can see the same trend. The desires for wealth and sex have guided men in their lower mode through the millenniums. In this sense also life is dichotomous since men normally have to sacrifice a large part of wealth to acquire women. Karl Marx said that only economics, that is, wealth acquisition, governed the human life and proceeded his argument on that premise. It was convenient for him and enabled him to proceed with his forceful dissections of economics. He did not even see that the men's sexual drive was such a strong inclination as to sacrifice a large part of wealth. Men normally spent more money in women and family than the amount of money Marx claimed that the employers exploited from them. This reasoning alone almost nullifies his whole argument on economics, though he also investigated into and revealed his opinions on politics in conjunction with economics.

Sex, which is a part of life, is also dichotomous in many other ways. Men desperately want good-looking women yet men try to curb the sexual desire under certain circumstances. Sigmund Freud put up the theory that disgust, shame and morality coming from heredity rather than education causes this repression. Sex has the universal appeal for men but it is not that men spend all the money and all the spare time on sex. They seek other low pleasures of life, such as drinking and gambling. Sometimes the two feelings on sex alternate: the desire dominates at one time and the restraint predominates at another time. Once a man has the desired woman, he normally loses an interest in her in no time and looks for another. Also men feel strong sexual desire towards women yet the former feel strong aversions to the nature of the latter. The opposite sexes sometimes pull together and sometimes push away. The opposites here are not so much contraries but the continuum of changes. Each sex has the strong attraction as well as the strong revulsion on the other sex. Just after intense sexual orgasm, men often feel aversion to the female body which has served them sexually. I remember clearly that even when the strongest sexual drive gripped my mind something in my heart told me what I was about to do was not right. Sex is a dichotomy in another sense. Since the average-looking young women can have sex at any time they want to, they can be choosy. However, the final say if they have sex or not depends on men having erection.

These phenomena are the reflection of the universe on the human life and the human sexual behaviours. Many people do not even know which of the two trends, the desire or the restraining feeling, is the good guy in the dichotomy of sex.

We may be able to explain the above dichotomy of sex psychologically. Freud made the following psychoanalytic theories in *The Ego and the Id* (1923). According to it, our thinking has three phases or conceptualised framework of mind:

- ego; our ordinary conscious self
- superego; conscience
- id or it; biological and instinctual drives of libido

The ego works on the reality principle and develops at an early stage of childhood and keeps the id from taking its own course.

Superego tries to curb and battle against id or it, one of whose manifestations is sex drive (Guntrip 1964, p. 14). It works as a mediator between the id and the ego by providing moral support (conscience).

Id motivates the mind in lustful drives, crude appetites, love and hate. Id is present at birth and works on the pleasure principle: human beings, especially if they are untrained religiously, naturally want pleasure and avoid pains. (Spielvogel 1991, p. 874)

The above three phases of human mind have a semblance to the Plato's postulate though he theorised from the different origins and purposes. According to him we can divide the human soul into three parts:

- the rational part or intellect
- the spirited part or will
- appetite and desire

The underlying tone of Jean Jacques Rousseau and Adam Smith is naturalism in everyday life of the former and in the field of economics of the latter. However, men have to suppress their innate sexual desires to certain objects such as their daughter or the wives of other men. We can make the similar statement about the desire for wealth. I am sure that the above two thinkers would agree that the desires for sex and wealth must be curbed under certain circumstances, otherwise universal chaos would result annulling even their favourite theories.

The age-old virtue that a man should be satisfied with his wife is hard to reconcile with the man's strong sexual urge. Perhaps this moral teaching came about for the social stability and happiness of the family members. We know that men do not act as their sexual drive dictates under normal circumstances. That does not mean the wild desires do not exist but rather, the various restraining powers are at work, preventing the full execution of the impulse. Internally, morals restrain men. The authorities such as parents and teachers taught men while they were at school age that sex in its extreme expressions is wrong. These teachings, in due course, become their conscience and try to behave themselves sexually appropriate and curb their tongue. Externally, men are constrained by the punitive measures of the society, such as social pressure, fighting and the legal sanctions.

Saint Augustine narrated that he had a serious sexual problem but he overcame the problem more or less suddenly by the divine intervention. He acquired a concubine when he was 17 and remained faithful to her for the next 15 years, and had by her a son whom he reared and cherished. (Lloyd 1964, p. 447) In love with his sweetheart, he was scourged with jealousy, suspicions, fears, angers and quarrels (St Augustine 1907, p. 32). He wrote after enlightenment that he still felt the temptation of the lust of flesh, though he did not keep any concubines (p. 236). He further wrote that he had to daily strive against the desires for eating and drinking, though he was not tempted by alcohol; he was still assailed by the tongue of men (pp. 172, 233, 242).

The yogin's effort for concentration and control of mind can be applied to any matter they direct their mind to. Many of them try to suppress the base desires, especially the hunger drive and the sex drive.

Men, under certain conditions such as war, sexual fantasy or absolute authority, tend to carry out what they desire sexually in their deepest thoughts. Many act according to the sexual desires and the restraining forces cease to operate partially or totally: The external constraints simply do not exist in these circumstances and men discard the conscience for the enjoyments.

The sexual laws of this book are mainly derived from my sexual experiences in their widest sense and the resultant analyses. Readers will find after reading this book that the moral laws of our society are in considerable variance with the sexual laws of this book. I merely state the results of my analyses as they come out: I do not encourage or discourage readers to adhere to the proposed law. I do not try to impose any moral judgement or any preconceived ideas on the conclusions: I do not say one conclusion is ethically right or wrong. Many readers would say that the two laws are completely different on many points. The former is recommended or accepted codes of sexual conducts, while the latter exposes what are the sexual thoughts of men and may make some people repugnant. This is the familiar contrast of 'ought to' and 'is'.

The ethics on sex is the normative statements that people ought to follow. Whereas the sexual laws being formulated here are positive statements that people tend to behave if unhampered, and are based on the principles of large numbers. An individual chooses which set of rules he should follow every time he has an opportunity to express his sexual arousal. The economic books often quote normative and positive statements. The moral laws may be the targets the moral teachers set for the general public: that does not necessarily mean these teachers behave sexually as they teach. The constraints in some way or another must be enforced in the sexual matters otherwise the society will experience universal chaos.

The moral laws in respect to sex are part of the overt culture. They are taught at school and discussed in the open. The sexual laws are part of the covert culture. People practise them in the hiding and do not often admit it. Decent people and literati maintain veneer of silence on the topic; however, silence does not solve the problems of sexual nature. It is better to discuss the problems openly. This book is an attempt to close the gap between the overt and covert cultures in the sexual matter.

We know from our experiences that men always desire beautiful women, whether the men in focus as well as the desired women are married or not. However, according to the socially accepted code of conducts, married men should want only their wives and should not approach any other women for sexual purpose. Single men are allowed to court only single women of their own age group and no other. Consequently men try to direct the sexual drive to a socially acceptable target at least publicly, though they want to go to bed with every good-looking woman even if she is married and outside their age group. A young man, for example, should understand that if he says he wants to make love with his friend's wife, he will often get into strife. Hence he learns to keep his mouth shut and also his desire secret. The breaker of the moral laws in regard to sex is in fact true to his innate feeling. However, if he follows his intrinsic urge, he may experience from mild social pressure to outright condemnation, depending on the perceived nature of his conduct which in turn greatly depends on who he is. He may alter his conducts or carry out his intentions under certain circumstances.

The average men are capable of pushing the sexual desire as well as the desires for food and drinks out of their mind while attending the matters important for them. If they cannot, they are not normal almost by definition and consequently not treated in this book.

Some men are interested in honour, fame and power the perceptions of which are abstract rather than concrete, though they may be displayed concretely as on paper or as their profession. Many men are devoted to obtaining the various material objects or money which have, as they perceive, solid basis. Whatever the men's main social interest may be, men cannot give up one infatuation of sex, which men can obtain through the various mediums above mentioned.

The ancient to classical Greeks in general are regarded to be ethically high, though they followed their own inclinations in the sexual matters. In fact their moral standard is said to be as high as or even higher than the modern civilised people except for sexual matters. It is interesting to note that in spite of the above assessment of general agreement the theme of *Odyssey* by Homer, whom all the ancient to classical Greeks looked as their cultural originator, was marital fidelity. Socrates freely admitted that the sexual attraction of young men fascinated him, though he was married and had three sons. People in the ancient to classical Athens, especially among the leisure class, love between males was regarded perfectly natural and was an unembarassing topic of conversation either for serious or jesting purpose. (Guthrie 1969, p. 393)

It seems that the ancient Spartans reached sexual indifference as the product of their social system (Toynbee 1962, p. 184). Some Greek states encouraged love between males; others like the Ionians forbid it under Oriental influence; for Oriental rulers were tyrants who regarded strong personal attachment as a threat to their power, like intellectual and athletic achievements (Guthrie 1975, p. 369).

When we look at sexual culture of Western civilisation, the Westerners adopted Judaic tradition and discarded Hellenic practice. The position of the Bible is clear about illicit sex: it condemns utterly, saying that the due punishment for carrying out the illicit sex is death. For example, it says, 'Whoever lies with an animal shall be put to death' (Exodus 22:19). Hence, people in the modern West esteem illicit sex, such as homosexuality, incest, bestiality and adultery as evil. In the Hellenic world the foregoing sexual practices were freely carried out. As a matter of fact, the ancient to classical Greeks did not have any guilt feeling about what we regard as sexual abnormalities. The modern Westerners regard sex within marriage is quite acceptable, which may not come from the Christian tradition but any way is in accord with the biblical teaching. Many highly religious people, be they Buddhist or Christian, want to live without sex altogether.

Holy Scripture (e.g., Matthew 5:27) repeatedly mentions that a man will be punished if he looks at a woman with sexual desire, though it does not say what sort of punishment will be meted out on the offender. The offence of this nature does not cause any social disruptions but rather it is a sin committed against the words of God. Masturbation and sexual fantasy may belong to this category of trespass. We may have to pay for the offences of this nature simply because they are pleasures. I expounded a theory in Section 1 that we are punished for any pleasure under the heading of 'Sex and Pleasures'. Majority of men and also many women habitually look at the opposite sex with secret longing, but they do not know in what way they are punished though most of them feel certain they are paying the price in some way. Some Christians would argue strongly that they have to avoid sins of any kind whether they receive punishment or not and in the same logic they have to carry out what God tells them whether they receive reward or not.

Interestingly there is some evidence in the book *The Imitation of Christ* that the author, a most devout Christian, masturbated regularly. He made frequent references that he suffered from carnal desire. While I pray, a multitude of carnal fancies occur to me! (Thomas a Kempis 1980, p. 234) If I love the flesh, I shall fancy oftentimes those things that are pleasing to the flesh (p. 236). For I feel in my flesh the law of sin contradictory to the law of my mind and leading me captive to the obeying of sensuality in many things; neither can I resist the passion thereof, unless thy most grace, fervently infused into my heart, assist me (p. 256). But with the flesh I serve the law of sin, while I obey sensuality rather than reason (p. 257). Though he was faithful in many respects to Holy Writ, he failed in the matter of sex. It seems that the author had to justify himself in a manner of mortal humans who had a bad habit they could not get out from.

I wonder if any human beings, men or women, can be free from the sin of looking at the opposite sex with sexual wish. The sexual laws do not say that men should not look at women with lust, which is the domain of the moral laws. The sexual laws state that majority of men look at beautiful women with craving. The proposition in Section 13 to follow further states, without moral judgement, men should get high degree of satisfaction when they masturbate.

Montaigne wrote in his *Essays* (begun in 1571) that popes died in bed between the thighs of the females (Montaigne 1965, p. 59). This reference suggests that some popes must have made love frequently in spite of celibate vow. Montaigne himself seems to have had sex parties at times, though only the careful readers can make this inference from his works. His admission on both accounts is extraordinary if we learn that he was a Catholic and the religious wars were raging when he was writing the book. Without a doubt he was an honest man in that he did not intentionally mislead readers, though I have some reservations about his philosophical statements. He was accepted as a forthright writer by the contemporary society; hence the people did not attack him in spite of the foregoing extraordinary revelations. I have found by reading many versions of his *Essays* that the above references--and also some references not related to sex I quote in this series of books--are deleted in some versions, being too touchy to some people.

According to the Old Testament, King David slept with a beautiful married woman and later got her husband killed in a battle in order to hide what happened from the public scrutiny (2 Samuel 11:2-27). The king had many wives and concubines available to him as the customs of the day allowed. In spite of the crime of a serious nature, he has been regarded as the greatest king ever governed the Jewish people by both the Jews and the Christians. Another sin by King David concerning the census (2 Samuel 24:1-17) is hard for us to understand: Why taking the census in his kingdom was against God. In point of fact the later book of the Bible (1 Kings 15:5) removed the reference. Keeping a harem by kings is actually against the biblical teaching. The Bible makes clear that the kings of the chosen people should not amass women, silver and gold (Deuteronomy 17:17). King David and King Solomon acquired a large number of women and great wealth: particularly splendour of Solomon based on the fabulous riches is legendary.

King Solomon preferred not to use military force to establish peace on Israel's borders; rather he relied on clever diplomacy to safeguard the state. One thing he did was to marry or take mistresses from the ruling class of the neighbouring states. That is why he had so many wives and concubines of the foreign origins as the Bible narrates (1 Kings 11:1-3). He imposed forced labour and heavy taxes to complete the extensive building programmes. After his death, during the reign of his son Rehoboam, the people in the realm revolted against the harsh treatments and the United Kingdom was spilt into northern Israel and southern Judah.

I remember seeing a painting which depicted Socrates, one of the four sages of the world, playing naked with his wife at home. Nobody today would be able to ascertain whether the degrading painting was based on fact or not. What happens to all his fine sayings which inspired millions of people through the centuries if he had acted as shown in the picture? I simply do not know the answer.

Buddhism teaches that all perceptions through the senses are unsubstantial; hence naturally it leads to the teaching that people should not be entangled in the five senses. Accordingly, people should avoid making love, eating good food, drinking alcohol, making pictures and sculptures, listening to music, using perfumes, wearing fine clothes and living in fashionable houses.

Resolve

Readers must keep in mind that I am not married. Married men may not be able to practise sexual restraint because their wives may passionately object to it.

When I started studying Buddhism at my youth, I came upon the following twin verses from *The Dhammapada* which was popular among a large number of people, laymen as well as monks. This book was written in Pali hence belongs to Theravada tradition; however, both Theravada and Mahayana Buddhists shared this canon. In Sri Lanka, every monk is said to recite all the stanzas from memory. The setup of the twin verses in *The Dhammapada* is similar to Proverbs of the Old Testament in that the sayings are usually two lines in parallel thoughts.

> Not even with a rain of golden coins is contentment found among sensual pleasures.
> Sensual pleasures are of little delight, are a misery. (Carter & Palihawadana 1987, p. 45)
> In so far as the underbush is not cut away, even to the smallest bit, of a man of a woman,
> in so far as is he one having [his] mind tethered, like a suckling calf to its mother (p. 60).

I had been very much intoxicated with the book and these verses impressed me so much that I immediately resolved to stop all sexual activities. A few hours later, however, I went out to the street and as soon as a pretty girl came into my sight, my determination disappeared like a burst bubble. Readers may well think this episode comical, seeing my initial seriousness and subsequent easiness in the change of the determination.

I tried to abstain from sex for many years, on many occasions without much success. Every time I read into religious books extolling the virtue of no sex, I was determined to give up sex but I was defeated every time and resumed the sexual indulgence. At that time I even had the knowledge that the sexual abstinence did not do any harm to my body from medical point of view. At times I felt my determination was curtailing the frequency of masturbation and the number of visits to the brothels where the prostitution was available. At other times I felt it did not make any difference. On one occasion I had a wet dream three nights in a row to abandon the restraining effort. It occurred to me, very so often, that if the resolution to forgo the sexual orgasm had not diminished the amount of the semen discharged from my urethra, I would have wasted so much effort which should have been directed to more useful purposes. Apparently the foregoing assessment is emotional. On cold reflection, the restraining must have decreased the volume of semen emitted to some extent, though lewdness did not decrease at all. I am sure that if the amount of semen ejaculated at masturbation, wet dreams and sexual intercourses had been collected and measured, it would have been less under the suppressed condition than the free conditions such as unrestrained or married.

I believe myself well disciplined. I have never indulged in smoking cigarettes or using any kind of drugs. Gambling and drinking habits are quite moderate and I feel I can stop either of them any time. I do not have any difficulty in controlling my weight. I had been addicted to caffeine contained in tea and coffee for several years. First I tried to limit the amount of tea or coffee intake, and failing that, I completely stopped drinking tea and coffee. Since then, the smell of tea and coffee stirred my desire but I easily refrained from drinking a cup, and I grew out of the addiction. I now occasionally drink tea or coffee as people normally do.

Encouraged by the above success, I went on suppression adventure on sex when I was 42 years of age. I made a determination not to have sex thinking I would be a better person if I had lived without sexual pleasure. When I had a wet dream at night I clearly felt the semen spurting strongly out of my abdomen, which resulted from the large amount of semen stored in my body. Sexual desire towards women was as strong as before, if not stronger. The problem with this approach was that the abstention was not natural and relied on shear willpower. I was still committing sins by looking at good-looking girls with desire, though I did not engage in any physical act of sexual orientation. According to the religious dogmas, Buddhist and Christian, from which I acquired the idea to suppress sex, people are judged and destined by their mental activity. If I applied this teaching to the state I was in during the forbearance, I was no better than in free indulgence. Thinking along this line, I stopped abstaining after seven months, during which period I had several wet dreams. The number of wet dreams I had during the abstention is incomparably less than the number of sex I would have had under non-inhibition, and also the same thing can be said about the volumes of semen discharged though an individual orgasm under the restraint would have discharge a lot more. I had hoped before embarking on the abstention exercise that I might forget the sense of sexual pleasure after sometime. The fact that the desire stayed with me all along explains that the sexual urge comes from within me rather than from without as such addictions as gambling, drinking or drug taking are. If I had been fighting the addictions coming from outside me, refraining the habits for seven months would have produced some results and possibly cured me.

It is interesting to note the following observation. Though I could not stop having sex, the willpower developed in the process seems to work in controlling any other activities, good or bad, such as learning, drinking, gambling and weight control. I don't have any problem in controlling these activities.

I have come to believe that people approach the problem of overweight in the wrong ways. They should develop their willpower to restrain overeating after acquiring basic dietary knowledge. They can use the willpower thus developed for any other purposes.

Hamlet in the play by Shakespeare advised his mother not to sleep with his step-father and further told her that the separation would become easier as the day goes by. Hamlet talks to his mother, Gertrude, Queen of Denmark, when they are left alone:

> Refrain tonight,
> And that shall lend a kind of easiness
> To the next abstinence, [the next more easy,
> For use almost can change the stamp of nature,
> And either master the devil, or throw him out,
> With wondrous potency.]
>
> (Shakespeare 1985, 3.4; pp. 166-71)

I have found that was not the case with me: abstaining from sex a long period did not diminish my sexual urge at all.

I can imagine an isolated small community where there are no gambling, nor drinking, nor drug taking; however, I cannot think of any society, however isolated and small it may be, where there are no illicit sexual activities such as adultery, incest, bestiality and homosexuality.

At one time I thought I contracted venereal disease from a prostitute. The thought of having VD so horrified me that I swore to myself I would never approach a prostitute. It turned out to be a false alarm. After a while my sexual drive overturned my sacred oath.

With all my tried discipline on many other matters and with all my determinations over many years, I could not stop having sex. There must be something peculiar in sex and this alone is a good reason to delve into the natures of sex.

Appendicectomy

As far as I can recall, I had mild sexual desire up to the time I lied on the operating table to have my affected appendix removed. Once on the operating table there was no time to think about but the operation and the anticipated pains. Though I had been diagnosed as having appendicitis 10 days earlier, the operation had been delayed such that I could sit for the university examinations in Tokyo. After the surgery which was unbelievably painful because of locally administered anaesthesia, I was to remain in the hospital bed for 10 days.

The sexual interest was totally absent from my mind for several days after the operation. At about the time I started looking at the young nurses with some affection I was discharged. This experience shows that sexual urge comes from a healthy body, and when we are sick, the surplus energy in the body is directed to combating the physical illness, not to sexual thought or act. There was no will to suppress sex on my part. This observation clearly indicates to me that the proposition that sex is energy is correct.

Ill-treatment

Just after graduating from the university in Adelaide, I, together with two of my friends, paid a visit to the nearby brothel. A young and pretty girl answered the door. I was a bit frightened but my companions urged me in. I went in while they sat in the waiting room. She had a most beautiful body matching her facial beauty. She with her graceful manner did all she could to make me comfortable and happy. After thoroughly enjoying her and leaving her room, I told to my friends in the waiting room what she was like. Then one of them wanted the same girl and went in borrowing some money from me. As we were leaving the house, he commented that she was a really nice girl, adding further that it was better than making love to his girlfriend. That was my first lovemaking session in five years, during which time I had been studying.

A few weeks later I went back to the same brothel and went inside alone, with another friend of mine waiting outside in his car, expecting nothing but to have a wonderful time. A woman who showed up at the door told me the nominated girl did not work there anymore. Expressing disappointment, I wanted her nevertheless and was led into the same room. The way she treated me in bed horrified me. She behaved exactly as the Bible describes how the ways of the harlots are, though I had an opinion that many prostitutes were more respectable than many politicians. I did not realise at the time that she felt she was insulted because I made her my second choice and possibly she had observed what had happened in my previous visit, and she was really angry with me. Anyway she allowed me to have an ejaculation and I left the premise disgusted, telling her I would never come back. After this incident I lost all interest in sexual matters, feeling no sexual urge--none whatsoever. This shows how shocking my experience was with my high hope of enjoyment dashed by the ill-treatment of the prostitute. I thought that the sexual apathy would last the rest of my life; however, several weeks later the sex drive returned to me. This incident indicates that it is possible to suppress sex by mental training, though a great deal of learning may be required before anybody can formulate the training methods.

Vasectomy and Castration

Readers must keep in mind in reading the following observations that I am a confirmed bachelor in order to terminate my issue.

The sexual crave and consequent shameful practice distressed me so much in my youth that I thought of the surgical means of removing my constant longing for women, failing to suppress the urge by willpower. I searched for the right kind of operation to achieve the purpose.

Vasectomy makes men sterile. The operation is simple and the doctor blocks, choosing one most suitable out of the few methods, the vas deferens which is the passage duct for sperm from the epididymis to the urethra. The epididymis is a tube situated along the posterior margin of each testis. After the operation sperm does not show up in the ejaculate. Sperm and male hormones are still produced hence vasectomy should not alter the sexual drive appreciably and should not decrease 'maleness' of the operated. It is popularly believed that the surgery does not diminish the level of sexual pleasure. The operated men can carry on the sex life virtually intact and most say that there is no change in their sexual satisfaction. It is not clear that the pleasure at orgasm is a few per cent less corresponding to the blocked sperm. Spermatozoa make up only a few per cent of the ejaculated semen. They do not notice the ejaculate is less after the operation unless they carefully measure repeatedly over many ejaculations: a few percentage decrease of the ejaculate can be hardly noted in addition to variations of amounts of semen discharged. Some men even reported that after the vasectomy operation their sexual potency improved (Wright 1977, p. 19). Sperm are still created in the testes and stored in the epididymis; however, since the vas deferens is blocked the sperm is dissolved and reabsorbed into the body: the ongoing process that takes place within the body with other dead and unused cells (Westheimer 1994, p. 275).

After vasectomy, testosterone levels in the blood go up, since testosterone secretions are absorbed back into the body instead of being ejaculated. This may explain the initial increase of the sex drive after the operation. However, about 10 years after the operation, testosterone levels decrease, which may result in the decrease of the sex drive. (Brewer 1997, p. 19) Some men reported that many years after the vasectomy operation they felt depressed, helpless and impotent: the doctors claimed that was because the operation reduced the testosterone production over the years. This result may be expected because the operation interfered into natural arrangement developed over the millenniums. Vasectomy is suitable for the men who do not want their partners pregnant for whatever reasons. This surgery obviously did not suit my purpose; hence I turned my attention to castration.

I thought of rather drastic way of solving the problem by having both of my testicles surgically removed. I was sure that absence of my balls would eliminate considerably my longing for the opposite sex, if not altogether. I would not be obsessed with sex and would live happily ever after, being in harmony with the religious teachings. Jesus Christ taught that if our body part makes us sin, it is better to cut it off (Matthew 18:8-9). My testes made me sin, hence I was prepared to cut them off. However, one crucial drawback came to my attention. The testes secret not only sperm but also a high level of male hormones, androgens, as well as a low level of female hormones. Male testes are homologue of female ovaries which produce eggs and a high level of female hormones, oestrogens, as well as a low level of male hormones. These sex hormones are responsible respectively for the secondary sexual characteristics of men and women. For men as well as for women, the libido or sex drive is largely due to testosterone, one of the androgens. Testosterone is also responsible for the secretion of spermatozoa.

Normally a person has one of the two hormones predominant. From unknown reasons my testes have secreted excessive amounts of both male and female hormones. I have come to the above conclusion from my unusually strong sex drive and my feminine body structure.

The normal male has 44 autosomes plus one X-chromosome and one Y-chromosome, which we can express as (44 + xy). My feminine body structure may be due to my abnormal genetic combinations. The normal female has 44 autosomes plus two X-chromosomes, which we can express as (44 + xx). The genetic abnormalities are possible. In my case I suspect that I may have one extra female chromosome, which we can express as (44 + xxy). A boy with one extra X-chromosome is said to have Klinefelter's syndrome; however, I have no other medical conditions characterising the syndrome. My testicles enlarged at puberty. I have unusually strong sex desire which must come from a large amount of testosterone produced. A boy with Klinefelter's disorder should give below normal testosterone secretion. One's genetic make-up determines one's hormonal state and one's body reaction to the hormones.

Without testes, the sex problem might have been solved, but my masculinity would have decreased drastically due to the absence of androgens. Since the androgen level is lowered, the production of female hormones may decrease. However, I concluded that the loss of maleness may be more pronounced than the loss of femaleness. Any loss of my virility was utterly unacceptable to me hence I decided not to go ahead with castration.

My assessment at the time that I would be without sex desire and without sexual function after castration was in fact wrong. Castration results in marked increase in the secretion of both LH and FSH from the anterior pituitary. Inhibin from sertolic cells and testosterone from interstitial cells, both of the organs are located in the testes, work as inhibitions. The castration removes these inhibitions. (Arthur, Sherman & Luciano 1986, p. 562) After castration with the penis retained some men will retain normal sex drive for decades to come. They can carry on sexual intercourse with ejaculation of some sort. Some men report that their desire and capacity rapidly wane. A third group claim that they have a sex drive but are unable to satisfy it. (Smith 1968, p. 77)

Testosterone controls the function of the reproductive organs and glands; hence the removal of the testes impedes the proper function of these organs and glands. The glands will reduce the rate of secretion, and erection and ejaculation may become deficient. (Arthur, Sherman & Luciano 1986, p. 564)

Sex and Dualism

Without doubt sex is dualistic: sex needs mind and body for its satisfactory function. We also know we have to have healthy mind and healthy body for the full enjoyment of life. Cleobulus wrote: Safeguard the health of both body and soul (Harbottle 1897, p. 377). Malfunction of either our mind or our body makes our life miserable. It is often said with a good reason that a healthy mind dwells in a healthy body.

Both idealism and materialism in their extreme forms exclude the other ideology and insist that one is primary and the other secondary. Seeing the duality of sexual performance and enjoyment of life, monism may not be correct after all to explain life or the world. There is no doubt that idealism is important for humans and so is materialism, though the two ideologies may be in their essence mutually exclusive. Judging from dualism of sex and health, though some people may say our body is not matter as referred to in materialism, it is logical to say that only when mind (idealism) and matter (materialism) function satisfactorily do we get the full benefit of life. Book One *Idealism and Materialism* places an equal emphasis on the two ideologies.

Section 3 Three Conversations about Women and Sex

I have had numerous chats about women and sex in my life and I believe the following exchanges give the good insight into the natures of the subjects, though the topics of the conversations are restricted in scopes. They are all really a series of questions and answers; I was the one who started the questions being anxious to know about the matter.

A Conversation on Cohabitation

I had the following chat in the foyer of the YMCA, Adelaide, with a stranger, a man of late twenties. I was a student at the time. The chat started rolling because I was curious about what the girls wanted to get out from living with the boys without marital bond. It was obvious to me that the boys wanted nothing else but sex from cohabitation.

He said, 'It depends on the girl. Some girls want money, some friendship and some sex. I lived with so many girls over the years but none of them had any money. I had to give them financial help in some form or another'.

I asked how the girls behaved sexually.

He answered in the following manner. 'Once we live together, the girls want sex as much as we do. They often ask for sex intercourse.'

I said, 'When you live with a girl, don't you always think what she is doing, whether she is at work or at home?'

He said he always did.

I asked if he had any interest in girls other than the cohabiting girl.

'I was always on a lookout for a good-looking chick. I always ogled girls; ogle means eye or eye up. As soon as I found one, I told the cohabiting girl to leave. She did not have any choice but to pack up and go. If she, on her part, found a better place to go, she left. She was just as cunning as I was.'

To my question if the girls knew what we really want from them if we try to take them out on the pretext of watching movies or dining out or whatever, he gave me a definite yes answer. To my question that when he dated with a girl he always had a thought of having sex with her, he answered positively. To the further query if the young women knew there was monetary value attached to their bodies, he gave me another convincing affirmative reply. To my question of how they got to know all these, he said that they learned from their experiences in life up to that time.

Encouraged by the smooth running of the conversation, I wanted to know even more intimate things.

I said, 'Beautiful women don't look like they fart and defecate. Don't they fart?'

He said, 'Of course they all do. When it comes up, they push it back if somebody is around and let it go if nobody is in sight, hoping no one would know about it; they often go into the toilet for that purpose. That's the way they all do. Sometimes we catch them in the act'.

I made a similar question, 'Don't they defecate?'

He replied similarly, 'Of course they all do. One girl used to pretend to go out in order to go to toilet. Another girl used to have a shower after every defecation'.

I said, 'How do their farting and defecating smell? Do they smell any better than ours?'

He said, 'They smell as bad as anybody else's'.

I said, 'When they fart and defecate, you sometimes can hear and sometimes can smell; don't you lose an interest in them?'

He said, 'It puts us off for sure but we still have sexual desire. The desire pushes away that and everything else. Let's keep away from them for a while after their excretion'.

Conversation about Girlfriends

On a fine day in the government ammunition factory where I worked, the following conversation took place. I spoke with a young tradesman, whom I knew only by sight, on the concrete floor outside his workshop. There was nobody else around.

After the exchange of the greetings he told me he had gone out with his girlfriend on the previous weekend.

I said, rather hesitantly not knowing if I could get through, 'Doesn't she make you wait?'

'They all do. Unless I wait I don't get what I want', he replied. This exchange established the rapport between the two and set the pattern of the interchange.

I further asked if his girlfriend was pretty.

He said, 'Not really' with a grimace on his face.

I followed up the last question, 'If you get to know a pretty girl, will you take her out rather than your present girlfriend?'

He said emphatically, 'Of course I would. We all want good-looking chicks. We cannot get better ones and that's the reason we have to stick with our girlfriends. Even married men, if they get better ones, they all will change over'.

'When you are with your girlfriend, don't you get at times annoyed with her and feel like grabbing and shaking her?' said I.

He replied, 'We all feel that way often but we are not allowed to do that. Besides, if I do she may leave me and I don't get what I want'.

Conversation about Daughter

I had the following conversation with a middle-aged tradesman in the munition factory, as we walked towards the workshop to have a look at the component of our mutual interest.

We were talking about his family and he said he had a teenage daughter.

I said, 'Is she pretty?'

He replied she was.

I asked if he felt sexual desire towards her, learning that she was young and good-looking.

'We all do', he said casually.

I said, 'Does your wife know about it?'

He replied in the affirmative.

I further said, 'So your wife makes sure you and your daughter are not left alone at home. When she goes out, she takes you or your daughter with her'.

He said, 'She always does that'.

Section 4 Sexual Orientations or Preferences

Everyone has one's own sexuality. One's true sexuality or sexual orientation is hard to establish even for one's satisfaction, let alone by somebody else. One may have to look for the sexuality which probably would vary as one goes through the different partners. (Taylor 1996, p. 14)

The above paragraph is the poetic expression in regard to a small number of people. Everyone is born with a gender, that is, as a male or a female. I do not treat the genetic abnormalities in this book. Gender identity, that is, the sense of maleness or femaleness, is set early in a person's life, probably by the age of four. The sexual orientation of a person is set during childhood and not to change throughout life time under normal circumstances. (Westheimer 1994, p. 53)

Only the penile-vaginal intercourse between fertile individuals can be the reproductive sex; however, there are many other forms of sexual practices. There are solitary behaviours and socio-sexual behaviours. They refer only to the number of persons involved in the sexual activities, that is, one person for the former and the multiple persons for the latter. Masturbation can be effected solitary or socio-sexual. Heterosexuality and homosexuality refer normally to socio-sexual behaviour but can be effected in the solitary behaviour. Fantasy and sexual stimulation can be practised not only in a solitary activity but in a socio-sexual relation. Possibly the uncertainty of the sexual desire in the process of sexual maturing for boys leads to the establishment of sexual preference when the uncertainty meets the requirement of pleasure maximisation at orgasm. Men, if normal, have constant sexual urge after puberty. Majority of men would want to make love to young and good-looking women in an attempt to calm the desire and to derive maximum pleasure in the process. They are heterosexuals and considered to be normal. Women behave similarly towards men with less vigour.

Heterosexual men have some cause to feel they are normal, since their sexual conducts are in accord with what nature originally intended for sex, and culture supports their view. Some men have sexual affinity for immature girls and some for old women. These men are still considered to be deviates though their sexual objects are the opposite sex. Some men fancy men, animals or inanimate objects as their sexual targets. These men are thought to be perverted in their choice. The deviates or perverts are no different from the heterosexuals as far as their desire to derive maximum pleasure from sex is concerned but their choice of object is different. Their sexual organs function in the same way as for the heterosexuals. Some of these deviants acquire the habit by born preferences and some through circumstances. Some homosexuals want to penetrate into the partners with their penis and are thus popularly called givers: some want penile penetration into their rectum and are called receivers. The act of the giver is sometimes called insertive, and that of the receiver, receptive. Some gay men specialise in the former and some in the latter, and some practise both.

Interestingly the recent observations have revealed that a significant number of non-human animals are unmistakably homosexuals. Homosexual activities for both males and females are commonplace among mammals, birds, reptiles, amphibians and fishes. (Taylor 1996, p. 79)

Statistically speaking, roughly one in 20 persons in any society is attracted primarily to members of his or her own sex. This set figure indicates to us that there is something more than arbitrary choice in homosexuality. In fact a recent research in the United States advocates that the homosexuals are born with the gay genes in a particular area of the brain, but this theory does not explain all cases of homosexuality (Westheimer 1994, p. 139). It is well known that homosexuality was a common practice in the ancient to classical Greece and

Rome, which the non-existence of sexual inhibition supported. Consequently the population in these states who practised homosexuality must have been much higher than five per cent quoted above.

In the ancient to classical Greek world, male homosexual love was as common as heterosexual love and was even encouraged particularly among students and soldiers. Young men were encouraged to submit to the advances of the old men, and the bonds and communications were thought to be the integral part of the education. The bonds of love between the soldiers were thought to guarantee the solidarity and bravery in combat. (Mercer 1996, p. 91) It seems that lesbianism was not encouraged nor as common as the male homosexuality in the ancient to classical Greek world. Also in today's prison, armed services and monastery, there is no doubt that the high percentage of people, males and females, practise homosexuality. These facts suggest that the gene theory accounts for only some homosexuals.

Dr AC Kinsey found that slightly over one-third of all men experienced a homosexual encounter in their life, and slightly under one-third of all women did (*Encyclopedia of Love & Sex* 1972, p. 124).

It is interesting to note the following observations. The homosexuals do not necessarily fantasy homosexual activity when masturbating, and their content of erotic dreams are not necessarily homosexual plays (p. 153). Though the heterosexual men masturbate invariably thinking about beautiful women, the contents of their erotic dreams are not necessarily pretty girls and are even men at times. Although the sexual desire is often aroused in the night dreams as for the waking times, the objects of the dreams are unsubstantial and removed from the realities. For more details of this aspect, refer to 'View of Sex According to Mind Only (or Emptiness)', Section 12 Various Views of Sex.

The following conclusion on homosexual origin seems reasonable to me:

- Some people are born with the homosexual genes and behave as gays under any environment.
- Some people acquire the habit under the environment they are placed, though many of them may have had an affinity to their own sex.

The gay gene theory amounts to the notion that biology decides homosexuality. In contrast culture may explain the behaviour. The interaction of biology and culture is the complex focal debate not only in the determination of sexual orientation but the development of various other aspects of life such as racism, history and personality. (Taylor 1996, p. 70)

Democracy is based on numbers, whether the majority is right or wrong; morally, politically or in any other measures. Many cultures support the view that the heterosexuals are the norms; however, this opinion seems to me to have come about by sheer weight of numbers founded upon the principle of democracy. Certainly the sexual deviates go against what nature planned but it is hard to establish the normalcy since all people, men and women, do their best to maximise sexual pleasure.

It is worthy to observe the following differences between homosexual men and homosexual women. More lesbians are engaged in monogamous relationship than gay men are. More gay men carry out cruising looking for partners than lesbians do.

It seems that the homosexual men have a great deal of freedom of choosing partners, provided they go to the right place. They can have on average 3 to 4 partners a week, which is virtually impossible to achieve for the average heterosexual men.

Section 5 Preferences of Heterosexual Men

In the popular movies or novels, love or sex is almost always one dominant theme. A romance between a handsome male and a beautiful female is intricately interwoven in the main plot. People with the subconscious longing to make love to the beautiful opposite sex identify themselves with the chief characters while watching movies or reading novels. The movie makers or the novel writers are well aware of this law of the large numbers and use the romance and sex to attract the maximum audience and readership, since money making is an important consideration to their businesses apart from the artistic zeal.

The movies and novels have the tendency to portrait marriages as happy and successful, though that portrayal goes against the harsh reality of life. The depiction comes from the judgements of the movie makers and authors that is what the people want, thus maximising the audience and readership. If the movie is based on a true story, the marriage is normally portrayed as good so long as the marriage is irrelevant to the theme of the movie. This comes about partly for the courtesy to the couple of the real life and partly for the contract the couple may sign in making the pictures. Watching movies are in one sense an escape from the harsh reality of life: if the movies show real life, not many people would bother to watch them. The movies and novels also distort the real life of crimes and criminals and tend to give romantic presentations of them. If people know precisely what the criminal life would be, not many people would commit crimes in the same way if people know precisely what the married life would be like, not many people would marry.

Once people enter into marriage or the criminal world, they cannot get out easily from the various reasons: the sexual pleasure and children for marriage, and the committing pleasure and proceeds of crimes for crime are the obvious reasons among others.

We have to note that people got married and committed crimes before the 19th century when the entertainments in the forms of novels and movies became available or fashionable. The European novels are usually said to have begun with *Don Quixote* (1605) by Miguel de Cervantes, though we can find the forerunners of the genre in many parts of the world. The novel as a literary genre surged ahead in the following centuries but the greatest period is said to be the mid-late 19th century. The movies came into existence since the late19th century. These forms of entertainments are characterised by adaptability, and bound by no rule of structure, style and subject matter. The effects of these entertainments on the people's attitudes may not be as great as the previous paragraphs indicate.

The food preferences of people seem to be random and the question why some people like some food seems to be nonsensical. A large number of people appreciate to eat such food as chocolate, prawns and stakes. I met a female who did not like prawns and also a German man who used to eat boiled potatoes with so much delight, saying, 'Potatoes are the best thing God created'. However, the question why this is so does not make much sense.

Majority of men want young and pretty women as their sexual partners rather than intelligent or rich women though if the latter has the former quality it is even better. This inclination is so universal that its acceptability is not questioned, though it is really peculiar if we reflect philosophically. It is also interesting to note that this strong inclination on the part of men has a mirror image on the part of women that women want to be attractive to men, that is, young and beautiful. The average-looking women, if young, should not have much difficulty in obtaining husbands seeing that men are sexually starved and have to deviate considerably from their ideal women if they are to be successful in obtaining wives. Similarly the wealthy, famous and powerful men would not have much problem in finding beautiful wives since women appreciate wealth, fame and power. These practices are virtually a part of all cultures. Is there any reason ascribable behind this preference of men?

One reason why men are impressed with female beauty may be that men do not expect anything else from women and think that women are useful only as bed-mates: the intelligent or rich girls are rare. This assessment is rather negative and also insulting to women but men have not progressed much in this respect since the immemorial past.

The proposition why men want young and beautiful girls may lie in men's wish to have strong and beautiful babies is hardly convincing at first. In the first place, sexual arousal does not come from an intent to have a baby. In the second place, men normally do not feel strong sexual desire to an old woman who was pretty when young, though logically speaking she should be as good a bet as a pretty youthful woman to have a desired offspring. However, I have come to the conclusion that men and women are aesthetically inclined in many ways and do not offer any opposition when it comes to sex. Men want young and pretty women as their sexual partners, in the first place to appreciate them in lovemaking and in the second place to have strong and beautiful babies in their subconscious minds.

I was anxious to touch the breasts of a young virgin, and after begging many times I got to fondle her breasts with so much delight. A few months later I got to know a widow, who asked me to touch her breasts. I did it only under obligation. It is really strange to think why I felt the ways I felt. I would not be able to differentiate the two sets of breasts from the touch; only difference was the age.

There is biological evidence to support the behaviour that men want to have sex with young women, though it is not on men's conscious mind to have babies when they are sexually aroused. Women's ability to conceive declines as they age; men's ability to impregnate also declines as they grow older (Burnett 1990, p. 858). The parenthood for the older mothers increases the health risks of not only the mothers but the babies. Also the chances of miscarriage increase as women get older. Specifically, as women age, the risk of the babies born with Down's Syndromes dramatically increases. At 30, it is estimated to be about one chance in 1000; at 40 about one chance in 100. (p. 855)

It is statistically proven that the older women have less chance of bearing healthy babies than the younger women have.

Chances of miscarriage also dramatically increase as women age. According to the Danish report, the risk of a woman miscarrying at the age of 22 is 8 per cent, at the age of 35, 20 per cent, and rises to more than 84 per cent by the age of 48.

It seems that men, from intuition or instinct, sense these facts; leaving healthy descendants is a critical decision, and go for young women, though all straight men feel is that the young women give more sexual satisfaction.

Men like to have sex with young and beautiful women primarily to maximise sexual gratification. However this notion faces a challenge when we think even the boys before adolescent adore pretty girls with whom they are eager to make friends, and also the old men without sexual activities still appreciate the presence of beautiful women. We can express the matter in the following manner. The fact that majority of boys and men want beautiful girls must originate in seeking beauty around them, which is a fundamental characteristic of human existence. In 'Introduction to Series', Book One, I cite necessities of life, sex, religion, idealism, materialism, racism, nationalism, sexism and arts as fundamental means of survival for humans, and the concept of beauty comes not only under arts but under any discipline. People, men and women, want to surround themselves with everything beautiful, such as clothes, household appliances, scenery, houses and paintings and they are ever eager to see and own these beautiful things, though the judgement of what is beautiful varies enormously among the people. This theory still falls short of explaining why men are so much keener to look at or possess pretty and young women than these inanimate objects.

There is definitely a common notion about female beauty. However, if we step back and think about the beauties among different objects, for example, females and scenery, we are at a loss. When we compare the beauties of women and rural scenes, we are surprised to find that no logical connections exist. There must be some common threads running everything: thus Socrates wondered. Plato thought that the sense perceptions were false as the Buddha did, and we cannot get the true insight into the external world through our perceptions. Plato devised the concept of 'Form' or 'Idea' which like beauty exists independently of the particular objects as the universal feature. He believed that the concepts such as mathematical proofs, beauty, bravery and goodness exist as essence of each thing, eternal and uncreated, available to be comprehended through reason. He posited the everyday physical world of changeable things which people come to know through the senses is a world of appearances or phenomenal manifestations. He believed that we cannot gain knowledge of things through our senses, and also the knowledge is constantly changing. He also posited an underlying timeless and unchanging reality, an immaterial realm of Forms or Ideas that are knowable only through intellect. Plato's Forms or Ideas are absolute and eternal in contrast with individual appearance, and manifest in such quality as justice itself, goodness itself and beauty itself. He later abandoned this idea altogether. (Freeman 1996, p. 231)

Another explanation may be to define the perception of beauty and ugliness as like and dislike respectively. When a man likes a female or scenery, he thinks it is beautiful.

Immanuel Kant (1724-1804) thought our knowledge has limitations. We can get to know the world of appearance by sense experience and scientific investigation. However we cannot know the world in itself, that is, things-in-themselves. Kant's idea gives out the following formulas:

Appearance = empirical world = phenomenon
Also, things-in-themselves = true state of the world = what really is = noumena
(Janaway 1994, p. 11)

Kantian thing-in-itself or noumenon is beyond the limit of human knowledge, whereas Plato's Forms or Ideas are the object of knowledge (p. 13).

When men masturbate, they are dreaming of idealised beauty of women as for Form or Idea who;

do not fart and defecate,
do not age,
do not show any defects, bodily and mental.

There are two separate questions in the phenomenon where the heterosexual men want to derive greatest pleasure by making love to pretty females. Both questions are hard to give convincing answers by their nature but I believe they hold the keys to explaining not only male sexual behaviour but human existence.

Why do the majority of men think (at the conscious level) that the young and good-looking women would give maximum sexual pleasure? The reason probably lies in a high probability that human beings are in essence beauty seeking and act accordingly. The beauty consciousness manifests in all facets of human life: consumer goods, arts, scenery, racism, etc.

Why do men want to maximise sexual pleasure in the first place? Men must eat and drink to satisfy their hunger and thirst. Apart from this biological need, men want to enjoy eating and drinking and spend enormous care and money in so doing. Men do likewise concerning with their clothes and houses. The same thing can be said about sex. Lovemaking is a physiological process in essence but men want to increase its pleasure as much as possible.

Desire to enjoy sex is greater than that to enjoy eating and drinking for most men, particularly if they are young. In their eagerness to have good sex, it is known in this age of AIDS that many men do not practise safe sex in spite of wide public campaign. Some men even insist on anal intercourse with women many of whom vehemently resist such an advance.

During wars people value to store jewellery more than anything else, though in this case economic security rather than sense of beauty that plays the major role.

Men have certain specifications on women to satisfy their sexual desire in the same fashion the employers have certain specifications on persons to fill the job vacancies. Men seek the usefulness in women of satisfying their sexual desire and the employers seek the usefulness in the applicants of serving the firm. The survival of the entities ultimately governs both.

Peculiarities of the male preference to the particular females has a corresponding peculiarities of the employer preference to the particular applicants: both prefer certain age group and some characteristics based on usefulness and functions.

Functional requirements for employment may be in general terms, not including the specific requirements for the particular jobs:

- one measure; educational or trade qualifications
- one measure; job experience, related capability and language command
- one measure; compatibility judged by nationality, mannerism and characters
- one measure; any personal relationship with the members of the employing firm

All these measures are intricately interwoven and the firm, particularly managers, feel the successful applicants must have, in the same way men feel some measures women must have for their sexual gratification. Functionally, the women who are not young and beautiful should satisfy men sexually. The desire to employ people for specific jobs does not necessarily match with the capacity of the applicants to do the jobs: the employers look for the usefulness of the applicants for the firm. The age and other features of the applicants often play crucial roles in the selection process though doing so is illegal in many countries yet its reasons are largely suppressed and undocumented like the male selection criteria of the female sexual partners.

Men have to keep trying to get good-looking women in the same way men have to, to get good jobs. They must have something to offer in securing satisfactory positions, such as the qualifications or the experience in a particular field. The same thing can be said about obtaining women. Men normally have to have something to offer--wealth, education or physical beauty--to entice women. They normally stop when they have the best they can get of women and jobs. However, men's nature is such that after a while they get sick of the women and the jobs, and majority are prepared to change for better women and better jobs.

If we turn our attention to the opposite ends of the affairs, the similar difficulties are encountered. It is a rule that the employers have problems filling in the professional vacancies with perfectly suitable applicants. Normally many people apply for the advertised positions but the applicants who have all the requirements are rare. Similarly the girls find that among the boys who want to take them out the really good ones are rare. The pretty girls would have high expectations hence they would have some difficulties. Even the average-looking girls want reasonably good boys who are hard to find among their suitors.

If men want young and pretty girls for sexual purpose, they can hardly blame, when they miss out, the employers who want certain age group and characteristics for the advertised positions.

I am sure that the foregoing explanations do not satisfy the curiosity of many readers and there has to be a lot more speculations needed to give good answers to the question why men want to go to bed with good-looking and young girls in an effort to maximise the pleasure.

Apart from two requirements of beauty and youth when selecting women for sexual purpose, there is another requirement we have to consider: The women should be compatible with men. Somehow a man feels that a girl is right or wrong for him when he sees or converses with her. He often expresses the non-compatibility by saying, 'She is not my type'. This recognition under the ordinary course of life is so subtle that some men may not know it affects their choosing process. However, I am sure that this selection criterion is at work on most occasions. Compatibility may be said to be some degree of fondness or love. Friends are made between compatible people. Many companies have a policy to employ compatible applicants once their capabilities are established. Love between a man and a woman can be defined as high degree of compatibility recognised. Love at first sight may be said to be this recognition at the first meeting. The old or ugly women can be sexually attractive to men when high compatibility is established.

When a man likes or is compatible with a woman in the general context, it does not mean he wants her sexually. However, in this book where sex is the subject, it can be equated with the sexual desirability.

In the course of everyday intercourse, the good look and youthfulness (both are basically objective qualities) play prominent role in the affairs of sex. After the initial contact, the compatibility (chiefly subjective quality) plays the prominent role and eventually wins out, pushing away the above two objective qualities. That is to say, once the compatibility is established men do not care if the women are pretty or young. In other words, the high compatibility negates the requirements of beauty and youth. As for the relationships between the races, once the compatibility or acceptance is established, this fact plays the major role pushing away the other requirements.

When men say that a girl is young and beautiful, men have certain criteria of common measures, that is, objective terms. The movies and popular magazines provide men with some standard men are supposed to judge. However, there are also subjective judgements involved in assessing the girl's youth and beauty. One man's perceptions can be quite different from that of another and often the male friends are surprised to learn so much difference. It is often said that beauty is in the eyes of the beholder. Ultimately this subjective term decides the issue. A man may prefer a woman who deviates considerably from the society's norm but that is not important for him. He in his mind assesses that his sweetheart is young and pretty.

Beauty is in the eyes of the beholder. An intelligent man said that cockroaches were the most beautiful creatures in the world. He did not mean a joke but really believed in his assessment.

In the deeper psychological field, all the requirements are subjective. Men do not have any concrete objects and measurements they can work with. The women--their figures and ways of thinking--are continually changing and also the men as the measuring sticks are changing. When a man loves a woman, he thinks she is most beautiful, though other people may think otherwise. He is judging solely on his perception. According to the Mind Only (or Emptiness) concept, his opinion and other people's opinions are all unsubstantial: they all believe erroneously their views are the truth. Suppose after a few years he does not love her any more. This happens for most of love between men and women, which is another substantiating evidence that all the requirements are subjective. Most likely he does not think she is beautiful any more with absence of deep affection. Still he does not comprehend that he is wrong on both occasions--during and after the love affair--regarding his opinion on her appearance.

Suppose two men meet two women in a confined social setting. It can happen that one man prefers one woman and the other man, the other woman. In this case, it is either both men are using the requirements of beauty and youth with different results or the compatibility perceptions are different. However, it happens often that the two men want the same woman with consequent fighting. In this case the two men are applying all the criteria with the same result.

Even savages recognise women are beautiful or not. However, the uncivilised men may choose stout women rather than pretty women as their wives: this is because of sheer necessity in the survival economy in the jungles. Similarly the civilised young men may marry old or ugly women because the women have something else to offer other than youth and beauty, such as wealth, prestige or love.

Men's sexual urge is pressing and immediate. They are obsessed with the idea of making love to pretty girls. Men do not care if the girls were fat in the past or they will be old and no longer attractive in the future. It is the human nature to judge the objects according to what they are at present, rather than what they were before and what they will be. It is not the nature of men to contemplate that since the beautiful women they want will become old and ugly and no longer attractive, they refrain from the effort to secure them for sexual purpose: men's desire is immediate. Similarly men do not think logically that beautiful women cannot be adorable because they fart and defecate. Women do these things in the hiding; hence it is convenient for both sexes to forget about it. When men adore women sexually, there is no telling them that the female attraction is an illusion. When a beautiful woman gets seriously injured, a man loses sexual interest in her straight away. If she regains her features, he also regains his desire. However, if the high compatibility is there the disfigurement should not affect the relationship though his sexual urge for her may be still diminished.

Another peculiar feature about sex is that men invariably lose interest in the women after going to bed with them. This loss of interest is one manifestation of sexual restraints. The greater disappointment corresponds with the greater expectation. In some cases, it occurs abruptly--even after the first lovemaking, and in other cases gradually. This inclination is also a characteristic of larger frame of men or human beings. Humans always lose some interest in the desired things such as wealth, fame, honour or whatever else after acquiring them. Men are prepared to go to any length to satisfy hunger and thirst but once sated men are no longer interested in food and drinks until the next round of hunger and thirst. In the same way men are prepared to go to any length to satisfy sexual desire but once sated men are not interested in women until the next round of desire. It is a general rule that a man loses a sexual interest in a woman after making love to her repeatedly. It is popularly said that happens after six months or one year. This is in a sense a learning process. A toddler loses an interest in a particular toy after getting to know it, to pay attention to something else. Even an adult loses an interest in a book, a home appliance, food, attire, a house, and so on after fully getting to know them.

The movies or novels do not emphasise this aspect and the story unfolds sexual love between young man and young woman, not telling the audience and readers that the love would evaporate under the normal course of events. Similarly, beautiful women sexually arouse men; however, the notion that men would soon lose interest in the women after going to bed with them is absent. It is normal for men wanting to see the naked girls if they are young and pretty: however, it is abnormal if men want to see the naked bodies of the same girls after months or even weeks of cohabitation.

The above feature is also observed in the animal kingdom. Montaigne wrote:

> I have put out to stud an old horse who could not be controlled at the scent of mares.

> Facility presently sated him towards his own mares; but towards strange ones, and the first one that passes by his pastures, he returns to his importunate neighings and his furious heats, as before. (Montaigne 1965, p. 464)

Men invariably lose an interest in women sexually after making love. Men want change. Change in all things is sweet [Euripides] (Harbottle 1897, p. 414). This desire to change sexual partners comes about from the mammalian origin: A strong male with a large harem must lose an interest in a particular female so as to approach the other females for the maximum spread of their semen and offspring. That is, the loss of interest on the part of the males comes about from the instinct of survival and the maximum multiplication of their species. The females on their part are prepared to submit to the strongest males for the best chance of survival of their offspring. This mammalian behaviour also shows up among the human females and they are prepared to submit to a desired male when a chance gets their way. The mammalian males must develop a strong physique to secure a harem. If they don't, they don't have a chance to leave their descendants. If they become weak because of injuries or old age, a young strong male wrestles the dominant position from them in the same way they themselves did when young and strong. In the animal kingdom, the strong muscular bodies contribute most to the survival and that is what the females want in the males.

In the human world the similar story unfolds with one notable difference. What women want in men varies a great deal and the physical strength is only one of them. The good look of men may be another. The youthfulness may be another. Men developed so-called culture to satisfy the female preferences on men. Men have to be well-educated, have a good job, be rich, be famous, be powerful and be good-natured among other desirables. The sexual desire is energy in the biological sense and the drive to acquire women also becomes energy in itself. Hence the strong sexual desire on the part of men naturally promotes culture. The female preferences on the desirability of men probably, though certainly strong, do not set the pattern of culture because the men's sexual desire is, though strong, only one of the life aims of men.

Men erroneously think that good-looking women have good body and mind as well. However, in the course of intercourse this expectation is often betrayed and consequently contributes to men's loss of interest. Men start looking for another woman. Anatomically beautiful women are no different from ugly or old women.

Men judge the females for the sexual purpose on the basis of appearance, which is not in accord with God's decrees. God (Truth) judges men and women through their minds. Therefore the men's preference on women based on compatibility may last longer.

Doing research and writing books are absorbingly interesting to me; however, after working for a while I get tired and do something else, to repeat the same process many times. If such activity as research and writing requiring a lot of imagination can get me bored temporarily, isn't it natural that men get bored with the same women after repeated love-makings which are essentially the same process. I have a strong desire to write books; men have a strong sexual desire. Both desires are there on the permanent basis but both can get people bored temporarily if they dwell on the same subjects too long.

Herodotus wrote, 'When a woman lays aside her garments, she also lays aside her modesty' (p. 321), expressing his disapproval and disappointment. 'The daughter-in-law of Pythagoras used to say that the woman who goes to bed with a man should put off her modesty with her skirt and put it on again with her petticoat' (Montaigne 1965, p. 71), thus teaching the ladies how to behave.

When men want something, in our discussion women, they feel they must have them. In the process men do not think that since they will be tired of them after a while they want less.

Even if a man may lose interest in a pretty girl, there are always a large number of men who want her, so she should not be overly worried about it under the normal circumstances.

A single man may believe that he will be totally satisfied sexually with his sweetheart after marrying her. People may think that a man whose wife is young and pretty is sexually gratified and does not cherish any desire to another woman. This opinion--one observing his future married life and the other observing the married couple--is wrong. Once men have their dream on any matter fulfilled, it is not a dream but a reality with less enthusiasm and with some problems. After acquiring girlfriends of their dream, men often say, 'There is too much problem' or 'I have all the problems of the world'. Men were originally in an idealised state where they wanted beautiful women and moved to the real world of having them. This universal phenomenon places every man on equal footing in terms of what they want--including sex. Haves and have-nots of beautiful wives or pretty girlfriends are all in the same mental status since the haves get dissatisfied with their beautiful women after a while. This observation puts a king with a large harem in line with a lonely masturbator. All men--kings, married men, and single men with or without girlfriends, if they are sexually normal, are in the same boat and ever want a variety of beautiful women at a time or in a succession.

If men have food preferences for the day, apart from the basic likes and dislikes, isn't it expected that men have female preferences for the night, apart from the basic likes and dislikes? If men can get sick of the same food after feeding so many days, isn't it expected that men get sick of the same women after so many nights? If men look for a variety of food, isn't it natural that men also look for a variety of women?

Men (and women) want a variety of food to satisfy their desire; this stems from the bodily need to satisfy a variety of nourishments. Men want a variety of women to satisfy their desire; this stems from the need to spread their semen as widely as possible for the survival of the species. In both cases nature or God (Truth) works on the desires of men to lead to the survival of the humans.

All in all there are four sexual preferences for men who boast they are normal. When men get old their preferences may change somewhat but the following preferences remain the basic pattern. The female sexual partners must be (the following terms from firstly to fourthly refer only to the numerical orders and do not indicate the orders of preferences):

firstly beautiful,
secondly young,
thirdly compatible,
and fourthly men always want more of the above specified woman.

The first three preferences refer to the quality of women and the fourth to the quantity of women. These preferences are also revealed in the vast amount of pornographic pictures available in the market, and men ever want to see a variety of naked girls not just being satiated with the same young and pretty girls. Another strong human desire to be rich refers only to the quantity of money in the absence of competing sets of currencies. The above preferences of men support the view that the sexual objects are illusions.

When men are really hungry, they eat almost anything to satisfy their hunger. In the similar logic, if men are sexually starved, they are prepared to go to bed with almost any women they can get hold of, disregarding the aforementioned criteria. Married men do not have much choice but to carry on the lovemaking with their wives even after losing sexual interest in them. However, some men have extra marital relationship; some pay visits to the brothel; some masturbate; and some opt for divorce.

In choosing a sexual partner, men prefer to use the foregoing requirements. However, it seems that men do the selection by the subconscious process, which is more accurate, efficient and faster than the conscious process. (Bader 2002, p. 12)

All of the above requirements are fundamental for men and at the same time they all come from the survival and multiplication instinct of men as a biological entity. Men want their offspring as beautiful as the beautiful female they want sexually. They want their seed impregnated in the young female to ensure the maximum survival. They want the women and the possible offspring to be compatible. They want a large number of women for the maximum spread of their sperm.

Men's primary interests in women are their physical features, and the intelligence and adherence to idealism are only secondary interests, in the similar way the employers look for certain characteristics of the job applicants: some characteristics are primary and some secondary. This comes about because men want their progenies to have good physical features, and men can teach them the intelligence and adherence to idealism after birth. The emphasis on the primary interests as a sex object is changeable and varies from man to man and also from one time to another for the same man.

The foregoing preferences do not have any restrictions of the marital status or the blood relationship: Men feel sexual desire according to the rules mentioned even if the men or the women are married, and to their own daughters. Young and pretty girls would testify about the validity of this observation. As far as my experiences go, there is no truth in that men get more sexual satisfaction from non-prostitutes than from prostitutes. The girls must satisfy the foregoing four criteria.

The strong hostility against the homosexuals from the fair number of straight people may come from the belief that the sexual conducts should be in conformity with the instinct of survival. The heterosexuals follow the survival instinct but the homosexuals do not in the selection process of sexual activities. Many heterosexual people believe that the homosexuals are different culturally and in the life views.

Economists assume, as a first approximation, that tastes do not change or that they change slowly, and that they are independent of all the other influences on demand. These preferences may be the measures men gauge women in sexual terms: these measures are more or less independent of the each others and are, so to speak, competing for men's attention. Sometimes one preference dominates and at other times a few preferences combine to make a big impression. Deepest psychological forces make these decisions and possibly men do not have much control.

Apart from the foregoing gauges men judge women sexually, if it comes to marriage men take into account of the further attributes: educational qualification, wealth, family, profession and nationality.

The fourth requirement goes against the moral teaching that men should be content sexually with their wives all their life. Strictly speaking we have to measure all the dimensions of engineering components before we can be sure if they are all satisfactory. Every woman is an independent experience for every straight man. Even if a man goes to bed with 10 000 women, which an average man is capable of having orgasm in his life time, the other women are new experience for him. In reality we should be able to use a sampling technique for engineering components as well as for women to know what they are like.

Men lose a sexual interest in women after repeated lovemakings, though men try to prevent this tendency by such means as the improvement of the lovemaking techniques or the professional counselling. This tendency is similar to the aging process, and humans try to prevent aging by such means as exercise or drug taking. Both tendencies are there irrespective of what people do though they can be checked to some extent.

The loss of interest by men in the particular women may also be compared to the process of the machine depreciation. The total value of the machine, which is the purchase price, is used up bit by bit on use. The sexual value of a woman may be used up every time a man makes love to her until the total value is consumed. We cannot quantify the depreciation of women as we do for the machines. We make only qualitative assessments concerning women. Even after this, the woman can be used sexually by habit energy in a similar way the machines can be used after the use-up date.

The concept of depreciation may be the reason why women are reluctant to make love to men. Depreciation is not so much the wearing out of the female bodies or the cheapening of their flesh though women may feel this way, but is the amount of desire men have on particular women. For the machine the depreciation is caused by aging and wear and tear, and the machine goes through this process only once. For women, depreciation here means for one man only and women can repeat the same process by another man if women are young and pretty. Wearing out of the female bodies and the cheapening of their flesh are caused by aging and possible injuries.

The loss of sexual interest on the part of men in their wives induces the various strains to the marriage, which shows up as boredom, frustration and even fightings. Counselling can reduce these problems to some extent. The humans are remarkably adaptable animals and when men appreciate women sexually, men push aside the various problems but as soon as men stopped appreciating women sexually the problems come to the fore.

In an effort to enhance the degree of sexual gratifications, men may read the various magazines or books; however, they will not help much. Also men may take the various postures of lovemaking; however, they will find that they don't make much difference.

Visiting brothels on numerous occasions I at times met an exceptionally beautiful woman. I still remember clearly a conversation with such a woman of rare beauty and good personality. Leading me into her room, she said that she had been lying under the heater for these hours waiting for a client. Sure enough her back, on touching with my hands, was really hot. It seemed rather strange to me that a good girl like her had to wait for a customer for such a long time. By the nature of the setup--waiting for the clientele at the premise rather than picking up strangers on the street--however beautiful a prostitute may be, she has to wait on and give adequate service to the customers to make a good living: This system relies on the regular customers. She was tall and had well-proportioned body matching her lovely face and in addition, to my delight, there was a conversational rapport between us. She impressed me so much that I proposed to take her out some time. Rejecting my proposal outright, she said, 'You will soon get sick of my body'. I was sure that she took my feeling as it was, that is, a genuine adoration for her.

To think back the conversation later, I figured that I would have lost an interest in her after a while—the only question was how soon it would have been. I got impressed with her who satisfied three preferences of desirable women; she was young, beautiful and compatible with me. What she stated was in fact the fourth sexual preference of men of my definition. The fact of life for her was harsh in this respect too. She spoke the truth which she learned from her bitter experience: she had let her admirer close to her life in the past only to find one day in her dismay that he was no longer interested in her.

Generally speaking, however a prostitute may be beautiful, her clients will lose an interest in her after a while. So she has to change the brothels often to attract the new clients to her, in a similar way we have to change the fishing spots after one spot is fished out. However, occasionally a prostitute and a client make good friends lasting for quite some time.

If the sexual laws in this book deal with what the prostitute takes for granted, readers may say what is the use of writing a book of this kind. I don't have any theoretical background to claim to be an expert on sex, and all I do in this book is to put some regularity to the common notions of sex. However, I have found over the years that learning and practising the common sense in any fields, such as sex, making money, becoming healthy and climbing the corporate ladder, are more useful than a sophisticated knowledge and its practice. This also agrees with the common notion that the experienced people without the relevant qualifications are more useful than the inexperienced qualified people. We also note that the contracts between God and the people in the Old Testament are quite easy to understand and practise: they are more or less the common sense. The Old Testament says: Now what I am commanding you today is not difficult for you or beyond your reach (Deuteronomy 30:1); and no, the word is very near you: it is in your mouth and in your heart so you may obey it (Deuteronomy 30:14). The difficulty of the Old Testament, as I refer in 'Introduction to Series', Book One *Idealism and Materialism*, lies in the deep understandings and implications. Montaigne wrote that the essence of virtue is so easy that even children can master it: Virtue's tool is moderation, not strength (Montaigne 1965, p. 120).

The following is another experience with a prostitute. I still remember my disappointment when I went through her body, which was flabby. Her skin did not have the firmness or elasticity; her skin gave in easily, reminding me of muddy ground surface which collapsed under the weight of my body. She was reasonably pretty but she said she was 29 years old. It is well established that as a girl gets older her body surface loses elasticity, probably corresponding to the loss of mental vigour. I can imagine that the brain tissues also lose elasticity as we get old. Though the soft yet firm skin is what men want on women in the lovemaking session, I would class this aspect of desirability under youth of women, rather than setting up an independent criterion because the above desired skin is found only in young women.

When men say that a woman is pretty, beautiful, nice, gorgeous or whatever else in sexual terms, they normally mean that she is also young and compatible. These qualities hit men in aggregate and there is no need to analyse what quality of hers constitutes sexual attractiveness: in fact men do not know and do not care. In describing the above requirements, it is assumed that the girls have no physical impediments such as crooked bodies, skin diseases, venereal diseases or AIDS. It is expected that men lose a sexual interest in the girls straight away if men learn they have the above disorders even they may be attractive in other respects. If the women are compatible with the men, the physical impairments should not make much difference to the men as in lack of any other desirable features.

I would imagine that absence of any one of the aforementioned four requirements in the general public would cause tremendous change to our way of life and hence would have produced an entirely different human history. This fanciful notion is only imaginary and would not happen in our real life except in a negligible number of people because all the requirements are, as I take great pains to explain, deeply rooted in human nature and in fact are parts of the human existence.

The following story may be valid when the Third Prophecy is in full swing and people don't want to have babies and the act of sex is carried out only for pleasure. The pregnancy preventive techniques became in the wide circulation since the 18th century in the West, a very short time indeed in the evolutionary terms. Men have not adjusted to this new phase of lovemaking. The sexual desire is the instinct to have children and hence they want young and pretty women as bed mates. If men do not want to preserve the offspring in the future, men may forgo these requirements and try to satisfy their desire on the available women, that is, the women who may not be young nor pretty. Besides, at that distant future men as well as women will have learned not to judge people on the basis of appearance, and the selection criteria of the females as sex objects will reflect that attitude.

Further the following way of life may become prevalent in the next few centuries, though many people of today's outlook may dismiss it as a mere fantasy. If a man takes a fancy on a woman, whether they are walking the street, doing the shopping or dining in a restaurant, he proposes to make love to her. She, on her part with the outlook of the future lady, does not refuse the offer as the wives normally do not refuse the offer of sexual intercourse from their husbands today.

Section 6 Difficulties Arising

One serious problem of heterosexual men may be lack of women who satisfy the criteria as I expounded in the last section. Young and beautiful women are scarce to start with and the compatible women among them are hard to come by indeed. This shortage creates intense competition among men to try to obtain the suitable women and also deep division among women to attract the best men. A beautiful woman cannot stand a more beautiful woman. The mass media sometimes report race related incidents in the shops; however, it seems that the female related incidents are more often than the race related. The female shop assistants at times do not want to help beautiful female shoppers.

The best men for women may have physical beauty, wealth, power, fame, or whatever else womenfolk think desirable in men. The words 'competition' and 'division' are used to point out the widely observed differences of approach between men and women. Traditionally men make the first moves towards women: Men try to get women and women try to attract men. Women respond to men depending on how the women feel about the move. For an average-looking young woman it is not hard to find a man who supports her financially since among the multitudes of sexually starved men she has to find only one man satisfactory to her. If a man wants a woman sexually and makes an advance, it means she is desirable for him and under normal circumstances she is flattered and feels happy. However, if she dislikes him from some reason she can hate his advances.

My assessment of the sexual desirability of young women says,

- One in 10 women is pretty.
- One in one hundred women is very beautiful.

If we take into account of the compatibility among the above desired young women, the really desirable women are hard to find indeed.

Gold and beautiful women are very much sought after but they are rare. John Maynard Keynes wrote a reckoning in his book *A Treatise on Money* (1930) that the world's total accumulation of gold could be put into a single ship (Galbraith 1987, p. 232). Are there any reasons for this scarcity? Why don't we have the abundance of gold and desirable women in the world? Are they rare by the definition, or nature has a difficulty in creating them?

Gold and precious stones disproportionately command high prices against practical uses. The beauty people place on them pushes up the prices in proportion. If the people place high value on the beauty of the jewellery, it is not unreasonable that men place so much value to the beautiful women, which have practical use in solving men's sexual problem.

In the early ancient Egypt silver was more expensive than gold, in fact twice as much for the same weight during the Old and New Kingdoms. That came about obviously from the supply and demand, and has been an exception than the rule in the course of human history. The above phenomenon also goes against the chemical fundamentals. Gold is more stable chemically and more rust resistant than silver thence the demand for gold outstrips that for silver.

In the 18th century, the Europeans exchanged one gram of gold for 14 or 15 grams of silver from the Spaniards, who in turn exchanged one gram of gold for 9 or 10 grams of silver from the Chinese. This discrepancy happened in the 18th century when comparatively easy communications and transport became available. We cannot even speculate what amount of discrepancies were on the market in the earlier centuries for speculative investment.

Pu'er tea is very expensive in China. This tea, strong aromatic when brewed, from Yunnan Province has been prized for medicinal properties. Its effectiveness is considered to improve with the age of the tea. In 2005, half kilogram of 64-year-old Pu'er tea was sold at auction for 155 000 Australian dollars, six times more expensive than gold. Gold, crystal of wealth, and beautiful women have had universal appeal for men, all nationalities beyond any era, but Pu'er tea has had appeals only for some Chinese. Gold and silver, neither beautiful women nor Pu'er tea, have been the international currencies from the obvious reasons.

Pearl Buck in her popular novel *The Good Earth* (1931) reveals the following social custom in China of the early 20th century. Her parents were missionaries and she grew up in China though she was born in America. She returned to China after attending American College. It was customary in China that when an idle son of a wealthy family became unmanageable because of sexual heat, he was given a slave girl to console him. The author wrote that after that the things passed easily. (Buck 1953, pp. 207, 308, 309) She further gives the following account. The farmers at the time of famine sold their daughters as slaves not their land, thinking their land was more important than their daughters. These slave girls, if pretty, were ravished by their young lords as pleasure. (pp. 8, 110, 111, 268, 270, 320, 338)

The Arabian Nights' Entertainment (*The Thousand and One Nights*) refers to the custom in the Muslim country in the medieval era to buy a slave girl in the market for the son of the rich family when he reached puberty.

Unattractive women in respect to appearance (mainly physical and of age) are fairly easily available to most men. Hence if men learn to satisfy themselves with ugly or old women, they do not have much competition and should lead easier and happier life. Self-discipline or psychological training may induce men to choose unattractive females. However, this line of thinking, though interesting as an argument, goes against human nature and possibly does not go beyond a fancy proposition at this time of human development.

I often heard that though women may be highly successful in their chosen careers, they in their deepest thought want to be beautiful more than anything else. Beauty is the quality men want in women. We can see that what women want comes from men and is the mirror image of men's universal sex drive. Here is the women's problem: what women cherish is an attribute that men want in women rather than what women can acquire by effort for their own sake. Being sexually attractive for women is more important and possibly more profitable than being strong or smart, hence they are more concerned with their make-up, their clothes and their mannerism. If this observation is correct, women in general are fated to think that men are primary and do not see any sense in striving for excellence. The view that men are primary is advocated by the Bible and in fact the universal opinion expressed by the pre-modern writers.

It is unfortunately a fact of life that young and pretty women stay that way only for a short span of time. The husbands may find their wives no longer attractive after several years of marriage. The wives, knowing this, may be at a loss what to do. Whatever they do, for example, they use expensive cosmetics or do vigorous exercises, they cannot stop aging process. In addition to aging we have to take into account the fourth preferences of men: Men lose interest in the women sexually after a while even they are young and pretty. Wives must learn to live with their husbands' sexual disinterest in them as well as sexual interest in other women in the same way husbands must learn to live with their wives' peculiar thinking and farting and defecating process, if they want to remain in marriage.

Female prostitutes will learn the fourth preferences of men's sexuality in no time in the course of their trade; probably they do not know the reasons. They have to understand that their customers want to change girls frequently; otherwise they may be perplexed or even hurt every time they see a familiar client goes into a room not of their own. The wives of ordinary men have to accept the sexual laws in such a way the prostitutes have to, and live with them rather than feel resentment against their husbands or feel guilty of themselves. This book may help average women in locating the problems and trying to assess the root causes.

In case of married women, they may have a considerable difficulty in comprehending their husbands' sexual longing for other women in an apparently happy marital relationship. Men, on their part, had believed that they could quench their sexual thirst after marriage but they found that their continual sex drive for beautiful women was as strong as before marriage. Virtually all married men fancy women in a similar way as single men do: This is a sexual law people have to learn to live with. However, there is a big step from fancy to adultery. We know not all married men try to sleep with the fancied women who are not their wives. Social custom constrains the married men to start with. Secondly, not many people are rich enough to attract and keep another woman. Thirdly, most of them would be reluctant to risk to lose their families--wives and children--they have built up over the years for the sheer joy of sex. Fourthly, the wives they agree to marry were the best available to them at the time of marriage hence it is fairly hard for the ordinary men to get better ones after marriage. Fifthly, adultery goes against the vow of marriage.

It is not possible for any man to sleep with all the women he wants. The sexual fancy of an average single man goes something like this:

> He wants the pretty girl next door. He fancies a movie star who appeared in the movie he really enjoyed. He dreams about a few beautiful girls in his favourite novel. One day he succeed in taking out a girl he likes and while dining with her he looks at a pretty woman at the next table with desire. He may fall in love with a woman and he believes that his desire towards her is as genuine as it can be. However, as far as my observations go, this man in love does not mind going to bed with another girl provided he does not hurt or lose his sweetheart.

If a virtuous and married man cannot suppress his sexual desire and go after the other women, does this fact annul all his integrities in the other respects? If he feels sexual desire towards his daughter or the married women, is he to be punished by the God's law in some way or another? I don't know the answers for these questions.

Section 7 Harem

Harem may be a multiple number of beautiful women kept in a segregated quarter who are to serve exclusively the master, not only sexually but in many other ways, for example, as a company for talks and amusements. If a woman with marital bond is kept in the house, she is a wife. If women are kept separately, not in the segregated quarter, they, though multiple in aggregate, are girlfriends or mistresses. The girlfriends are kept by friendship with undefined financial link, and mistresses, by monetary bond with undefined friendship.

The masters choose a woman or women from the harem for the day as their fancies dictate. Men have caprices apart from their discernible pattern of likes and dislikes of their tastes for such matters as food and women: I have come to understand even the fish have their fancies as to what they eat for the day apart from their broad pattern of likes and dislikes. I still don't know why men and fish have such fancies for the day in these matters. Both the fancy for the day and the pattern of likes and dislikes are made in the deep recess of the mind and possibly the most intricate psychology of today cannot unravel their workings.

I am certain that psychologists cannot predict which girls a man may prefer as his bed mate before he sees them. He himself is certain which girl he wants only after he inspects the girls.

Since resistance characterises women, they are material and come under materialism in scrutinising the various aspects of women. It is often said that men want wealth and sex as the low desires dictate; however, the two desires may originate in materialism. Men want to collect as much wealth and as many women.

Kings and emperors through history often owned the harems matching their wealth and authority. But the rulers were not the only men who had the fortune to indulge in this enjoyment. Aristocrats, rich merchants and even rich farmers had the harems whose size and extravagance depended on the money they allocated. Whoever the masters may have been, I would say the existence of harem depended on money since without money they could not have maintained women with the necessary expenditures. Stated in reverse, any man who was prepared to spend substantial wealth could have set up a harem for himself. In this sense harem was money and not the power or fame. Certainly the powerful or famous men could have obtained women for sexual purpose without much difficulty but could not have kept a harem without huge expenses. In prostitution where sex and money are exchanged, only money can buy sex and nothing else can. Political power or fame in itself cannot obtain sex in the sex market.

Jahangir, Akbar's son, ruled the Mughal Empire in India from 1605 to 1627, inheriting a harem of 5000 (Davison 1993, p. 128). Ivan the Terrible was only eight years old when his mother, regent, died in 1538; his father had died in 1533, and Ivan himself became Grand Prince of Moscow, in effect, a ruler of Russia. He was left to defend himself surrounded by a court of power-seeking minor princes and boyars or landowners, who insulted and neglected him. During his youth, Ivan was allowed to assault and rape any girl who took his fancy. (p. 131)

The harems for the rulers played important roles in shaping the history of the various parts of the world. We may think that the harems were established for the sole purpose of satisfying men's innate dream of securing a lot of young and beautiful women for the whims of the rulers. However there were more in the establishment of harems for the rulers. The following speculations seem to be generally valid for most harems all over the world through history.

The children thus born were appropriated as officials within the realm, thus securing the rulers' authority at present and in the future. This facet played the role as the self-preservation or survival of the rulers.

It was often convenient for high-ranking officials that the monarch neglected his duties, indulging in such pleasures as sex, drinks and amusements, so that these officers could exert greater influence in the state's affairs and could get away even if they made serious mistakes. Thus the high officials, especially those who were close to the ruler and aware that they were incompetent, lazy or corrupt, encouraged the ruler to keep a large number of beautiful women with the state expense. It is more often than not through the human history that these people have pushed away the upright and competent people, not only in the ruling administration but in the various organisations such as families, firms and military. The system also gave the opportunity for the officials to present attractive females for the service in the harem, thus giving the successful officials greater power and in some cases making them the relatives of the ruling family.

Kings wanted not only good-looking women in their harem for erotic pleasure but for alliances with important families within or even outside the realm to consolidate their dominance. Many females and their backers were in a fierce competition for the affections and consequent favours from the ruler. The harem was always a place for plots and intrigues. Oftentimes, the conspirers in their hottest rivalries tried to remove and even murder the ruler. This piece of history sounds odd to us since the harem was founded for the enjoyment of the ruler; however, this facet reveals both the fascinating nature of history and the strange behaviours of human beings. For example, the Harem Conspiracy Papyrus details the trial of a group who plotted to murder Ramesses (Ramses) III (1182-1151 BC), an Egyptian king. The majority of the conspirators were personally close to the king and many were officials in the harem. (Clayton 1994, pp. 164-5) Also we find in Ottoman court the shocking example revealing the nature of the harem. Political intrigue was focussed on harem, where ambitious people schemed to put their woman on the throne. There was no rule of succession and hence the sultan chose the heir by ordering the murders of all the rest of the half-brothers of the chosen heir.

Kings and emperors in the East as well as in the West, more often than not, kept courtesans or concubines in the special quarters: this is nothing but the harem. It is interesting to note that the monarchs were ever on guard against any flirting of these special purpose women: the jealousy of the husbands and the flirting of the women have been known through the history at all levels of the social strata. These rulers of all people under their realms spent enormous sums of money to try to satisfy the apparently unquenchable sexual desire. The harem has continued to be seen as the ultimate setup which has remained only a dream for the vast majority of men.

The average men will rather have a large number of beautiful women than a single most beautiful woman. The single most beautiful woman may have been the subject of the various stories but has had a few limitations. She grows old and no longer attractive and caters for only one man at a time. Besides a man will soon get sick of her however beautiful she may be. I put forward three most beautiful women through the history of the world in Section 9 Three Ultimate Beauties in History, to try to get into the insight on this matter.

Every woman is an independent experience for men. As a consequence of this proposition, a powerful ruler with a large harem was ever on the lookout for a beautiful woman in the same way the ordinary men have been ever on the lookout for a pretty woman. When men look at a good-looking woman, they cannot be sure about her sexuality until they go to bed with her. Until men sleep with all the beautiful women in the world, they cannot say categorically what all the women are like, since there is always a possibility that some women behave differently sexually and give different impressions.

There is another twist concerning harem. According to the testimonies of many rulers, the possession of harem did not give the degree of happiness they had hoped to be theirs. For example, the preacher (possibly King Solomon) in the Bible (Ecclesiastes 1:2; 2:8) found that all was vanity in whatever he did, including acquiring wealth and concubines. The monarchs must have thought before the possession of the harem that they would be submerged in a perpetual bliss owning a harem in a similar fashion a young man before marriage tends to think that he would be submerged in a perpetual bliss in the marriage with his sweetheart. The reality is different for these men. Many kings and emperors, though their wills were absolute in many matters, experienced various problems in the maintenance of the harem--of money, of management and of intrigues--in a similar fashion mere mortals have had with their wives and girlfriends. We know that even the ordinary men have spent enormous (for them) amount of money on sex; for prostitutes, woman friends and wives. The rich husbands have money to spare and can attract young and beautiful women; hence they have more opportunity to have sexual relationship outside marriage. The differences are only the amount of money and prestige involved and subjectively speaking there was possibly no difference.

The fact that ordinary married men as well as kings with a large harem are not sexually sated suggests to us that there is something wrong with men who dream possessing all beautiful women for sexual purpose.

Many of the books in the Bible advocate consistently restraints in many matters, especially in sex. For example, Proverbs (Proverbs 31:3) goes: Do not give your strength to women, your ways to those who destroy even kings.

The following passage refers to the Persian Empire:

> A major component of the court was the harem. The Achaemenid [Achaemenian] king always had several wives, one of whom was his principal queen, and many concubines. While such a set-up had the advantage of ensuring numerous relatives for appointment for imperial offices, it also provided endless opportunities for social and political intrigues. As the book of Esther makes clear, the woman of harem often played important role in imperial decision making. (Cotterell 1993, p. 157)

Natural consequence of the harems as a social institution where a small number of wealthy men owned a large number of beautiful women was the depletion of women available for poor men since the population of women was approximately equal to that of men as it is today. We have to also consider the degradation of women in this system. In modern times this inequality or injustice is well recognised and the bigamy, possibly not harem, is illegal in most countries of the world today. The Bible does not condemn the custom of harem as an institution as it does not with slavery. The vast majority of people in the ancient and classical world looked at harem and slavery as a matter of fact or necessary evils of the society. The women who went into the sexual service to the rich men were sometimes forced; sometimes willing thinking they were better off than staying with their families. The situation would not have been much different for the people who went into slavery.

> And he [a good king] must not acquire many wives for himself, or else his heart will turn away; also silver and gold, he must not acquire in a great quantity for himself (Deuteronomy 17:17).

The above verse in the Bible is a part of the verses attached to the way of the kings.

Aristotle wrote, 'Through insolence of women many monarchies have been overthrown' (Harbottle 1897, p. 351).

In Chinese history, beautiful women, when looked as sex objects of the rulers, were known as castle levellers or country levellers from obvious reasons. The Chinese sovereign often possessed a thousand or more resident concubines. It was what we call a harem. (Harris 1999, p. 128)

The eunuchs were required to remove the penis as well as the testicles as the Chinese imperial tradition dictated. The majority of the eunuchs came from the poor family and performed a range of duties in the emperor's private quarters. They usurped the authority when they can, taking great risks. They showed solidarity as palace eunuchs who were mutilated, despised in the society and had to rely on the palace for the only support they could count. (p. 130) The eunuchs lived with the imperial family often from the emperor's infancy and served and became friends with him who appreciated their dedication and loyalty.

The following descriptions of the Chinese court during the decaying period of the T'ang dynasty (618-907) are bizarre to us but still are true and a part of history:

> By the early ninth century the eunuch palace servants gained control of the court, to the point where they and their henchmen enthroned and dethroned emperors, even murdering them with impunity (Murowchick 1994, p. 137).

The following is an account of eunuch servants of the Ming dynasty (1368-1644). The first Ming emperor, being conscious of the harms done in the past by eunuchs, restricted the number of eunuch servants to one hundred who were illiterate. During the 277 years of the dynasty the number of palace servants grew enormously and at the end of the sixteenth century as many as 70 000 eunuchs were employed at the imperial palace in Peking alone. Each eunuch was allowed to keep three retainers. The imperial family, especially the emperor, found that the eunuchs were loyal and useful for the various administrative jobs. The eunuchs in turn needed the favour of the imperial family for their sheer social existence, being despised in the society and having no power base outside the palace. During the last one hundred years of the Ming dynasty, the eunuchs (the inside party) controlled the palace administration to the exclusion of the scholar-officials (the outside party) to such an extent that Emperor Wan-li (1572-1620) did not have a single audience with his senior officials in 25 years, conducting all his business through eunuch servants. (Milston 1978, p. 214)

Even if men--kings, emperors or rich men--were convinced that they could lead a better and happier life without harem, most likely they would have carried on with their lives so as to get maximum sexual pleasure, thus keeping the harem. This result was universal and inherent in men and possibly in women too. Every man tried to secure the best girls he could get hold of, kings, emperors, the rich, the famous and the powerful having the best choice.

I have found that men can have a harem of their own by adjusting their outlook. They can look at a large variety of prostitutes as a harem. Just like a powerful monarch, when men become horny, they go out and choose the girl of their liking. If men pay well, the prostitute normally behaves well like a woman in the harem.

In conjunction with paying for the professional service of prostitutes, men must be worried with high expense as well as the contraction of various diseases. Standard rate for half hour service was 70 dollars in Australia in 1980s. The average wage earners had to work as much as six hours to make this amount of money. Thus, the income ratio of the wage earners and the prostitutes were 1 to 12. Even if the prostitutes had to pay half of the earnings to the brothel owner, the income ratio was still 1 to 6. The above reckonings do not take into account that the prostitutes, even beautiful, must wait for the clients to turn up.

Some people may object to the idea of sex for money; keeping harems or buying prostitutes. They must realise that the majority of men, whether they are married or have consenting girlfriends, have to pay for sex. We can say that a married man keeps a prostitute or one woman harem in his household. Not only do men pay financially but they have to pay in many other ways: most women make their men wait and angry by their peculiar way of thinking.

The Chinese intellectuals through the ages dreamed that China be unified under one native emperor in a similar fashion the ancient Greeks dreamed that the Greeks be governed by the independent city-states where only the Greek men participated in politics. The intellectuals of both nationalities no longer cherish the above dreams today. The Chinese dreamed the empire as the political ideal with no democratic concept, possibly from around the establishment of the Ch'in Empire (221 BC) to the early twentieth century. The Greeks had the foregoing political dream from the late ancient to early classical era with no concept of equal opportunity for women and foreigners. These contents of the idealised political state were different, stemming most likely from the different geographies and races, and the consequent different social setup.

However, men, young or old, married or single, rich or poor, of not only these nationalities but all over the world, have dreamed through the ages to the present day of owning the harem though almost all adult men have thought that women were inferior and evil, excluded them from the decision-making process, and oppressed them in the family and employment. Most men suffered from women in the domestic context but did not get rid of women from men's life since men needed women for their conveniences. Women served men sexually, did the domestic chores, and bore and raised children. When men dreamed harem, men were thinking of sexual aspect of women pushing aside the other aspects, helpful or unhelpful. Men confined women to domestic life depriving women of social life. By studying the history we can get to know the idealised political institutions of the peoples above mentioned. How do I know that men through the ages dreamed of owning the harems and more generally the sexual laws being developed in this book are applicable to virtually all men? I am devising the laws that are true today, and through inference, human nature and fragmentary information I conclude that they are the eternal truth. A few powerful women, not necessarily empresses, through the Chinese history obtained a number of men for sexual service who were called 'white face'. I have not come across any instance where an emperor was homosexual. I read a few stories of male homosexuals but none of female homosexuals.

Section 8 Sex without Concept of Woman (or Bitch)

Suppose a baby boy (or a puppy dog) is left in the jungle and brought up by some wild animals, in a way JR Kipling narrates in *Jungle Books* (1894; 1895). Obviously the baby (or the puppy) would grow to show his physical characteristics which the genes decide. However, we know from the instances of the similar cases in the real life which were reported the world over that he would think and behave like wild animals with which he came into contact. At puberty, he would feel a sexual need if he is normal, and would either have a go at friendly animals or masturbate. He still does not know what a woman (or a bitch) of his kind looks like in a proper physical form.

When we watch a suburban dog masturbate on our leg for want of a bitch, he does not appear to be fantasising an intercourse with a bitch, though he knows what a bitch looks like: he gives the impression that the act is of a desperate physical nature. Admittedly men are no better than this dog and the reason why submitting women are not frightened by the desperate act of men is that women are fascinated themselves.

The boy in the jungle is expected to behave sexually in the similar fashion as the wanking suburban dog because his thinking faculty is not well developed. He most likely does not need fantasy to achieve orgasm. Men brought up in the civilised world are no better than the wanking suburban dog or the jungle boy (or the dog), as far as the sexual drive is concerned. However, the reason developed in the civilised men alters their behaviour somewhat: they would do the sexual act in the hiding to give semblance of dignity in public.

Suppose the boy (or the dog) in the wild is brought to civilisation and a girl (or a bitch) is presented to him. I can imagine the situation where the boy (or the dog) tries to have sex with her in the presence of people. However, the most likely scenario would be that he is at a loss what to do. Probably he does not look at her as a sexual object, and has to learn about her in the same way about many unfamiliar things around.

Section 9 Three Ultimate Beauties in History

The ultimate physical pains, the ultimate mental anguish and the ultimate female beauties: they are all hard to convey in any language and art forms. The ultimate severe physical pains are likely to cause unconsciousness or even death. The unbearable mental agony can lead to suicide for the sufferer but in my case led to the development of new philosophy as I expound in Book Four *The Third Prophecy*.

Many artists drew what they thought were ideal female figures but I doubt if they are as good as the females men create in their fantasy during masturbation. I would bet the average men would pick 10 beautiful women as their possessions rather than to have one ultimate beauty. Besides we don't know if these beauties are good natured, intelligent or not. We do know for certain that they all fart and defecate, though they give us the impression that they emit gas perfume and solid perfume now and again from their arse. We also know they grow old and die, though Cleopatra committed suicide in her middle age and Yang Guifei was killed while young.

Seduction story of Helen is described in *Iliad*, and the subsequent return journey by Odysseus in *Odyssey*.

It is also often quoted that Cleopatra was the most beautiful woman that has ever trodden the earth. She was a Greek by blood, descending from Ptolemy who was a general of Alexander the Great. When Alexander and his army marched into Egypt, the Egyptians had been under Persian rule for nearly two hundred years and the Egyptians welcomed Alexander and his army into their land as conquerors in 331 BC. (Wells 1925, p. 201) By the life time of Cleopatra, the Egyptian kingdom was disintegrating and she had to look for the outside support. Cleopatra became mistress of Julius Caesar, who restored her as the ruler, queen Pharaoh, of Egypt (Freeman 1996, pp. 281, 368). Women were held in high esteem in Egypt and a female head in Egypt was not rare, though it was extremely rare in the classical world that women became the rulers in their own right. There were three or four female pharaohs in Dynastic Egypt and a number of queens in the Ptolemaic Egypt. (Wells 1925, p. 130) The matrilineal nature of ancient Egyptian society was evident from very early times.

The Chinese have regarded Yang Guifei (Kuei-fei) as the most beautiful woman in their history. Her beauty was enhanced when people got familiar with her tragic story as the favourite concubine of the Brilliant Emperor, Xuan Zong (Hsuan Tsung), who lived in the 8th century.

Story of Helen

The Trojan War and its aftermath became the subject of the *Iliad* and the *Odyssey*, whose authorship is attributed to the Greek poet Homer; and the *Aeneid* by the Roman poet Virgil.

The two epic poems, *Iliad* and *Odyssey*, became the basis of Greek education and culture throughout the late ancient to classical age to be replaced by Christianity in the classical years. The Greeks esteemed the two epics as more than works of literature and knew much of them by heart. They were the symbol of Hellenic unity and the source of moral and even practical instructions.

An alphabetic writing system had reached Greece in the 9th or early 8th century BC. One theory asserts that Homer fixed *Iliad* and *Odyssey* based on the oral traditions sometime after 750 BC. *Iliad and Odyssey* were committed to writing on Homer's creations since he was known to be blind. Homer added his creativity and spontaneity to the traditional and formulaic style of the oral stories.

Pentateuch was translated from the original Hebrew into Greek c. 250 BC and the rest of the Old Testament was translated in Egypt in the second century BC. These Greek versions of the Old Testament was called Septuagint and presumably intended for the Greek speaking

Jewish community in Egypt when the Greek was the lingua franca throughout the region. The New Testament was originally written in Greek. The majority of the Jews read only the Old Testament and discarded the New Testament.

According to Greek myth of Trojan War, the Greeks laid the seize to Troy, in order to recover Helen, and to avenge the wrong done to Menelaus, king of Sparta. Paris, son of King Priam of Troy, had seduced Helen, wife of Menelaus. Helen was reputed to be a rare beauty. Agamemnon, Menelaus's brother, led the Greek army against Troy to win back Helen. Paris was killed during the battle. Helen then married Paris' brother, who was also killed. After a 10 year siege, Troy which was protected by high stone walls was finally captured by the ingenious use of the Trojan Horse. (Reader's Digest 1983, p. 70) After the capture of Troy by the Greek army, Helen and Menelaus were happily reunited.

Some critics say the story of Troy was only legend and did not take place in the real life. Michel de Montaigne (1533-1592) did not think that the Trojan War ever had taken place (Montaigne 1965, p. 570). Some modern writers speculate that the Mycenaean Greeks assailed Troy in order to secure a trade route to the Black Sea through the Hellespont which the Trojans controlled (Wells 1925, p. 110).

The city of Troy yielded the extensive ruins the oldest of which date back to 3000 BC, and is one of the most important archaeological sites of the ancient world. The Turks knew the mound at the site to contain the ruins. Charles McLaren identified the site as the Homeric Troy in 1822.

Heinrich Schliemann confirmed the city of Troy, and by digging the site in 1870 he found that several cities were built on the site over a long period. Troy was an ancient city in Asia Minor, about 6 kilometres from the southern entrance of the Hellespont, later called the Dardanelles. The prosperity of Troy depended on the trade commanding the strategic routes between Europe and Asia. After the founding of Constantinople (present day Istanbul) in AD 324 at the location 250 km north-east of Troy, Ilion, a transliteration of the Greek name for ancient Troy, faded into obscurity.

After Schliemann's death in 1890, the excavations continued. The excavators established that there were nine principal strata, representing nine periods during which houses were built, occupied and destroyed. Troy VIIa, destroyed by fire some time about the 13th century BC, is probably the city of King Priam described in Homer's *Iliad*. Many scholars believe that the poems of *Iliad* and *Odyssey* were composed between 800 and 700 BC because they match with the social conditions of the era.

Cleopatra

Plutarch (?46-?120) wrote that Cleopatra was not particularly beautiful but had the most beautiful voice reminding of singing, drawing this conclusion from the eyewitness accounts. He further wrote that she was proud of her charms and possessed with the opinion of the power of her beauty. (Gwinn 1990, pp. 757, 769, 775) Plutarch's uncomplimentary remark on her appearance matches with her portrait in the contemporary coin: she had an unusually large nose and is not beautiful at any stretch of imagination. The coin makers must have done their best to make the portrait look better than or at least faithful to the real life, as we can easily conjecture from today's coin making practice.

Herodotus called Egypt the gift of the Nile. He also made his another famous remark concerning Cleopatra: Had her nose a little flatter, the world history might have been different. This proposition assumes that Cleopatra was very beautiful with her prominent nose heightening her beauty. However, this assumption goes against the contrary evidence of the last paragraph. It also does not take into account the fact that Egypt remained the most powerful state among the successor states of Alexander's empire and hence in the

Mediterranean world, only to be eclipsed by the rise of Rome. Rome played, at around the time of Cleopatra's life, the dominant force in Mediterranean politics. Ptolemy XII (80-58 BC and 55-51 BC) legitimatised his rule with Roman approval during his first reign. He regained the kingship again with the help of the Romans after having been driven out of the office.

Cleopatra became the co-ruler of Egypt together with her 10 year old brother, Ptolemy XIII in 51 BC, after the death of her father Ptolemy XII. Cleopatra and her brother were in fact married. The Ptolemy's guardians seized power for him and drove Cleopatra from the throne. Caesar, after defeating Cleopatra's opponents, set Cleopatra back in the throne along with another brother Ptolemy XIV; Ptolemy XIII had died by this time. Cleopatra gave birth to a boy Caesarion, which she claimed as Caesar's. At the time of assassination of Caesar, Cleopatra was in Rome. The Caesar's association with Cleopatra was unpopular in Rome; it seems that the assassins knowing the above fact murdered Caesar while she was in Rome. On returning to Egypt she had Ptolemy killed.

In 41 BC Mark Antony and Cleopatra met in Asia Minor and fell in love. They conspired to rule Rome; however, the defeat at Actium by the hand of Octavian's general put paid to all their schemes.

Around Cleopatra's life time Egypt was a country of great wealth, possibly exceeding that of the Roman Republic; Rome was not an empire at this time. Strength of Rome is said to be the democratic form of government which the Greek cultural predecessor originated, as well as its huge and well-disciplined army. Cleopatra was, with all her wealth, well aware that Egypt was no match to Rome militarily and desperately manoeuvred for her survival as a monarch of independent Egypt.

She must also have expected that the issue was ultimately to be decided by the military conflicts rather than other factors such as economics or politics. Julius Caesar and Mark Antony in turn coveted the grains and the wealth of Egypt not so much for their own gains but for the control of the Roman Republic. Hence these men wanted to acquire Cleopatra as a lover whether the living legend that she was the most beautiful woman was true or not. Being a queen in the men's world of governing in the classical era would have helped to nurture the legend. Certainly nurturing the legend would have helped their cause. If the powerful man such as these men had said in her presence with some convincing tone and surprised look, 'I heard you were the most beautiful woman in the world but you exceeded all my expectations', she, being conscious of the legend, would have been greatly flattered and prepared to submit herself, thus saving them enormous expenditure and human lives in subjugating Egypt. One story goes that Caesar and Antony were the only men Cleopatra knew in her life.

There is another story. Cleopatra set the price with her night in bed as the lover's life, that is, the man was to be killed after one night with her. There was no lack of volunteers, which must have promoted the idea that she was most beautiful. I am to develop the psychological profile of both Cleopatra and her subject lovers since, I hope, this development may assist the understanding of sex. Certainly not confirming the truthfulness of the story--in fact nobody can--may give the impression that the profile is only a fantasy; after all sex is mostly fantasy.

Cleopatra was to be revered as a god in her realm as the tradition dictated of the pharaohs of Egypt. However, she knew she was only a human with all her desires and defects. Her body functioned physiologically in the same way as any other females. If she spent a night with a lover, he would certainly know that her body was no different from any other women and most likely be disappointed in the same way a bridegroom would be in the first night with his loving bride because of high expectations. Cleopatra's lover, after the night, would tell people what he discovered about her body and mannerism in bed, which she must have detested.

We do not have to resort to economic theory to work out that one of the measures of a commodity price is the availability of the commodity: the difficulty in obtaining it forces its price up. If Cleopatra had slept with a large number of men, she would have become cheap most definitely among these men and possibly in her queendom. In spite of her above reasoning she still wanted to go to bed with a large variety of men. She solved the problem by killing the lover after a night with her. She took only willing and consenting lovers such that she was not guilty of murdering her subjects, though she, as Pharaoh, had a power to kill any of her subjects.

Being voluntary gave a few more advantages to Cleopatra. The male participant was prepared for death; hence he had to make the most of his night in lovemaking. I would imagine that a forced lover would be frozen stiff from fear of dying in the morning and unable to function as a useful bed mate. In addition, the voluntary bed mate would not have noticed even if she had some physical defects. Everything would be crystallised like a dream since his hours on earth could be counted with his fingers. He would have seen the queen and lovemaking as the most beautiful. If he had expressed his opinion to the jailers, his family or his friends just before he died, he most likely would have said that Cleopatra was the most beautiful woman, believing that was the truth. Thus the legend of Cleopatra was further promoted.

The foregoing sexual indulgence by Cleopatra probably did not have much to do with her personal fate: even if the story had been true she would have been hardly to blame from moral viewpoint.

After all her political and military intrigues Cleopatra eventually felt that everything was lost and killed herself in 30 BC when she was 39 years of age, and Egypt lost her independence and became a province of Rome. It is on record that she even tried to seduce Octavian (later Augustus) without success. This confirms the earlier two propositions. Cleopatra was not beautiful and the wealth of Egypt was in the hand of Octavian at that time and he did not need her on both accounts. It is said that Octavian brought so much wealth from Egypt to Rome that usury substantially fell (Robbins 1998, p. 42). Egypt became a Roman province as Cleopatra had been afraid, and Roman domination of Egypt lasted from 30 BC to AD 642, when the Muslims from Arabia conquered Egypt. It became a personal estate of Augustus at one time. Egypt's vast quantity of grains was shipped to Rome to feed the Roman citizens. However, the legend that she was the most beautiful woman has lived to this day. The legend was born from the circumstances and her possible contrivances but the evidence suggests she was not beautiful. I now believe that Cleopatra's look was average at best in her contemporary society: I do not think that the judging criteria of female beauty among the Mediterranean peoples and the peoples of the Western world have changed appreciably in all these centuries.

Story of Yang Guifei (Kuei-fei) and Emperor Xuan Zong (Hsuan Tsung) (Reigned 712-756)

Emperor Hsuan Tsung was the sixth emperor of the T'ang dynasty and China achieved its greatest prosperity and power during his reign. Hsuan Tsung became emperor in 712. He was the last of the three great T'ang rulers. During his reign China produced the best poets, Li Bo and Du Fu, in her entire history. The emperor's economic programmes greatly increased China's wealth. In 747, China reached its peak of influence in Western Asia.

In 736 the political dominance of the aristocracy was firmly established, and Li Lin-fu, the chief minister of aristocratic origin, became a virtual dictator. The emperor withdrew from the affairs of state and indulged in the pleasures and Daoism (Taoism). The emperor, now 60, became desperately in love with Yang Kuei-fei, a concubine of his son, in 745; and forced his son to discard her and took her as his mistress.

The story centres on love and tragedy, not on sexual nature (Ebrey 1996, p. 121).

Yang Kuei-fei became the favourite concubine of Emperor Hsuan Tsung. An Lu-shan, as a military governor, made frequent visits to the capital and became the favourite of the emperor and Yang Kuei-fei. He was appointed to the royal court through her influence. Though he was a general in China, he was a Turkish descent. By the time of Minister Li Lin-fu's death in 752, An Lu-shan was the most powerful general in the empire. However, after the intrigues, Yang Kuo-chung, a brother of Yang Kuei-fei, was appointed as the first minister of the empire. An Lu-shan got enraged when he did not get the post of prime minister and launched a rebellion in 755, proclaiming himself an emperor. In 756, Hsuan Tsung turned the throne over to his son, who became Su-tsung. It was rumoured that An Lu-shan and Yang Kuei-fei were in fact lovers and also she encouraged his ambition. The revolt seemed to succeed and the emperor had to flee from the capital Ch'ang-an. On the way the palace guard demanded the execution of Yang Kuei-fei and her brother for further loyalty; so the emperor had to comply. The rebel leader An Lu-shan was murdered by his own son and the government forces restored order in 763 after painful battles. Hsuan Tsung himself nearing 80 had died of exhaustion and his grief over the death of Yang Kuei-fei in Ch'ang-an a year earlier. (The Editors of Time-Life Books 1988, pp. 116-8) Though the rebellion was contained in the end, the prestige of the T'ang dynasty was broken. The T'ang emperors had to appoint military governors to protect the northern boundaries. These generals formed virtually independent kingdoms and appointed their sons as successors. The rebellion started the decline of the dynasty, and the weak governments and emperors followed, though it lasted another 150 years. (Milston 1978, pp. 161, 163)

We can see the elements of tragedy in the above story. The old emperor loved beautiful Yang Kuei-fei who was not faithful to him as both a lover and a subject. The emperor did not see the absurdity of his love and he had to agree to her execution not understanding what really happened. Unless Yang Kuei-fei was really beautiful, the story does not make sense.

Section 10 Instinct of Young Lovers

When inexperienced adolescents fall in love, they, unlike in the movies, often too timid to talk to each other, much less to go out for a date. We may attribute it to shyness. Or it may be that a feeling inside--some people may call it an instinct--tell them that they do not want to violate the sacred emotion by coming to terms with the reality. They perceive that the physical contact, not necessarily of sexual relation, would degrade their platonic love. The girls sense that once they reveal what they are to the boys, the boys may lose interest in them. Hence the girls are reluctant to show everything to the boys. Both sweethearts know intuitively that the feelings they have each other are not real and built on imaginations. They secretly cherish that their fancy does not end by facing the fact of life. They know that their bodies are not as good as their sweethearts may be imagining and also are aware that they have all sorts of desires and defects which they want to hide from their beloved. Thus they avoid each other though they desperately want to converse.

It may happen that two young persons in love are united by some circumstance which is beyond their control: Apart from the foregoing remarks about the young love we have to take into account the strong sexual desire of the boys. They passionately engage in a romantic infatuation to the exclusion of everything else. It is expected that after a while they become sober and lose interest in any more affairs. They may be totally alienated and left with bitter and sad memories. Why did they not live happily until the ripe old age as they had hoped? I may say that God (Truth) does not approve all consuming passions in whatever human activities: they excluded God (Truth) hence were punished. Their love contains a large amount of conceits as I mentioned in the last paragraph, which goes against truth.

God as the Old Testament portrays is anthropomorphic and shows various human emotions such as anger, pity, regret and jealousy. In the New Testament these traits disappear completely. One prominent quality of God in the Old Testament, which we feel strange, is that God has one imperfection of being jealous, if expressed in human terms. God was jealous of the young couple because they devoted exclusively to each other hence God inflicted some pains on them befitting to the circumstances. I may add that the two people were deluded into thinking that they could satisfy all the sexual and other needs with each other. According to my research men and possibly women too get bored with the same partner after so many repeated sex. Also humans had to satisfy the other needs apart from love and sex. Many parents do not want their children to go through the similar traumatic experience of the love affairs as they did when they were young. The youngsters, in their turn, feel the urge that they have to have their sweethearts, irrespective of the parents' feeling and what may lie ahead of the relations. Thus they normally repeat what their parents went through. Here again we can see that love between sexes is fundamental to humans and exclusive of another fundamental inclination that humans want to be happy.

The above observations reveal that the sexual love among young people is in fact a fleeting emotion in spite of their genuineness. Young lovers may know by instinct that their love is an illusion and they do not want to shatter the illusion by coming contact with their sweethearts thus try to avoid them initially anyway. Jesus Christ said that the highest state of mind achievable by the philosophers is manifested in the toddlers (Matthew 11:25-6; 18:3-4). Similarly we may observe the concept of Mind Only (or Emptiness), the Buddha arrived at after many years of asceticism, in the young lovers' mind not contaminated by base emotions. Mind Only (or Emptiness) teaches that everything, in this case human bodies and sexual love, is an illusion.

Section 11 Sexual Taboos

When the written history started in a few places of the world around 5000 years ago, there had already been the set sexual patterns in the human society. A prominent taboo against incest was established. Women were considered as property with sexual and reproductive values. Men were free to have as many sexual partners. The prostitution was widely spread. (Masters, Johnson & Kolodny 1985, p. 11)

Most mammalian males behave sexually in a similar way human males do; after all humans are mammals. Both of them always want the females around for sexual purpose and when they are sexually aroused they seek penile penetrations into the females. Thus we are justified to seek mammalian origin for many of the male sexual behaviours. Yet one feature strikes me that both are quite different. Mammals copulate in the open whereas humans today under the normal circumstances try to hide their sexual activities. It is not easy to give reasons to such a matter of fact as human's making love in the utmost secrecy. It seems that in the so-called primitive human societies, the primitive human animals did not have sexual taboos and practised unrestrained and uninhibited sex activities. (Kinsey, Pomeroy & Martin 1948, p. 222)

Humans have learned to wear clothes for warmth and social intercourse. They normally take off their clothes only in the hiding. Hence, naturally, when they make love, men and women undress, while mammals do not have to disrobe since they do not wear any clothes.

There is another difference between mammals and humans in the sexual term. Mammals' sexual urge is seasonal, whereas men's sexual drive does not depend on the season. Some men and women prefer to have sex at a certain time of a day by their habit; some want in the early morning or in the afternoon or late at night. Mammals' seasonal nature of the sexual activities can be easily ascertained by the need to have offspring at the time of warm weather and abundance of food, that is, spring and summer. Most of the mammals mate for reproduction purpose only and the males approach the females for copulation only when the latter are ready with their reproduction cycles. (*Encyclopedia of Love & Sex* 1972, p. 185)

Mammals can be considered in three groups: subprimates, primates and humans. Primates include humans in the normal use but this paragraph and the next make use of the different classification for easy explanation. Subprimate females do not have menstruation but have estruses and the sexual coitus is seasonal. In oestrus (estrus) the ovulation is taking place and the copulation can lead to pregnancy: the males can tell by smelling the female genital organs. Human females have menstruation but menstruation does not regulate sexual activities. Primates such as monkeys and apes are between the above two extremes. Some primate females have estruses and some menstruation, though the copulation habits are not necessarily dictated by estruses or menstruation as above mentioned. (Zubin & Money 1973, pp. 190-1)

Dogs, one of subprimates, are peculiar in that they have a genital lock during mating. The swollen penis within the vagina makes tight connections until the transfer of sperm is complete. The transfer finishes in 15-30 minutes and detumescence begins.

Inbreeding (breeding mammals that are consanguineous) is a serious problem even for animals in the zoos. Hence zoo managements throughout the world exchange animals to avoid inbreeding. Inbreeding of animals as for the humans can produce birth defects and eventually weaken the entire population.

When people are submerged in a culture with some taboos, they don't think these taboos are strange until they come across a culture of different taboos. Hence contact of two cultures make people think about their own culture. Thus one benefit of travelling is without any doubt a pleasure, which is often emphasised: the travellers do not suffer from the local problems. Another benefit would be to think about themselves in the light of the various aspects, say, taboos of another culture.

The Bible says that men should not approach their wives during menstruation for sexual purpose, and people should not work on Sabbath in order to dedicate the day for worship. Both prohibitions are taboos, though people submerged in the Judaic tradition may have resistance in acknowledging it. The reason for the former taboo is probably women are unclean during menstruation. The reason for the latter is clearly stated in the Bible: God rested on the seventh day after creating the world and the Sabbath day is holy and belongs to God (e.g., Genesis 2:1-3; Exodus 20:8-11); also many Christians believe that Jesus Christ resurrected on Sunday. Sabbath comes on every seventh day for the believers. Sabbath is Saturday for the Jews; many Jews still believe that Sabbath lasts from sunset of Friday evening till night fall of Saturday, strictly adhering to the prescribed rules. Sabbath is Sunday for the Christians, and Friday for the Muslims.

Sigmund Freud explored the taboos of the Aboriginal people in Australia. In Australia in the early dream time as in many other places of the world, the group marriage where a number of men exercised conjugal rights over a number of women was the norm. However, the individual marriage had to come about to prevent incestuous relation, though some form of group marriage still exist to this day in a few tribes in Australia. Among the various taboos, the clan places the strict incest taboo in conjunction with totem. A totem is an object; an animal, a plant, or natural phenomenon symbolising a clan and representing a common ancestor. This is a simplified code and in practice the relationship of totem and clan is more complicated. Marriage within the clan is prohibited, and the penalty for sexual intercourse with a person of forbidden clan is death for both the man and the woman with some exceptions granted. A clan is a large unit of people many of whom do not share the consanguineous relationship, which also reflects the excessive degree of horror of incest by the majority of the Aboriginal people. A tribe is a still larger unit consisting of clans. (Freud 1960, pp. 2, 4-7)

Taboo is a Polynesian word. Taboo is invariably expressed in the form of prohibitions or negatives. Taboo is a social custom prohibiting a particular practice. The taboos generally come about when people feel sensitive about the subjects (sexual and otherwise) and do not know what to make or what to do on the issue at hand. Taboo operates in a compulsive fashion: people do not ask why but feel they have no choice but submit, and defies any logical explanation except for incest taboo. Aristo used to say that the words men fear most are those that uncover them (Montaigne 1965, p. 643). It is a natural withdrawal symptom of humans from the highly sensitive matters.

There are other dimensions of taboos apart from the social taboos. For example, it is a taboo by the nature of the beliefs for the Christians to criticise the Bible and Jesus Christ, and for the communists to criticise *Capital* and Karl Marx. We are told that we should not discuss politics or religion, particularly race and woman issues, at work. This is not a taboo but more a recommendation for avoiding the conflicts. In case of sex there are other considerations. It may be because humans, being intelligent, are aware that the lovemaking process is not a pretty sight to see for the non-participants--especially for their children. It may be because they want to hide their ecstasy accompanying copulation. 'Do not lie' is not a taboo, though expressed in a negative but is a moral stricture, seeing that the prohibition is universal and in the open. 'Love thy neighbour' is a positive statement referring to the moral and definitely not a taboo.

Sex has been, until recent times, a taboo subject in most cultures--at least in the overt cultures. Sex ceased to be a taboo subject in the Western world after World War I, particularly after World War II. The subject of death also came to be discussed freely after World War II: it had been a taboo subject earlier.

Masters and Johnson found that a considerable proportion of women are sexually aroused during the breast feeding of their babies, some to the so-called plateau level that immediately precedes orgasm, and a small number of women even experience orgasm. The mothers who are sexually aroused during breast feeding will, if they are normal, hide that fact from the family and disclose it only under a specific circumstance in the similar fashion they do not disclose their occurrence of menstruations under normal circumstances. Both of these prohibitions are taboos, seeing that though both are universal both are not in the open.

Breast feeding, as for sexual coitus, is essential for the survival of the human race hence pleasure accompanies both activities. Even the infants feel pleasure suckling the breasts in the process of receiving the nourishment, and the erection of the penis is common in male babies. (Zubin & Money 1973, p. 82)

The parents normally do not discuss their sexual habits with their children. Sex is a taboo subject between parents and children. The parents often relate their sex life with people other than their children. The children in turn talk about what they see or hear concerning their parents' sexual activities among themselves or with their friends. We often hear that the toddlers, not being aware the parents' embarrassment, disclose the sexual conducts of their parents in the open. These toddlers learn quickly not to talk about it under some circumstances as they grow up. Also they learn in no time the taboos associated with their private parts.

All societies have a concept of incest, and all societies have a prohibition or taboo against it. Definition of incest varies according to the definition of who is close kin. The incest taboo is perhaps the most binding and ubiquitous social restraint known to man. (Sadock, Kaplan & Freedman 1976, p. 415)

Most societies forbid intercourse between the family members; father and daughter, brother and sister, mother and son. These intercourses are more often than not crimes punishable by laws.

It happens quite commonly that the parents feel sexual desire towards their offspring--especially a father towards his pretty daughter. The father and mother, if normal, keep the desire to themselves, do not discuss with anybody, and do not dare to make it a reality. It is a taboo to carry out sex between the parents and their children and also a taboo to talk the desire in the open. The society severely reprimands the offenders, though they are only honest to follow their innate feelings.

Closely tied with the incest taboo is the practice of endogamy or marriage within one's own tribe or similar unit; and the practice of exogamy or marriage outside the group. Incest refers to sex; and endogamy and exogamy refer to marriage.

In conjunction with incest which does not necessarily produce offspring, there is a problem of in-breeding which produces offspring. The nearer the relationship the worse effect of in-breeding. The offspring born from the near relationship have the greater chance of premature death and severe abnormalities. This trend has been statistically proven. (Smith 1968, p. 263)

There is a general agreement among the researchers that parent-child incest does not occur in stable, loving families (Westheimer 1994, p. 155). As a matter of fact, brother-sister incest is the most frequently reported form and is almost five times more frequently reported than that of father and daughter. Incest, particularly parent-child sex, has been forbidden in nearly all communities since the people entered the cultured state from the natural state. Sex between brother and sister was permitted as a social practice in a few cultures especially among nobility. For example, in the ancient Egypt, the pharaohs had to marry their sisters to keep the blood royal. The pharaohs were thought to be so divine that they could not marry commoners. It was customary for the pharaohs to marry blood relatives within the degree of consanguinity, and the pharaohs often had their sisters and daughters in their harem. Among the commoners in Egypt, brother-sister marriages were almost unheard of, although marriages between cousins, uncles and nieces were quite common. (Freeman 1996, p. 53)

Royalty in ancient Egypt and the Incas of Peru did not have any restrictions of close blood marriage. In fact in-breeding in these royal families was encouraged. Ramses II (?1292-?1225 BC) had at least 50 daughters and he married quite a few of them. (Smith 1968, p. 259)

In the Egyptian society, especially in the New Kingdom, love was often the important subject people elaborated upon (Burguiere et al. 1996, p. 133). The universal taboo about marriage and sex was not strictly followed in the Egyptian society, which was so contrary to Greek and Roman cultures that the root cause is sought in the Egyptian practices (p. 134). Ptolemy II (285-246 BC), an Egyptian Pharaoh, married his full sister, who became Arsinoe II (p. 134). This marriage set the precedence for the consanguineous marriage among the royal families, which became famous among the Mediterranean peoples. Akhenaton married his father's wife. (p. 135) The effect of the marriage of sister and brother is unknown in Egypt.

In the royal marriage in the Egyptian society, the open reason cited is to keep the royal blood pure. However, the true reason seems to strengthen or legitimatise the royal succession by combining two lineages of the royal blood. (p. 134)

In the Ptolemaic Egypt, the indigenous and occupying Geek communities coexisted while remaining separate. Of the 14 Ptolemies who reigned in Alexandria, eight married their own sisters. Their marriages were prompted, apart from the fundamental reason to secure the throne as stated in the last paragraph, by economic, personal, and diplomatic considerations. (p. 138)

The period of Roman domination in Egypt saw a sharp increase in consanguineous marriage in the Greco-Egyptian population. In the AD first three centuries in Egypt, it was estimated that 10-20 per cent of all marriages were consanguineous. (p. 138)

The Bible prohibits the sexual intercourse among the family members. It prohibits not only sex between blood related people such as father and daughter, and mother and son but the family members by marriage or adoption such as father and daughter-in-law, and mother and son-in-law. (Leviticus 18:6-18)

I am trying, among other things in this section, to uncover the reasons for the sexual taboos most of which is still paramount in today's so-called civilised societies.

The nuclear family are related by blood (through birth), by affinity (through marriage), or through adoption. The nuclear family is universally practised in the world and forms the basis of the other types of family. The polygamous and extended family are also widely observed.

Many scientists looked into the sexual behaviours in apes in an effort to unravel those of our ancestors. However, one species of apes sexually behave differently from another; and even among the same species, the apes from one community behave differently from another. That is to say, the generalisation is hard to make based on the observations of apes. One observation is strange but consistent. If a male chimpanzee is denied the sexual knowledge before the age of six, he, after his sexual maturity, does not know what to do; even he and his mate are on heat. (Taylor 1996, p. 80)

The observations on the pygmy chimpanzees go like the following. They seem to be interested only in sex. They indulge not only in adult heterosexual activities but in adult and infant sex. However, the sex between mothers and sons over six years of age seems to be a taboo. (p. 81)

When the Europeans explored the various parts of the world in the modern times, they reported the open sexuality among the natives (p. 82).

Four million years ago in Africa, the proto-human ancestors started walking, making distinction from the chimps. They were covered by hairs. Females had large clitorises and small breasts. Males had small penises. They made love indiscriminately even with the members of their own sex or immediate family, though it seems their selection was based on physical beauty. (p. 4)

It was speculated that the Stone Age men or more generally the prehistoric humans, did not know the connection between sex and reproduction. They simply had sex intercourse for pleasure and did not anticipate the pregnancy and the birth of the babies. (p. 91) They would not have speculated a connection between incestuous unions and consequent physical and mental abnormality of the infants.

The survival cannot be explained from the surrounding environment alone but also comes from the sexual selection. Men wanted beautiful females which deviated considerably from the environmental adaptation, for example, lack of body hairs. The females on the other hand selected the males not only because they were strong but astute or beautiful. (p. 5)

Two and a half million years ago, the proto-humans, with the freed hands by walking upright, started culture, making various artefacts. The chipped stone artefacts have survived but the artefacts made of skins, bark and wood have not survived because of their non-durable nature. (p. 6)

It was conjectured that around 1.6 million years ago, the language and possibly clothing were invented. The language was used as a declaration of love, and the clothing was used to conceal and enhance the attractiveness of the genital region. (p. 6)

Between 1.6 million years and 150 000 years ago anatomically modern humans first appeared (p. 7).

The animals, as for the proto-humans in the past, are under the domain of Darwinian evolution, biologically adapting them to the natural environment. Natural selection is not mediated by conscious awareness on the part of the individual organism. (Sadock, Kaplan & Freedman 1976, p. 420) In the history of human kind, the evolution is made by culture. The culture, as learned information, is inherited and magnified from generation to generation and thus adapting the environment to ourselves.

Scientists believe that family life began among prehistoric people more than 300 000 years ago. Several families lived together to make a group. These prehistorical people did not know the technique of farming and engaged in hunting animals and gathering wild plants for food and moved from place to place.

The family started when a large number of related people by blood or adoption lived under one roof. They made love freely among members. When a woman got pregnant, the family did not know and most likely did not care who the father was. Consequently matrilineality had to develop where the descent of the family was traced through the female line. It seems that the matrilineality was the norm among all the peoples of the world during the prehistoric era. Probably the head of the family was a male by sheer necessity since it was established by this time that men were physically and mentally more capable than women.

This system of family had a serious flaw in that the offspring was mostly of related blood and hence tended to be inferior to the parents, manifesting a higher incident of death, mental retardation, and congenital defects. We learn at school that marriage of close blood has a high probability of producing inferior or even defective children in both physical and mental terms. There are ample evidence to support its assertion and nobody questions its validity in today's civilised world. However, I am at a loss how the distant ancestors got to that conclusion. In-breeding is a problem even among wild animals and it seems they are aware of that, trying to avoid under the normal circumstances. The civilised humans are also aware instinctively of the problem, and it shows up as the general but acute aversion to making love to the blood relatives.

Incest is universally condemned. As the immediacy of biological relationship increases, the sanction also increases. Highly inbred population have diminished reproductive success and become gene pools for hereditary disorders.

The prohibition of inbreeding signals the transition from the natural state where the mating between the close relatives was permitted to the cultural state. It seems that the major force of the transition is not the horror of inbreeding rather that a group wanted to avoid isolation by connecting the two groups by marriage. (Burguiere et al. 1996, p. 25) Thus the exogamy provides an opportunity to create relatives and the best means of living peacefully with one's neighbours. The endogamy does not give this advantage. (p. 26)

The oppression of women, which we still witness in the modern world, has its root in prehistory and more a product of culture than the biological characteristics. In a few parts of the world, the Neolithic revolution took place around 10 000 years ago. Its chief manifestation, farming, led to the division of labour between men and women, which heralded the oppression of women. (Taylor 1996, p. 9)

Every human being carries potentially harmful recessive genes. When the recessive genes mate the similar genes, the offspring produced has a high probability of the genetic defects. Brothers and sisters, fathers and daughters, and mothers and sons have half the genes in common. The fractions become smaller as the relationship grow more distant. On uncle-niece matings, one-quarter of the recessive genes is shared. On cousin matings one-eight is shared.

Wheat is an example of a plant that is predominantly self-pollinating. Self-pollination is the closest form of inbreeding, but the inbreeding does not progressively weaken the vigour of a wheat strain. Inbreeding decreases the vigour and yield with corn. Inbreeding and a prevalence of homozygosis is the normal state in wheat, whereas hybrid vigour is the normal state of a corn population and the humans. In the species and populations in which the reproductive biology is adjusted to outbreeding, consanguinity leads to decline in the average vigour and to the appearance of relatively many individuals with hereditary diseases and malformation. (*Encyclopaedia Britannica*, 15th edn, sv, Genetics and Hereditary.)

The inferior or defective offspring from inbreeding comes from nature or God. The people who live under the same roof can have sex comparatively easily. However, nature or God says that is wrong. It is hard to speculate the reason for the prohibition. Incest, if it does not produce any children, should not have any harmful effect. Sex between father and daughter-in-law or mother and son-in-law should not have any detrimental effect, even if offspring is born. The Bible uniformly condemns the incest which is punishable by death. Nature or God ordains that when an egg cell is germinated by a sperm cell of the similar blood, the fertilised egg tends to be defective. This is the way of nature or God to say that the egg should be fertilised by the dissimilar sperm for the better results. The above observation may be true for mammals but not true for some plants.

In China marriage within the same family was strictly forbidden by immemorial custom.

> In Yang-shao villages and cemeteries, houses and cemeteries were clustered in well delineated groups, suggesting that society was organised in unilinear kin groups that regulated the behaviour of their members. For example, members of a unilinear--either patrilineal or matrilineal--group were forbidden to intermarry. (Murowchick 1994, p. 63)

The Yangshao (Yang-shao) culture in northern China was at earlier Neolithic era and characterised by shamanism and reached the peak of its development around 3000 BC and was displaced by the Longshan (Lung-shan) culture. From the Longshan culture arose the Shang dynasty, China's first dynasty, during the 1700s BC. In dynastic periods, the empress had to be chosen from the females who did not have any blood connections with the emperor or crown prince. (Cotterell & Morgan 1975, p. 541)

> According to Ping-ti Ho, the societies of the Yang-shao period obeyed the laws of matrilineal descent. In contrast, the following period, that of the Longshan, indicates passage to a patrilineal society. (Eliade 1982, p. 5)

During the Zhou (Chou) period marriage among patrilineal relatives was not practised, so the king and lords of his surname had to marry with the families of lords of other surnames, linking virtually all of the upper ranks of the nobility through either patrilineal or affinal kinship (Ebrey 1996, p. 32).

During the Ch'in dynasty, if the children of the same mother but different fathers had sexual relations and they were brought to the authority, they were both beheaded, a punishment reflecting the traditional Chinese horror of incest.

We are aware that even with the modern technical expertise it has taken decades of research before the scientists established the irrefutable link between exposures to radiation or asbestos and high level of cancer incidents. It is hard for us to conjecture how the distant ancestors worked out in their conscious mind that the offspring born from the related blood have high incident of the inferior or defective offspring. Some animals seem to know the above fact from instinct. Apart from the probability that humans could have been aware of this fact instinctively, they must have worked out the adverse relationship by observing their life carefully.

I would say that it must have taken centuries or even millenniums before the primitive people realised that the children produced from the union of related blood are apt to be of low grade. Thus the marriage among close relatives became a taboo in their society. Most tribes must have placed restriction on marriage in order to prevent inferior or defective breeding. The tribes which did not conform to this practice produced inferior people and in the course of time must have been conquered or wiped out.

Many people feel strong aversion to the sexual relation within the family members, the spousal sex being excepted of course, though sexual desire of men does not distinguish between family and non-family. The repugnance may come from the memory of the ancestors which our body cells may store. The taboo of sexual relation between the blood relatives, still practised today, has a logical base and is the law among most civilised countries of the world.

Interesting enough there is much evidence to support that the sexual taboos, except for sex between related blood, have no sound bases and are not inherent in the human nature but rather dependent upon the cultures and circumstances. I am going to present some instances supporting this proposition:

The Kinsey report refers to cultures where the exposed sexual activity is a matter of course but the eating is done in utmost secrecy (Kinsey, Pomeroy & Martin 1948, p. 4).

In the battlefields, many people are seen copulating in the open.

Many people are willing to do the sexual acts for the shows if they are paid well.

In some communal families, the members often do not bother to go out but stay in the room to make love, thus the other members including their children can witness the acts.

The fact that the children do not discuss the sexual habits of their parents with them reflects the unexpressed wish from the parents. Provided the family is isolated from the other families, it is expected that the young offspring can be taught to talk about and witness the sexual activities of their parents without embarrassment.

It is well documented that the ancient to classical Greeks did not think sexual promiscuity was sin. Sexual intercourse within the family members and homosexuality were widely practised without condemnation. However, they still made love away from people in the hiding. The family members talked about sex freely for jesting or serious intent. In ancient Sparta, the boys joined the mess at the age of 20 and it seems that in the dormitories homosexual relationships were the norm. These boys could marry, but until 30 all visits to their wives were done stealthily by night. (Freeman 1996, p. 175) More generally in ancient Greece, love between men was as common as heterosexual love and was even encouraged among students and soldiers (Mercer 1996, p. 91).

Ruth Benedict, an American anthropologist, states in her book *The Chrysanthemum and the Sword* (1946) that it is a taboo to discuss romance and sex matters within the Japanese family (Benedict 1974, p. 284). She further states. The Americans have many taboos on erotic pleasure while the Japanese do not have. It is an area about which the latter are not moralistic as the former are. (p. 183) In America the practice of masturbation is condemned utterly and the parents pass this notion of guilt into their children when they misbehave (p. 188). It seems that she was not aware that masturbation is entirely harmless from the medical point of view according to the modern science, and widely practised in America as in any other countries. *Sexual Behavior in the Human Male* (1948) and *Sexual Behavior in the Human Female* (1953), both being known as the Kinsey Report, were published a few years after the publication of the above book by her. Hence she would have not known that both men and women in America widely practised masturbation. As an anthropologist she is acutely aware that their own culture has big differences to any other culture, the degree of which surprise the researchers. The American and Japanese cultural differences are no exceptions. (p. 10) Child rearing is a pleasure for the parents everywhere but in Japan the children give the status symbol to the mothers and at the same time ensures the continuation of the family (pp. 255-7). In America, being in love is the most approved reason for marriage. After marriage a husband's physical attraction to another woman is humiliating to his wife because he bestows elsewhere something that rightfully belongs to her. (p. 184)

Ruth Benedict fell deeply in love with and married a man in 1914. However the marriage faltered from the start; she wanted a child desperately to save marriage but could not conceive one. After several years of strained cohabitation they lived apart though they did not divorce. In 1922 Benedict got involved in a love affair with a woman. Benedict's husband died in 1936. Benedict's friendship with the woman lasted until Benedict died in 1948. It is quite strange to note that Benedict utterly condemned masturbation but she chose to live in a lesbian relationship.

Bertrand Russell experimented within his school such that the pupils freely discussed sexual matters without any sense of shame or embarrassment. He proudly reported that a pupil new to the school received unexpected response from the local pupils, who did not show any giggles or derision about sex and talked about it as a matter of fact. Russell may have derived a personal satisfaction out of this experiment but I do not see any gains for the pupils concerned. In fact, the young people can be taught to behave in a lot more than he, an educator, dares to experiment in a school environment. There is no doubt that education or training can remove the guilt feelings about sexual taboos. The main objection to this idea is that we do not have any benefits except to satisfy the personal egos.

People may argue that sexual acts involve emotional change and hence are done in secrecy. However, excretory process does not involve emotional change but is done in secrecy.

Section 12 Various Views of Sex

Sex as Means of Procreation and Survival of Human Species

The overriding basis of the decision-making process of all the living things is survival of the individual and multiplication of the species. Without this strong desire no living creatures would have survived the harsh living environments for the individual as well as for the species. The mammals achieve the preservation of the species by the strong sexual urge and consequent multiplication of the same kind. It is often forgotten in the prosecution of strong sexual activities accompanied by pleasure that sex is a reproduction process using the male and female reproductive organs.

Asexual (non-sexual) reproduction in the low forms of life gives the carbon copies of the solitary parent and has strength in numbers but not in diversity. Sexual reproduction gives the diversity of offspring; some are superior and some inferior. In the struggle for existence the superior seeds, though small in number, have the advantage in the long run as far as the survival of the species is concerned. (Smith 1968, pp. 54-5)

Whiptail lizards have done away with sex entirely. They lay 8-10 eggs, though unfertilised, which hatch as perfect replicas of themselves. (Fisher 1992, p. 60) Bacteria have no sexual distinctions. These organisms come together and exchange DNA. (p. 61) Strawberries can reproduce asexually (cloning) and sexually. Earthworms are hermaphroditic, having both male and female reproductive organs in an individual. Some fish are transsexual. (p. 62)

The females of bonobos--sometimes called pygmy chimpanzees--have a monthly period of heat, though extended, but the copulation is not restricted during oestrus (p. 129). Some bonobos copulate in the face to face position and some the rear entry pose. Also they like a variety of other, some are quite bizarre, positions in copulating. (p. 130)

Some female chimps are sexually insatiable and copulate several dozen times in a day and they even masturbate. Both sexes avoid coitus with close relatives, such as a mother or siblings. (p. 132)

The female animal species as a rule copulate only at the time of oestruses, but there are exceptions to this rule. Perhaps the greatest asset the females including human species have may be that they can copulate only when they want to. (p. 184)

The sexual desire does not come from the wish to have babies: the desire and pleasure are the way nature or God intended so as to result in procreation. Certainly the brain power characterises the humans and has been the chief survival weapon. However, the strong sexual desire of men makes people multiply enormously under the favourable circumstances, and replenish quickly the large number of the dead as the results of wars, diseases or serious crop failures.

Thus, the strong sexual drive of men stems from the self-preservation instinct or the survival of humans. The strong sense of pleasure must accompany lovemaking to repeat the act which is the means of impregnating women. Without pleasure most men would not have bothered to have sex even they knew that they must have sex to have babies. If there were no pleasures in sex act, women would have very low pregnancy rate and human race could have died out not surviving the cataclysms such as widespread diseases, wars and natural disasters.

All living things have high mortality rate through the course of struggle for existence. To compensate for high death rates, all the living creatures among the myriads of species have to devise the means. The penalty of not having the suitable means is extinction for the creature, which means on the reverse side of the coin that all living things now existent have devised the means of adequate method of procreation. A fish produces a huge number of hard roes and likewise a plant, of seeds. Birds and reptiles do not rely on a large number of offspring for the maintenance of the species: they lay only several eggs. However, to utilise to the utmost the comparatively small number of possible progenies, the laid eggs make the pregnancy period of the female parents short, thus allowing free and easy manoeuvring of the parents and resulting in the high probability of hatching the eggs and increasing the number of the offspring.

Unlike plants, fishes, birds or reptiles; the mammals, especially primates, do not have the above-mentioned in-built mechanisms, that is, a large number of possible offspring or a short pregnancy period. The mammals have the characteristic of a small number of progenies with a long pregnancy period. For primates such as monkeys, apes and humans, these restrictions are extreme. To overcome these difficulties the mammals developed a system by which a strong male tries to procure as many females as he can to make them pregnant. This arrangement will work only if the dominant male has strong sexual drive, which is the way nature or God ordained the preservation of the species. The mammals achieved the objective by the strong sexual urge on the part of the males, which in turn manifests as strong emotional attachment of the parents to their progenies to protect until they grow to support themselves.

It is a general rule that the higher the evolutionary stage of the species the longer the protection on the offspring by the parent. In the case of humans the protective period is extreme.

Men have another in-built mechanism by which a small number of offspring has a high rate of survival. A man ejaculates in lovemaking 80-300 million sperm, each of which is theoretically capable of impregnating an egg. This large number of sperm is in competition to impregnate an egg, and only one strong and no other sperm can get to the egg and achieve its objective.

It is beyond any doubt that without strong desire of men, humans would not have survived the high mortality rates of various causes such as delivery at birth, growing up, diseases, starvation and wars during the long uncivilised state. Upon entering the civilisation the strong male sexuality was, generally speaking, a serious cause for overpopulation. Sex has been on the stronger rather than adequate for the preservation of the human species. As the death rates at birth and from natural causes gradually decrease as the society advances, we have to learn how to deal with the men's strong sexual drive. Even we take into account of the occasional fierce wars such as World Wars One and Two, the foregoing statement is generally true.

Education and birth control have checked the overpopulation in the economically advanced countries in the recent years. People have learned through the education the futility of making large families and have achieved the end result of small families by the various birth control methods.

Sex as Necessity of Life

Sex is a necessity of life like food, clothes and shelter at least for men. Average men probably spend more time thinking about sex than any of the other necessities of life. Also average men possibly spend more money on girlfriends, wives or prostitutes in an effort to calm sexual drive than any of the other necessities of life, though this assessment does not take into account the probability that there is more to lovemaking than sexual outlet. A wife and children are more expensive than a house for the average man. In spite of the above appalling estimate, there is little information available on the book market as to how to deal with the sexual urge except either in the way of rousing the pleasure or how to make love, compared with a large number of 'how to' books for the rest of the necessities.

We normally don't say that addictive drugs, alcohol and gambling are necessities of life, though many men cannot live without these pleasures. Taking drugs, drinking alcohol and gambling do not come from the physiological need of men and they are only necessary in the sense of pleasure for addicted men. Gambling, not involving absorption of substance, has psychological hold on the addicted gamblers. It seems that the drug addicts and alcoholics are hooked bodily as well as psychologically. Certainly the addicted men would feel the compulsion to have them, even by disregarding the other necessities of life and committing crimes to feed the habit since the ecstasy gives men high-quality pleasure. It is interesting to note that we can see the different levels of necessities and also the different levels of pleasures coming from the necessities of life and the various addictions.

Only after meeting the urges for hunger, thirst and warmth, the ordinary men are interested in sex. It is not hard to satisfy the basic urges for survival mentioned above but the desire for women is hard to quench. With the necessities of life of a usual usage, most men would be satisfied with what they can obtain: however, they ever want a better sort of woman.

Sexual function as well as body function and brain power promotes by the moderate and proper use. Non-use of any of these functions leads to decreased efficiency, to malfunction and ultimately to atrophy; and overuse over a long period leads to exhaustion and to malfunction.

Men have learned myriads of skills over the millenniums for their survival; however, they have not learned to live without women, though I am sure many men tried. From this viewpoint alone, women and sex are necessities of life.

Sex as Disease

Sigmund Freud asserted that the two dominant drives of the humans are the hunger drive and the sex drive. He further stated that the human mind is not only dominated by the above innate drives but greatly influenced by the fantasies and wishes. (Westheimer 1994, p. 223)

Aristotle taught that hunger was in fact a kind of disease to be cured by food. This may be a right concept in dealing with hunger and food: we would be a lot more careful of what sort and quantity of food we should eat. We should weigh ourselves daily and decide what amount of which medicine or food we should consume. If we are not sure what sort of eating habit is desirable for us, we should consult a dietician. Instead of following the above line of thinking, it seems to me that many people recklessly eat whatever amount of whatever food they like. They eat for pleasure rather than for health and end up unbalanced nutrients and overweight.

The above observations apply to the people in the affluent societies. A large number of the world population are on the starvation level and it is apt to say that food is really medicine for these starving millions.

Can we say the same thing about sex? Should we look at sex as a disease to be cured by semen discharge? Do we have the right amount of sex and the right kind of sex in the similar way as for food? Traditional ethics tells men that men should not approach their daughters, married women and under aged girls for sexual purpose, even though these women may be agreeable. Men should not rape a woman under any circumstances. Also men should not go to bed with the women with sexually transmittable diseases.

There is an optimum intake of food for men's proper daily activity and health; it is wrong for men to eat as much as the food they like most. It is often said men should eat less fat and less salt and more fibres. By analogy there must be an optimum number of sexual acts men should have for a week; men should not have as many times as they like. Many wives often refuse the request for sex from their husbands, which probably produces more harmonious and lasting relationship.

When men are sick they go and see a medical doctor for treatment. Similarly men go and see a woman for alleviation when they have the disease of sexual longing. In this treatment process, men spend a huge amount of time, effort and money. They often ponder if women are worth all that trouble. Some, from the religious or other conviction, may become sexual ascetics who want to avoid the sexual pleasure altogether.

Sex is known to give men relief from tension and also to induce sleep. Men have various means of reducing stress, from physical exercise to drinking to drugs. However, sex is the common tension reliever and is thought to be natural. (Zilbergeld 1992, p. 79) Many men, when they are tense or needing sleep, often seek the affection of their wives rather than take the tablets, thinking that sex is healthier than medicine. Quite often, though, men, after orgasm, feel aversion towards women who offered their bodies for the sexual service.

Sex is more than a simple relief. All men long for temporal cure of sexual intercourse; rather all men have an incurable disease of sexual urge in the same way as of hunger.

Sex as Pleasure and Addiction

The sexual activities looked as a pleasure and an addiction is the main reason men think and talk about sex.

For most of the economically advanced countries, the death rates of humans are quite low today compared with the procreation rate. Even at the time of war, people may get the impression that a huge number of men and women die as consequences of battles, diseases and starvation. However, it has been proven time and again through history that the humans do not have any problems in replenishing the dead thanks to the strong male sexuality. The humans, like any other successful living things, are so good at multiplying the same kind under the favourable circumstances that it has come about that people look at sex as pleasure source rather than procreation means: People think sex as a well of enjoyment rather than the process of making progeny. Sex becomes an addiction when men are obsessed with sex to the detriment of their life.

It is a human nature that thinking about sex, as for thinking about dying, is far more often and enjoyable, more suffering in case of dying, than sex itself.

There is a fundamental problem associated with the above thinking. If women give only pleasure and nothing else, as men tend to wish, there is no point in enquiring any further. All men have to do is to enjoy the company of women. The fact of the matter is that men have a lot of trouble mixing with women, sexually and non-sexually.

I propose in Section 1 of this chapter under the heading of 'Pleasures' that one fundamental teaching of the world religions is that pleasures and sins committed by men and women have bad consequences stored for them in the future. Sex may not be a sin but certainly a pleasure. Accordingly the perpetrators of the sexual pleasure are expected to reap unhappiness in some way or another. The religious leaders of note teach people that one reason why they suffer is that they repeat pleasures (sex is one of them) and sins. The author of *The Imitation of Christ* exclaimed; 'How fleeting and deceitful are all pleasures of life!' (Thomas a Kempis 1980, p. 164), irrespective of what consequence may bring him in the future.

Sex gives men tremendous pleasures. Sex is a form of addiction for men, and sufferings and pains follow pleasures though some men may not realise it. The hard drugs give extreme pleasure to the addicts. However, the users have to go through the period of rejection after the period of ecstasy. It is also known that most drug addicts, not being wealthy, take big pains to procure the drug they are addicted to. They cheat, steal and even kill people to obtain money to buy the addicted substance. It is well established that the young and pretty female addicts pay for the drugs with their bodies. It may be obvious in this case to the observers that the addiction is as much or more suffering as pleasure; the addicts suffer as much or more as they have pleasure. The deep suffering negates the high-quality pleasure. We can see another example in the parenthood: the extreme joys of being the parent are negated by the deep fear that their children may be maimed, desert them or die in some way.

View of Sex According to Mind Only (or Emptiness)

Up to this point of this section, I have given and expounded a few theoretical reasonings for men's sexual arousal. They are all in accordance with the common notions about sex. Though I listed them separately, they all are true and in fact they all form what the average people think would be the reasons why people have sex. If men feel constant sexual urge towards women, we don't gain much in giving explanations for that feeling. Men may argue that these views are useless since men in any case want women at least for sexual purpose: men have to spend money on women who are the beneficiaries. Certainly women want other than money from men: they want sex, love, protection and friendship.

Under the above heading I am going to delve a bit further and try to pinpoint a common misconception behind such a strong urge using the Buddhist doctrine 'mind only (or emptiness)'.

Mind Only (or Emptiness) states that everything is an illusion. Still Buddhism does not deny that we need necessities of life, that is, food, clothes and shelter to sustain our life. We have to eat food, wear clothes and live in a house for the life to go on. Gautama (family name) Siddhartha (personal name) himself, who acquired the title of the Buddha after the Enlightenment, went through all kinds of mortifications to deny that food, clothes and shelter were necessities or realities. However, he realised the futility of the effort and abandoned the idea. Then he reached the Enlightenment and his first sermon was the middle path which recognised the needs of these material objects. However, Buddhism as for Christianity places the strict prohibition on enjoyment and luxury of these requirements. If everything in life and the world is an illusion, it is difficult for us to see the necessities of life are the realities and not illusions. Christianity poses the similar difficulty. The Bible states that God is the alpha and omega (Isaiah 44:6), that is, everything. Yet even the devout Christians need the necessities of life to sustain life. Christ, who is sometimes said to be God like and God itself, ate food and even drank wine as narrated in the Gospels. Possibly Buddhism and Christianity alike do not deny for the lay followers at least that they can have sex so long as they obtain sex in a proper manner such as in marriage.

In this book I am to separate the biological sex drive which is esteemed as a reality from the psychological sex drive which is esteemed as an illusion. In this process I am not going to project the concept as an unalterable truth as the Eastern philosophers tend to do but to present the concept such that it explains satisfactorily many of the experiences men have concerning sex.

The concept 'mind only (or emptiness)', as I interpret regarding to sex, tells people that sex is not something lying outside but is within people. In other words, sex is not the joining of two bodies as is generally thought, but lives in the minds of the subject individuals. A heterosexual man may equate sex with a young pretty girl, that is, he thinks sex centres around beautiful women and beautiful women centre around sex; however, this is in fact illusory. He does not know that he is seeking a pleasurable outlet of his longing, which happens to fall on the desired woman. Some men look at the same sex or anything else as sex object. The object depends on the fancy of men though they all have sex drive. The analogy may be found in food. Food itself does not have anything to offer in terms of taste but people appreciate the taste.

Mind Only (or Emptiness) holds the view that all human perceptions, seeing, tasting, touching, hearing and smelling, are false. The Buddhists train hard for many years such that these sense perceptions do not entangle them.

All perceptions are false, hence any way of thinking or life coming from perceptions is false as well. Buddhism puts out three independent faculties--mind, perceptions and physical

world. They deny the triple concordance. Mind does not have the true picture of the physical objects because the five senses do not give the accurate representations of the external world.
Mind Only (or Emptiness) answers in the negative for all the following questions:

Is masturbation better than wet dream?
Is making love to a prostitute better than masturbation?
Is making love to a girl friend or wife better than any of the above?

I got to know a 29 year old woman in Melbourne, when I was a few years older than she. At the first meeting she was quite attractive to me and I was eager to have a go at her. We lived in the same boarding house and her room was in the opposite of mine, sharing the same corridor.
She showed a few signs that she wanted to make friends with me. I grabbed the opportunity and occasionally we spent a few hours, chatting or watching the television. I found that she could hardly read the newspaper. I also realised that she was not as attractive as I had thought before. She told me many lies for the short duration of acquaintance. She was so boring and nasty that I always wanted to be alone while I was with her.
I kept with her only in the hope of having sex with her. One day I got to her bed after putting up many female ploys. I made love to her if we can call that love. It was finished in a few minutes without any sexual satisfaction on my part. Instead of staying in her bed, I opted to go to my room to sleep. However, on the following day I wanted her sexually and had a go at her. She vehemently refused my advance. When she was really annoyed, I saw in her face what she had been desperately hiding all these times--wrinkles all over her face. Then I left her room for the night. I did not spend much time with her since then. A few weeks later her brother came to the boarding house to pick her up.
I analysed the association with her. It cost me about the same to sleep with her as with a prostitute. The time I spent mixing with her was a lot longer. The sexual satisfaction I got from her was probably even less than I would have got from a prostitute. I am certain I would have been happier if I had kept away from her. I still cannot work out why then I felt I had to have her sexually for the second time. Probably this assessment is true for the majority of men in conjunction with their female friends. Men behaved similarly for millenniums not knowing the reasons why they have to have women for little satisfaction. It seems that there is more than the sexual act when men are under the urge to go to bed with women though I cannot work out what it is.

Sigmund Freud developed the following lines of thoughts. The sexual instinct seems to be independent of its objects with so many variations (male, female, young, old, animal, inanimate) in a similar way hunger is independent of its objet with so many variations (food). The thumb-sucking of the babies, a sample of sexual manifestation, simulates breast feeding. The babies' lips behave as erotogenic zone and sucking is autoerotism exhibiting rhythm and repetition and does not have the object of female or male for both sexes of babies. Reproductive organs are not developed for infants and their instincts are shown as erection, masturbation, and activities resembling coitus. However, sexuality and libido for both sexes are of a wholly masculine character. (Freud 1962, pp. 14, 44-6, 85)

Buddhism teaches that sexual orgasms are pleasurable illusions and hence should be avoided. However, in this book which deals with the conducts of the ordinary people, the orgasms are esteemed as reality since the ordinary people cannot go on without occasional orgasms. Women in this book are esteemed as illusions or phantoms since ordinary men are capable of having orgasms without the help of female bodies. If a man claims sex is an illusion though he cannot stop having occasional orgasms, he is conceited and has a misconception somewhere in his thinking.

More generally, Mind Only (or Emptiness) insists that the common premise that life and the world have substance is wrong. Everything is an illusion; life and the world have no substance and no value. The concrete manifestations of life and the world, such as wealth, fame, power, women, and even the abstract concepts of justice, freedom, equality and beauty have no substance, therefore all are illusions. Wealth, honour, beauty, women and the like have attractions only for those who appreciate them. They themselves have no inherent values. They are all empty and illusions. For example, even if beautiful women fart and defecate in the hiding, that does not make them inherently beautiful.

The premise that sex is not in women is in accord with reality, explaining many happenings concerning sex. After a love affair, the man loses an interest in the woman; however, it is more natural to say that the man had an interest in what was not there in the first place. After marrying the desired women, men often get disillusioned and lose an interest in them: these men do not understand that the adoration they cherished before marriage was in the first place misplaced on the illusionary objects. A man, looking at a beautiful woman, desires her, though he knows subconsciously that she will not be attractive after a while from familiarity or aging. This desire based on illusion is similar to those based on wealth, fame, rank or whatever else he cherishes, even he knows he must die and they don't mean a thing after his death. They are all illusions and he acts according to the illusions, which must be corrected, according to Buddhism and also to the Bible. The pursuits of these illusions become causes of a lot of woes. People are acting on the wrong premise, hence misery, fighting and pains of this world ensue. If people put aside the wrong thinking, they are free from all kinds of sufferings. Thus the Buddhists, Judaics, Christians and Muslims preach the world.

When men acquire women, wealth, honour, authority and so on, they rejoice for a while. However, after some time they do not derive as much pleasure and they want more of better things, and even start being worried about what they have. The rich people as well as the poor people are worried about money in a different way.

I now hold the view that hunger, thirst, the feeling of being cold or hot, and sexual drive are all real and not imaginary. Many Buddhists and Christians alike, including myself in the past, believed that the above human traits as illusions and tried to extinguish them using all kinds of mortifications. The Buddha himself tried the ascetic practice for many years without success to realise the futility. After the Enlightenment he preached the middle path recognising the above human traits to be normal and to have to live with.

The following observations may support the view that women are illusions but the sexual drive is real:

Kings and emperors with all the women available to them ever wanted to acquire beautiful women as the commoners with their wives did.

When a man goes to bed with a desired woman, he invariably does not get as much satisfaction as he anticipated. The higher his expectation is the greater his disappointment is. When lovemaking disappoints him, he should start thinking about the Buddha who taught that everything including women is empty and without substantiation. After a number of lovemaking sessions with the same women he is expected to lose an interest in her and fancy other girls in the same way as before the association.

A word which a man does not know carries some mystery and fascination until he knows its meaning and how to pronounce it correctly. In the same way a woman has some mystique and charm for him until he goes to bed with her.

Some men prefer men, animals or inanimate objects to women as objects of sexual desire. This observation supports the view that the sex objects are illusions. Men are endowed with sexual desire to preserve the species, and most go after women. Women as sex objects are unsubstantial and illusory; hence some men go after men. The objects of the sexual dreams are not necessarily the opposite sex for heterosexuals and not necessarily the same sex for homosexuals. These observations exhibit unsubstantiality of sex objects.

A man does not have to look at an attractive woman in the flesh to get sexually excited. A photograph, a film or even a hand painted picture are enough to arouse him. They may not even exist in the real life—photographs or films may be altered to be attractive and the model girls may now be old or dead. Yet the fact that he can be excited is quite strange if we think about it. This fact points to the conclusion that women as sex objects are in fact illusory.

A masturbator often uses a photograph of an attractive naked woman to aid the process. He gets sick of it after a while and obtains another photograph. It is hard for him to imagine that the same process would take place when he makes love to a pretty woman in the real life.

An idealist uttered a verse: how a building can be beautiful since it was built by the people who were ever jealous of the other people. If the same logic is used, how can a woman be beautiful since she farts and defecates. Though imagining what happens in the anus or even sexual organ of a pretty woman may deter a man temporarily, the sexual urge eventually takes hold of him. Logically speaking, there must be something wrong with men who adore and go after women who fart and defecate. The reason is that men do not understand that women as sex objects are nothing but illusions as for any other desired objects in the world. Sooner or later men have to face the reality in realising that they made a mistake in adoring the unsubstantial objects. Of course, it is possible to adore women in non-sexual contexts. A Buddhist scripture defines a woman as a bag of urine and faeces in an attempt to deter the disciples from women. The description may be apt; however, it is virtually useless to suppress men's sexual drive. The definition forgets the fact that sexual desire has in essence nothing to do with women.

Arch of Triumph (1946) is a novel about a German doctor who fled to Paris to escape the Nazis prior to the outbreak of World War II. The story ends at the start of the war. The story seems to be a fiction, but the author puts meticulous care such that it is true to the real life. Ravic (assumed name of the doctor) works illegally as a doctor in Paris.

Ravic examines the private parts of the prostitutes in a brothel in order to detect venereal diseases:

> One prostitute says: You still feel like sleeping with a woman when you do these things?
> Ravic says: I don't understand it, either. (Remarque 1988, p. 49)

Here the prostitute, the doctor and the author of the book by inference agree that the female private parts are really disgusting but men still want to have sex from unexplainable reasons. However, Ravic, hence the author, did not try to delve further into the reasons and he kept having sex. I would say the author, Remarque, did not know that women as a sexual objects were illusions.

The novel, true to life, also reveals how various problems Ravic has to deal with in mixing with his lover. In spite of his emotional resistance from the past, he still has to go through the excitement of love in Paris, to come out as a bitter loser again.

The same author wrote *All Quite on the Western Front* (1929), which was more successful as a novel in the book market.

Prostitutes urge clients to finish sex fast once they receive money. I used to think that this was because they wanted to see the next client quickly for maximum profit. This was true beyond any doubt. I also came to believe that they knew their bodies were an illusion and hence there were no gains for the client to know that. They want to leave the client unsatisfied for possible future business with the same client.

Sexual urge is mostly fantasy and imagination, hence a man's fancy on a particular woman can be broken by a trifle matter and the reverse can happen. Many women within marriage or outside marriage will testify that their men lost or gained sexual interest in them due to trifle matters. These interest or disinterest may be temporary or permanent. Their men may suddenly change their attitudes towards them. I clearly remember the disappointment I felt when I saw a few hairs sticking out from the nose of a pretty girl in the class room more than half a century ago.

I am sure that most readers would agree with the foregoing views of sex except the view of sex according to Mind Only (or Emptiness). I have been convinced that this last view is theoretically correct and matches well with my sexual experiences. People do not understand the concept of Mind Only (or Emptiness) and thus they have various problems in life. They do not understand the true nature of sex as I explain here and thus end up in a messy strait.

Judging from their behaviours, it seems that women are aware subconsciously or intuitively that their sexual attraction to men is an illusion and men lose interest in them in no time. Women know that there is nothing mysterious about their body—appearance and function—from their experience in their daily life, and may wonder why men want to see their naked bodies and touch them and have a go at them. This facet manifests in making men wait when mixing and having sex. Also many women do not go to bed with men until married. Women spend enormous amount of money on clothes and perfumes, and pay utmost attention to mannerism. Sex is the means for survival for women apart from being an emotional experience. Hence women have to know for maximum benefit that men lose an interest in them after going to bed with them. Men in their desperation push away the notion that women are illusions until they go to bed with them. The overriding concerns for men are that they have to solve their pressing sexual problem and want to spread their semen in as many women as possible in their intuitive urge.

The Mind Only (or Emptiness) view of sex opens a new outlook concerning masturbation, which is the topic of the next section. This proposition is probably the most important concept in this book in that it is the concept which this book, that is, the sexual guide for single men, was seeking from the start, and also compliments the idea of the Third Prophecy in the sexual term.

Section 13 Proposition about Masturbation

Proposition: Average men can get as much or even more sexual satisfaction by masturbating as having a sexual intercourse with their preferred objects; beautiful women in the following discussions but any other desired objects such as men, animals or inanimate objects.

Please note that the word 'can' indicates the potentiality and not necessarily present actuality of achieving the above degree of satisfaction from masturbation. Also masturbation is a sexual self-relief and satisfies only men's sexual need and leaves unsatisfactory of the other needs such as social and psychological requirements. This is another limitation the proposal expresses. The proposition says that autoeroticism can be better than making love to a desired partner. However, we don’t know even in the lovemaking how much contribution we get from the self-stimulation and how much from the opposite sex.

I expect quite a derision from many of readers concerning the above view:

> The statement is absurd. Masturbation is only a substitute for making love to a woman; substitutes cannot be as good as the real things. Wanking is a loser's game. A wanker is a stupid person in everyday parlance. Many things in life have adequate substitutes but women cannot be replaced by anything else.

Some people may say that mere philosophising about sex does not eliminate yearning for women, which is different from yet stronger in some way than yearning for wealth and alcohol. The proposition does not say masturbation eliminates the desire for women but concerns itself with the degree of sexual satisfaction.

Some people, while agreeing that with masturbation the penis head is stimulated and semen is discharged at the conclusion, may argue that men cannot be sated unless they come to contact with the female body.

It is certainly not a good sight for other people to watch a man, in some posture or another, stimulating his glans penis imagining that he is making love to a variety of beautiful women.

It seems a good idea that two opposite sexes, unsatisfied if separated, can get satisfaction together. The proposition about masturbation does not emerge in the atmosphere where men can get women freely in the similar logic many idealistic concepts emerged when people suffered enormously and wondered why they had to suffer. Getting consolation from masturbation when the females are not available has a parallel to getting consolation from solitude and religion when the worldly consolations are not available. Solitude and religion may give greater happiness than the worldly affairs by their nature, which gives rise to the possibility of the section proposition.

The section proposition also goes against, some readers with serious notes would dispute, the social conventions and phenomena:

- Why do people marry then? The fact that most men at suitable age want to marry is a strong evidence that masturbation is not an effective way of calming the lust.
- Men since immemorial times have wanted to acquire wealth and women as well as to dominate the other fellow human beings by hook or crook. How can we tell people that those desires are all false? The Mind Only (or Emptiness) theorem states that all is an illusion, which refers to wealth, women and dominating other fellow humans among other traits.
- Why are men eager to go to bed with beautiful and young women; spending enormous amounts of money, time and effort; often pretending to be somebody other than what they

are; and even at times using unethical means? Paul wrote, 'To the weak I became weak, so that I might win the weak. I have become all things to all people, that I might by all means save some' (1 Corinthians 9:22). With the similar enthusiasm men become 'all things to all women' in an effort to obtain them for sexual purpose.

- Since men were separated from women (sexes are divisions of labour), infinitely a long time before history, men, young and old, if normal, tried to acquire women for sexual gratification. Men spent a large part of their life, thinking about women, fighting among themselves, pillaging and even going to war to obtain women. The above scenarios are observable even in the daily life in the civilised society except pillage and war for women. The section proposition put a huge part of men's life null and void and makes mockery of men's effort to acquire women for sex. Is it possible that all men have acted on the wrong premise all these millenniums?

When men advise their friends to masturbate and save money, it is assumed that wanking carries less satisfaction than making love to their girlfriends or prostitutes. This assumption is supported by the culture which nurtured them since the cradle.

The sex drive is biological but the preferences of the sex objects are very much psychological, hence it is not strange for men to choose masturbation out of the choices open to them and exert self-education and practice in an effort to derive the maximum pleasure. I used a love doll in the hope of deriving a high sexual satisfaction but found it was useless.

Some people may hold the view that masturbation is unwholesome and unnatural and may bring some undesirable mental or physical consequences; however, the various scientific researches established beyond any doubt that masturbation is entirely harmless (Wright 1977, p. 155). Medical doctors argue that masturbation is healthy, natural and harmless (*Encyclopedia of Love & Sex* 1972, p. 221).

Contrary to the above medical view, modern psychology contends that if men keep masturbating thinking that it is bad, they may have bad effect in the long run: If they think the practice is harmless they may not have any bad consequences. Sex is pleasurable but often forbidden, which creates psychological distress (Bader 2002, p. 3).

The topic of sex often comes up in the course of psychotherapy (p. 3). According to Dr Michael Bader, the sexual problems are often the key to solving the other problems in life (p. 181). When we look inside the mind, we find the world. When we look at the world, we see the complex workings of unique and individual minds. (p. 221)

The sexual decline is often the first sign that there is a marital problem. Sex is often the window into our deep psyche, through which the therapists can get the clue as to the nature of the problems. (p. 3)

Sexual fantasies are day dreams to generate sexual excitement (p. 30). Since sexual fantasies are not constrained by prohibitions or compromises as the sociosexual behaviours are, the fantasies give us more accurate pictures of our sexual desires (p. 234). In fact sexual fantasies are a door into the unconscious minds (p. 94).

Day dreams and possibly even night dreams are from one angle the entertainments or recreations and the avoidance of realities. In night dreams the most powerful representation is done pictorially, though language and sound and other perceptions play parts at times (Freud 1982, p. 84). The day dreams or fantasies have a great deal common with night dreams. Both are wish or fear fulfilments, are often based on the infantile experiences, and yet give benefit by the relaxation of censorship. (p. 492) Some are openly so and some are unrecognisable as wish or fear fulfilments because the dream work as the displacement is operating (p. 550). The forgetting of dreams is to a great extent a product of resistance (p. 520). The couple in love don't normally dream each other but are often unfaithful in their dreams (p. 81).

In the prehistoric era the world over, the dreams were thought to be the revelations from gods and demons (p. 2). The dreams can be concerned with the future (p. 97).

The stories in *The Arabian Nights' Entertainment* (*The Thousand and One Nights*) are fantasies devoid of any reality. They are a collection of about 200 stories. The stories were gathered from the 1300s and written down in the present form in Arabic in about 1500. They were mostly performed in public by story tellers. The tales collected came from different cultural regions: Arabia, Egypt, India, Persia, even China and other countries. The stories are of popular literature and its backbones are Islamic and Arabic cultures. Their nucleus is of Indian origin, first translated into Persian and then into Arabic. *The Thousand and One Nights* takes the form of frame story unified under a repeated opening and closing construction: a maid avoids her death telling her king husband a fascinating story every night. The frequent sexual references are also pure fantasies, exhibiting awry explicit sexual nature. The stories as a whole seemed addressed to the people in the medieval era who were not happy with the daily life and had to resort to the fancied stories. Two main themes of the fairy tales are wealth (gold and jewels) acquisition and sex. The Qur'an expressly prohibits these two pursuits. The stories also make references to good food, fine clothes and magnificent houses. The authors of the tales, who, it was established from the poor writing skills though their imaginations were strong and vivid, were not even professional writers, made thinly veiled attacks on the orthodox Islam. They offer recurrent praise prayers of Allah as the Most High, the Almighty, the Glorious and the Great, contrary to the themes they deal, disguising criticism of Islam.

Materialists, though they may have the experience of masturbation, may not see the sense behind the proposition and reject the notion outright, arguing that the concrete objects, in this proposition the female bodies, are real, and the women in the fantasy are false. The female bodies, since characterised by resistance, are material and thus in a broad sense the women for sexual purpose are an object of materialism: men want to own as many women as possible in the same light as much wealth as possible. Idealists, on the other hand, may argue in the opposite direction that masturbation can be as good as making love to women, focusing the attention on the impact on mind.

It is established by the various researches that almost all men and most women have masturbatory experiences and many masturbate throughout their lives. In the *Janus Report*, a national survey published in the United States in 1993, 55% of adult men and 38% of adult women reported they masturbated on a 'regular' basis, ranging from daily to monthly. (Westheimer 1994, p. 174) According to the same report, a fair number of married men and married women masturbate regularly (Janus & Janus 1994, p. 159): married men who masturbate daily or weekly amount to 44% of the respondents; for married women, the figure is 16%.

The better educated tend to masturbate more than the uneducated. For some women, masturbation is the only way to achieve an orgasm; roughly 50% of women are unable to reach a climax during penetrative sex. (Brewer 1997, p. 28)

Masturbation though well carried out does not give total satisfaction in a similar way a man married with a beautiful woman and a ruler with a large harem don't have total satisfaction.

Since this book refers only to average men, we can drop 'average' from the section proposition. Men should reach a level of wanking competency to feel the section proposition is correct.

The section proposition corresponds to the proposition of the Third Prophecy and compliments the prophecy in the sexual term. Men should note the tremendous benefits accruing from the acceptance and practice of the proposition. If men feel that the proposition is correct, that is all needed for the proof of the proposal and no other arguments are required.

People have to study to get to the core theories of such creeds as Buddhism, Christianity and communism for years. In the similar logic people may have to learn about the proposition in the light of their experience before they get to know the core thinking behind.

Since the proposition is contrary to the public perception, it will take me a great deal of effort to overturn the preconceived idea about masturbation. So I am going to explain why the view is correct, in the remainder of the section in two stages: 'Preliminary Remarks about Proposition' and 'Direct Arguments Supporting Proposition'.

Preliminary Remarks about Proposition

Human beings often depart from logical behaviour. In fact humans are undoubtedly aware that their way of thinking and consequent behaviours are not based on logical inferences under certain circumstances. Sex is no exceptions and in fact contains a large element of unreasonableness. Hence there must be some room for seemingly illogical proposal under consideration: we are seeking superficially unscientific solution to the often irrational sexual problems. It is a logical approach to seek a seemingly illogical solution to the illogical manifestations of sex. The proposition may sound illogical to people with common notion of sex, but it is perfectly logical in view of Mind Only (or Emptiness). In fact, many happenings in life or nature are illogical. For example, if two tsetse flies are weighed just after birth, the baby weighs more than the mother.

There are no skills or techniques which we cannot improve with knowledge and practice, the level of proficiency depending greatly on the inborn capacity of the individual on a particular subject and also on the eagerness to learn. Proficiency in masturbating is definitely worth acquiring since men reap enormous benefits in the way of money, time, effort; at the same time in not feeling jealous or anxious about women. Instead of spending time in trying to improve the technique in leisure activities such as fishing, tennis, eight balls, men may be advised to improve wanking skill for sure reward. I have been convinced that men can overcome even the fear of death by a proper guidance and practice. In the same logic, men can achieve a good quality orgasm by masturbating only after accumulating proper knowledge and practice. There are a large number of sexual manuals on the market and some of them give out masturbatory techniques. There must be right and wrong ways of masturbating as in any other human activities. The prospect and benefit of reaching competency in wanking may warrant a series of training by an expert. Also men may even have to develop good imagination to get good quality orgasms since men rely on fantasy to carry on masturbating.

Average men would reach a socially acceptable level of competency on any skill, though possibly not on scholastics, of their choosing, though only a tiny number of them become virtuosos. In the similar fashion, average men would reach an acceptable (to themselves) level of competency on masturbation.

If men masturbate even once on an experimental basis instead of going to bed with a hooker or a girlfriend, they should have saved enough money to buy this book on sex.

Viral particles, bacterial cells, and cells of higher organisms can multiply autonomously, that is, asexually. Many organisms have a choice of either sexual or asexual reproduction. The asexual reproduction creates the identical offspring and hence there is no scope for change or improvement. Higher organisms such as animals or plants require sexual acts for multiplication. (Dulbecco 1987, p. 167) The sexual production gives the offspring the traits of two parents hence there is a scope for adaptability and evolution. Most one-celled organisms, such as viruses and bacteria, reproduce by splitting in two (fission), which is the basic form of asexual production.

Masturbation is a corresponding concept of a single cell creature dividing for reproduction in the absence of a mating partner. A cell probably feels the compulsion to divide itself to multiply in the absence of a mate in the same way a man has the compulsion to masturbate in the absence of a female. Masturbation is also parallel to the yogins' contention that they can find everything in the universe by looking into their minds: the aim of yoga is to train the yogins in self-control and power of concentration. (Kung et al. 1986, p. 155) Thus biologically and metaphysically, pulling oneself is not such a strange practice. Masturbation also has conceptual parallels in self-hypnotism and self-cures of mental illness. For want of food and drinks men are unable to satisfy themselves by pretension. In this sense masturbation is different from eating and drinking. Further, interestingly enough, masturbation does not have parallels in any other forms of what men desire, such as wealth, honour, fame and power, except for the dreamers teetering on the edge of sanity. Since these fantasy indulgers are exceptions to the general rule of society, we ignore them in this book which seeks laws of the ordinary men.

solitary sex = autoerotic activity = self-stimulation
A partner can effect stimulation (Masters, Johnson & Kolodny 1985, pp. 282-3).

Traditionally masturbation was condemned and discouraged, and people were taught the practice may affect physical health or emotional stability (p. 282).

We can find the practice of masturbation in the animal kingdom too. Apes, monkeys, elephants, porcupines carry out self-stimulation in the sexual sense, and dogs and cats regularly lick their private parts. (p. 283)

Medical authorities carried out research instead of speculating to assess the effect of masturbation in the middle of the 20th century. For example, LE Holt in the revised edition of *Diseases of Infancy and Childhood* states that masturbation by a child does not cause any physical harm but the problem may be worry and guilt a child may feel. (p. 287)

The clitoral glans or tip is so sensitive that women may not stimulate directly during masturbation. The clitoral stimulation, if concentrated in one spot, becomes less pleasurable for the woman; the spot becoming numb. (p. 290) A fair number of women prefer a vibrator to effect masturbation. They normally use the vibrator to the external genitals; however, a few women insert it into their vagina. (p. 291) A small number of men insert objects into the urethra or the anus when masturbating (p. 295).

The feminist Betty Dodson makes a strong statement:

> Masturbation is our primary sex life. It is the sexual base. Everything we do beyond that is simply how we choose to socialise our sex life. (pp. 282-3)

A fair number of women, possibly about a third of all women, experience orgasm during sleep. They are awakened by the muscular spasms in lovemaking during sleep, and notice that their vaginas are lubricated. (p. 298)

In the past it was thought that only men got sexually excited and their penis erected exposed to the erotic material in the market. Recently it was established after the research that women go through the similar process resulting in increased vaginal blood flow or lubrication. (p. 300) Repeated exposure to erotica leads to satiation and boredom (p. 301).

I like to remind readers of the fallacy held virtually by all the people in the world on the geocentric notion before the modern times. Also the general public in the pre-modern era believed erroneously that the earth was flat. They could not imagine the earth was a globe and the people on the other side were standing upside down. They could not accept the proposition that our planet was in motion because the rotating world was contrary to the perceptions of their eyes and bodies. It is now firmly established that contrary to people's perceptions people on earth are moving at a tremendous speed. Hence the intelligent readers may sense a possibility that the public notion concerning masturbation can be erroneous. I dare say that the misconception on the earth's movement had negligible effects on the daily lives of the people except in the sense that science developed unfettered freed from the religious constraint; however, the correction of wrong idea on masturbation can have tremendous impact on the lives of men and hence on women and the society.

In spite of the low esteem towards masturbation by the general public at present, they must agree that masturbatory practice by men has the following advantages over having sexual intercourse with women. Some of the benefits contribute to raise the level of enjoyment.

- The practice is of low cost and can be had at any time and is free from the association with women, which many men detest. The cost incurred may be on the purchase of the erotic magazines and films.
- Masturbation is the truly safe sex in terms of transference of sexually transmitted diseases. There is no chance of pregnancy for the masturbators, though this is also true to the homosexual lovemaking. Two virgins (two males or two females) are virtually free from both of the above problems, though in the real world the probability of two virgins of the same sex in a stable relationship may be really small. Besides, there is some possibility that the virgins may be carrying sexually transmittal diseases such as venereal disease and AIDS, transmitted by non-sexual means.
- Masturbation does not have any age restrictions and any extra sexual demand from women Many men who cohabit with women should know that the women's request for sex can be persistent and troublesome. They may nag for sex continually like the prostitutes do. When I was young I received many offers of marriage. A few men advised me that the sexual attractiveness of men normally ends around the age of 35. That was what really happened to me and I did not get any marriage proposal after I turned 35. I heard that the females have the similar difficulty after they reach 35. Of course, there are no age barriers if the couples get to know well and become friends. It is interesting to note the following research results: men's capability in job performance becomes greatest from 34 to 44 years of age.

Men can, and normally do, indulge in sexual fantasy of their creation while masturbating. Solitary fantasies do not have the kinds of compromise and accommodation as in the socio-sexual behaviours (Bader 2002, p. 9). It seems that many married men at the time of lovemaking to their wives fantasise that they are having sex with other beautiful women. A few married men confided to me that they do the above practice; I was sure they did not tell that to their wives. I suspect that some married women carry on the similar exercise in their secret thoughts. This observation leads to the notion that the masturbation is in fact superior to the lovemaking of the physical dimension. According to the theory of Mind Only (or Emptiness), all sense perceptions are illusions, and that means the sensual pleasures associated with lovemaking are illusions. More generally, all realities are unsubstantial and are nothing but the dreams, and the other side of the coin is that the fantasies the masturbators create are no different from the realities. The Buddha taught people that all sense perceptions were illusions hence the perceptions men's imagination create while masturbating should be no different from the realities. Dreams are real for the dreamers while they are dreaming, and upon waking up they realise they had dreams. It is up to the men who make the head or tail of the dream and the reality. During wet dreams men dream they are having sex normally with beautiful women, and orgasms are reached without any physical stimulation. When dreaming, sexual or non-sexual, our conscious minds are completely asleep (p. 14).

The boys who have no sexual experience may imagine that the sexual acts in the real world would be fabulous beyond measure but the experienced boys would think otherwise though they may still think that making love to women is better than masturbating.

To throw more light on the premise that dreams or fantasies by the masturbators are no different from the realities, I present the following paragraphs:

Sigmund Freud tried to connect the contents of the dreams to the happenings of the real world. *The Interpretation of Dreams* (1900) by Freud explains the meanings of the dreams we have while we sleep. He insists that the dreams have certain meanings connected to our experiences while awake. The dreams have fascinated people since the immemorial times; it has been a strong tradition in history that people tried to find meanings and even secrets of life in the night dreams. Freud asserts that dreams have meanings which he can establish with objectivity and certainty, that is, scientifically. Every dream has a meaning, though the meaning is often hidden, and it can be interpreted by techniques. (Freud 1982, p. 96) Freud rather surprisingly draws the following conclusion and set out to prove it. In all cases, a dream is a fulfilment of a wish, often under disguise. (p. 122) Many people believe that the above book, his early work published in 1899, is the finest work by Freud and in fact he himself wrote in the preface added in 1931: The most valuable of all the discoveries it has been my good fortune to make, insight such as this falls to one's lot but once in a life time.

He further wrote in *The Future of an Illusion* (1927) that psychoanalysis is his creation and has met with plenty of mistrust and ill-will, and it is a method of research and an impartial instrument (Freud 1989, pp. 46-7). Gregory Zilboorg comments that though Freud's works showed both originality and genius, he had many enemies because of his doctrines and his [pedantic and often confused] writing style, and in particular the idealists rejected him thinking he was a materialist and the materialists rejected him because of his alleged mysticism (Freud 1961, pp. viii, x).

Sleep is physiological phenomenon. Dream is psychological phenomenon caused either by mental excitation (psychology) or somatic stimuli (physiology). Dreaming might be called clustering in images. (Rico 1983, p. 70)

> Since the advent of psychoanalysis, all therapies have focused on the interpretation of dream images as keys to our mental states. For Freud, all dream images were at root sexual symbols. For Jung, all dream images reflected the archetypal concerns of the collective unconsciousness. And for Gestalt therapists, dream images represent parts of ourselves often in conflict. (p. 167)
>
> Dreams are our own code of life symbols. When we awaken, we find those same symbols. Do we really know dreams from reality? (p. 181)

The Bible makes a few references that a dream exposes the secrets of life. We can find the examples in Genesis Chapter 40 and Daniel chapters 2 and 4. Job 33:15-17 gives out the following verse: God warns people while they are asleep that they should turn away from doing evil. Further the prophets of the Bible try to interpret what these dreams mean. Also the

Bible warns of the false seer who foretells the future events correctly by dreams and tries to mislead people from true God (Deuteronomy 13:1-5). The thrust of the Bible is that our experiences are not random occurrences but have certain meanings behind them; good or bad occurrences happen with some causes.

The following record is an example where people tried to put some explanation on the dreams. In Mesopotamia, around 300 BC, there emerged the seers or soothsayers who interpreted the various signs occurring around the world. They even interpreted the content of dreams, which were seen as direct link to the divine world. (Mercer 1996, p. 129)

A man who fantasises of his harem while pulling himself is no worse off than a mighty ruler making love to the choicest girls in the real world: both are in effect dreaming about women for a little while in the light of the Mind Only (or Emptiness) concept, the difference being that the masturbator having more numerous of finer quality women. Both the masturbator and the ruler in their ignorance don't understand that the make-believe harem and the harem of the real world are no different and have no concrete substance behind them. Buddhism, being idealism, preaches the superiority of mind over matter. If men believe that masturbating is better than making love to girls, that is necessary and sufficient reason and no other reasoning is required.

I tend to forget the night dreams of a matter of fact and remember good or bad dreams for many years as well as good or bad real life experiences. As I get old, the dreams and experiences merge into faint memories. The Mind Only (or Emptiness) theorem states that there is no difference between the dreams and the realities. In the movies and novels, the facts and fictions are often intermingled and the viewers and readers normally do not bother to separate the facts from the fictions.

Suppose a king is deposed and no longer possesses the wealth, power and harem. For this deposed king everything including the harem is a past event, and no more than a dream. He may sometimes remember how he behaved in front of so many beautiful women. Still the harem he had before is only a memory and a dream. If this king dies after a while, everything including the harem is null and void. The king does not know anything and it is immaterial if he had a good harem in his life or not.

The sexual fantasies by their nature are practised in solitary situations as well as during lovemaking with a partner (Masters, Johnson & Kolodny 1985, p. 265). Imagining with a different partner is most common sexual fantasies (p. 277). The sexual fantasy does not necessarily reflect the real life situation. A married woman may fantasise a sexual liaison with another man but this does not mean that she wants to commit adultery in the real life. A woman may dream to be raped by a few men but that does not mean she wants to be raped in the real life. Sexual fantasies have many advantages overcoming boredom; the contents of the fantasies are idealised, and fantasiser and partner are also idealised. (p. 265) Even in the contents of sexual fantasies men and women are more similar than different. The gender roles set in the society seem to reflect the fantasies, and women in their fantasy follow the lead set by males. (p. 280)

Direct Arguments Supporting Proposition

Under the above subheading I am attempting to prove beyond reasonable doubt that the public notion about masturbatory practice is wrong and my proposition is correct, using the various reasonings which stem from the common sense and prevailing social customs. I am hoping that many readers after going through the arguments believe that the proposition is more like the theorem concerning masturbation and they are eager to put the theorem into practice.

My proposition broadly rest on the evaluation that the sexual urge is mostly psychological and fallacious. Sex for men originates in semen secretion (biological) and ends in semen discharge (physiological), but these non-mental contributions are not on men's minds when the urge to have an intercourse with women grips them. Sexual drive is in the main in the domain of mind, though the bodily functions form the bases of this drive.

The vast majority of men are not totally satisfied with their wives or girlfriends. They get hold of the best females they can and are, as a result, resigned to the notion that they cannot do any better. With masturbation men can have any women in their make-believe world: they may be their friends' wives, movie stars or entirely fictitious girls. When men masturbate they are dreaming the essence of idealised women, which Plato called Forms or Ideas. The masturbator has all the selection criteria satisfied to the fullest extent. A man not only can choose women of his dream but has full control of the fantasy contents. Stated in reverse, the women the masturbator dreams in his masturbatory dream are those he really wants as his sex partners. The availability of infinite number of beautiful women in the fantasy leads to high degree of satisfaction. In the real world, good girls are scarce and those who agree to go to bed among them are rarer still. The problem is that the masturbator does not know that he cannot do better in the real world and is conditioned to think by habit energy that he should get more satisfaction with the women of flesh and bones. Men with good imaginations who form the majority may be disappointed in sex with the females because the reality is not as good as they imagined. In fact many men express being let down in lovemaking with desired women. The greater the expectation before making love with a woman men have, the greater the disappointment at the lovemaking men feel. If the sex intercourse falls short of the masturbation, men naturally ask themselves a question why this is so. According to Mind Only (or Emptiness) we can make the similar observations to any other desired objects, such as wealth, honour, authority and fame.

Sex is not the union of two sexes, as the general public believe, but is the sexual instinct within the individuals. Copulation is an attempt to calm desire, believing that a certain objects (females, males, animals or inanimate objects) would give the highest ecstasy. My observations and analyses show that men do not need any physical objects to reach high degree of orgasm: self-stimulation is sufficient to achieve the same results. Sigmund Freud makes a definitive statement that religion is not truth but an illusion and poses a question that sexual arousal may also be caused by an illusion (Freud 1989, p. 43). He makes a clear distinction between sexual aims (the act towards which instincts strive) and sexual objects (the person, organ or physical entity eliciting attraction) (Freud 1962, p. 2), and the foregoing statements refer to the former making light of the latter.

All normal men want good-looking women as their bedmates; however, as soon as they have them they look at them in a different light. Many men told me that the sexual relations with women (within or outside marriage) brought all the problems of the world: they said they had too much trouble mixing with women. Some expressed the strong reservation that sexual pleasure might not be worth that much trouble after all. Masturbation eliminates all the hassles mixing with the females. Sexual desire is crystallised: a romanticisation of biological and physiological processes. It is a longing which men cannot be sure of. As soon as the males grab hold of the female bodies of their dream, they enter into the real world and thus often become disenchanted. The female bodies are always less satisfying to our touch than we imagined to be. Whereas, the masturbators, who may have had the experience of sexual intercourse, can remain idealised about their fancied objects and hence can achieve a high-quality orgasm. Certainly the beautiful women in their fantasy are idealised and have perfect bodies with charming personalities.

It is known that the young unmarried men have a tendency to pull themselves too often. This is another evidence that masturbation without the participation of female flesh is an effective way of alleviating the sexual problem. Most likely most of them do not realise that sex with woman carries less satisfaction. They should be on guard against excessive repetition of this habit in the same way they should avoid any other excess in whatever they do in their life except for special circumstances. Refer to C Middle Paths, Section 3, Chapter 7, Book One *Idealism and Materialism* for the enlargement of the last statement. My experience tells me that moderate sex gives more energy for the other activities of life. The sexual restraint causes irritability and the excessive sexual activity causes devoid of energy. I still remember a remark by an educator I read when I was young that the practice of masturbation is not dangerous for the youngsters as long as they do not despair with too much indulgence.

The Kinsey Reports analyse the orgasms of males and females statistically. The authors record orgasms are achieved or not at sexual acts and do not register their quality. The report uses binary system, however the orgasms are achieved--fantasy (masturbation), a nocturnal emission (a wet dream), a woman, a man, an animal or an inanimate object. The report does not consider the degree of satisfaction the respondents attained. They simply look at the physiological aspect of sexual climax. The binary system adopted is not the conclusion of the report that the orgasms obtained by various means have the same value but they simply did not differentiate beyond orgasm. In fact the authors are well aware of the different levels of sexual satisfaction men can have but did not choose to pursue this line of investigation as the following paragraph testifies:

> But we have no statistics on the frequencies of physiologic differences, or of the various degree of satisfaction, and in the present study, all cases of ejaculation have been taken as evidence of orgasm, without regard to the different levels at which the orgasms have occurred (Kinsey, Pomeroy & Martin 1948, p. 159).

The two books *Sexual Behavior in the Human Male* (1948) and *Sexual Behavior in the Human Female* (1953) were published originally for the sex researchers but became national best sellers in the USA. Both books are widely recognised as the pioneering works in the scientific knowledge of the human sexual behaviours and regarded still the best social data ever collected in this field. (Westheimer 1994, pp. 161-2) These two volumes are popularly known as *The Kinsey Reports*.

In order to prove my masturbatory proposition statistically, we have to measure quality of orgasms resulting from sexual acts of different modes. The orgasms would be graded according to the levels of satisfaction. A heterosexual man would register a high level of satisfaction with young and pretty women and would rate low with old or ugly women. A homosexual man would have a better quality orgasm to men than to women. A man should show the highest satisfaction with his preferred sexual object. Conversely, the preferred object would be inferred when the results are presented statistically, though a few results may deviate from the expected norm.

If someone develops a gauge to measure the quality of orgasms, I am sure that the results, appraised and statistically presented, will prove my proposition. With the absence of the gauge, we have to rely on our resultant feelings to assess its validity.

Masters and Johnson carried out thousands of physiologic experiments and reached the following conclusions. The basic physiologic responses for the males and females are the same regardless of the source of stimulation: in case of men masturbation and intercourse; in case of women artificial coition with laboratory recording device, fingers, or breast stimulation. (Brecher 1967, pp. 79, 84) Further experiments were carried out on mutual strangers instead of married couples but the results were confirmed to be the same (p. 79). Psychological (subjective) ratings were added for the females. The women were asked after the event if the sex was satisfactory in the scales of 1 (mild) to 4 (very intense) to 5 (multiple orgasms). (p. 71) Dr Ruth Westheimer recorded the results of the above experiment: For the females there were convincing responses that the mode of sex did not affect the sexual satisfaction (Westheimer 1994, p. 173). The results possibly come from the fact that women do not need any fantasy to achieve orgasm while masturbating. Men need invariably sexual fantasy to achieve orgasm while masturbating.

There is another report:

> Masters and Johnson reported the significance of masturbation for women: Through manual manipulation of the clitoral area or by the use of vibrators they might reach orgasm more reliably than through coitus. Kaplan devised innovative techniques to teach women how to overcome some sexual dysfunctions by becoming orgasmic through self-stimulation. (p. 176)

There is another report: Some studies made in 1980s have found that the reported frequency of orgasms for lesbian partners is higher than that for heterosexual women (p. 166).

When men make love to opposite sex, most of them prefer vaginal intercourse. It is also known that some men insist to use anus, to the disgust of many females, or other parts of female bodies. A man does not have to insert his penis into vagina to reach orgasm: he can get the same quality orgasm using any parts of female body though the female may be left unsatisfied.

In coitus interruptus, a man withdraws his penis just before ejaculation, thus trying to prevent pregnancy. Obviously the frequent users of this practice think that this method is better than any other pregnancy preventive measures. However, this technique makes us wonder about a few things. What happens to the semen discharged outside vagina: does it soil the bed or is it caught by tissues. What happens if the man misses the timing? What happens if the woman does not respond quickly enough to let the partner go from her firm embrace.

Coitus interruptus does not give coital satisfaction to women and besides it interrupts the sexual union with adequate satisfaction for both parties. Hence it should not be practised to achieve the harmonious and satisfying sexual relations. (Velde 1965, p. 134)

It is interesting to note that the Bible (Genesis 38:8-9) punished Onan for spilling his semen on the ground whenever he lay with his brother's wife. God was enraged with this practice and put him to death. Onanism derived from Onan means masturbation in today's language but the practice in the Bible was actually coitus interruptus. The Bible did not define onanism. God condemned Onan for not fulfilling his duty as the custom of Israel required at the time, not because God saw coitus interruptus as evil.

Among the multitude of reported rape incidents, it is not rare that the offenders masturbate instead of perpetuating penile penetrations. Some researchers found that the rapes are not so much sexual desperation of the culprits but rather violence on women from frustrated delinquents. The spread of the sexual assault victims further supports the latter finding. We may think that young and pretty women are most prone to sexual violation but statistically youth and beauty do not play an appreciable part in victim selection. The above first finding shows that the offenders are revealing their innermost desire to maximise the sexual gratification out of the situation they are in, and indicates the sex intercourse as we know is not a requirement for highest pleasure. The Rape Crisis Centre in London reported that only one rapist among one thousand rapes committed was actually convicted. The rape is used to express power and pleasure by rapists. (Taylor 1996, p. 85)

For sex therapists, who are more acquainted with sexual habits of people than the general public, the proposition that masturbation can bring more satisfaction than the real life intercourse is no surprise. For instance, Dr B Zilbergeld received many claims from his clients that they got their most intense orgasms through masturbation. The doctor ascribes the reason to his belief that no one knows or can know their bodies as well as themselves do. While masturbating men continuously adjust the movements of their various parts to heighten the sense of satisfaction: the way the glans penis is stimulated, the number of strokes per minute, and the amplitude of the stroke. Men's brain gets the feedback from the movements and don't have any difficulty in changing the stimulating motion. (Zilbergeld 1992, p. 153)

It is true that masturbation cannot give total satisfaction to men. However, we have to take into account that it is also true that the married men and even the monarchs with a large harem are not completely content with the women available for them: They ever want more of beautiful women. Thus the proposal is valid in relative terms only and does not promise unconditional contentment.

In the course of sexual relationship, many men get to know that the oral sex is more reliable method than coitus to bring women to orgasm (Westheimer 1994, p. 192). Oral sex is a form of sex: applying one’s mouth on the partner’s genitalia. Cunnilingus: the object of the oral sex is the female genitalia. Fellatio: the object of the oral sex is the male genitalia. (pp. 166, 191) The oral sex has the hygiene problem, particularly for men. The process even if the vulva is clean has the same effect as licking the urinal. Women are advised to clean the anus thoroughly after defecating and should wipe the anus from the front to the rear only, to prevent the vulva soiling with excrement.

‘While most men do not have any difficulties experiencing orgasms, the same is not true to all women. For many years the term frigid was applied to women who were not orgasmic, but that has been replaced with the word preorgasmic, because in most cases these women can be taught how to have orgasms, usually by teaching them to masturbate.’ (p. 194)

‘Masters and Johnson reported in *Human Sexual Response* (1966) that most women participating in their study felt that mechanical auto manipulation to the mons area with the aid of a vibrator produced the kind of stimulation that resulted not only in the fastest and the most intense orgasms but also in multiple orgasms during a single sexual episode.’ (p. 194)

‘Compared with the intensity of sexual excitation in women produced by cunnilingus, manual stimulation and the use of vibrators, rarely are there reports of multiple orgasms occurring from coitus alone.’ (p. 194)

It is not rare for married people, husbands or wives, to masturbate regularly: this practice happens most frequently while the spouses are away from home for some days.

Section 14 Sexual Differences between Men and Women

I commented earlier that women would behave sexually in much the same way as men do if the cultural inhibitions and economic restraints disappeared. Men and women have markedly similar anatomic, physiologic and neurologic responses to effective sexual stimulation. The fundamental anatomic response is of a vasocongestive nature. (Lloyd 1964, p. 460) However, men and women are not entirely the same in coping with sexual urge in the same way we expect some behavioural differences in sex between humans and mammals. We would say that as the present trend goes on--we do not have any reasons to believe otherwise--women's sexual behaviour would approach men's ever closer but never quite the same. We can express that the former should draw near to the latter asymptotically in dealing with lovemaking.

All women have the potential to favourably respond sexually, and the failure can be ascribed to the men's ignorance (Velde 1965, p. 7). It seems that many women fake orgasms during love session for various reasons. Women's orgasms have nothing to do with pregnancy. Some females want their partners to make love gently; however, some females insist on the dominant personality from their men and rough treatment during sex (Bader 2002, p. 4). It is well established that men want a variety of women to have a high degree of satisfaction. This has a parallel phenomenon that women want a variety of lovemaking techniques to obtain satisfaction: for example, rubbing of one spot of the female body eventually becomes numb after a while. Vaginal stimulation is not essential for sexual excitement and orgasm of women. Some women achieve orgasm during anal intercourse and many women reach climax as the result of stimulation of other erogenous areas. Pre-adolescent girls can have sexual excitation and sometimes orgasmic response. (Lloyd 1964, p. 455) Women tend to identify their sexual passions with the particular men—their boyfriends or husbands in contrast with men who can have sexual orgasm with personal or impersonal partners (p. 458), though some women also engage in one night stand as men do. We are going to magnify the unlikenesses of the two sexes in this section.

Sex is the manifestations of survival for men and women. The survival instincts in regard to sex show up as pleasure for men and stable relationship for women, though both sexes may not know the reasons behind. Sigmund Freud asserted that much of the people's behaviours (the sexual behaviour is only one of them) are rooted in the subconscious mind, and the reasons for many behaviours are covered up and people are not aware of. Sexual desire originates in the preservation instinct of men, and sexual act is the means for men to impregnate women. At the same time the men's preferences for particular women indicate the wishes for the beautiful babies and their better survival rate. Women, when dealing with sexual matters, also act in a way to enhance their value and their babies' welfare.

Biologically, sexual distinctions of men and women have come about to achieve the division of labour which is supposed to be evolutionarily at a higher ground than unisexual procreation. We can see the evolutionary traces in the bodies of men and women. Men still carry unfunctional nipples on their breasts and women have clitoris which may be said to be partial homologue of male penises in that they are functional in sexual excitation but do not discharge urine.

Sperm and ovum also show division of labour. Sperm, though in a huge number, are tiny and short-lived outside the male body but have mobility. Ova have bulky body with nutrients. They unite to become zygotes.

The sexual divisions of labour between men and women further manifest in:

- the gonads which are the testes for men and the ovaries for women,

- the gametes which are spermatozoa (sperm) for men and ova for women,
- sex hormone which is diversified into testosterone for men and oestrogen and progesterone for women.

(Arthur, Sherman & Luciano 1986, p. 551)

Masters and Johnson, while noting the differences of male and female sexual responses, were more impressed with the similarities of the sexual cycles between the two sexes (Masters & Johnson 1966, p. 8).

Women, as for men, want to enjoy, more fulfilling sex life. Enjoying sex is one of the best ways of diffusing stress, lifting one's mood and inducing sleep. It is also satisfying way of enhancing a long-term, lasting relationship. (Brewer 1997, p. 76)

The biological differentiations induce the traditional social division of labour between men and women to achieve the efficiency and the maximum economic gains for a unit of two sexes with children. That is to say, the economic gains of a married couple with children are greater than those of a man and a woman living separately carrying half the number of the children. Still a single man has a better economic advantage than a single income family with children and even without children. Traditionally men were given the task of going out and doing the jobs to make money; men were the bread winners. The masculine characters necessary to achieve the objectives are independent, aggressive, competitive, and men are to initiate to contact women. Traditionally women were given the task of staying at home and looking after the home, and bearing and rearing children. The feminine characters necessary to achieve objectives are warm, emotional, dependent, non-competitive, and women are to look after men and children.

Sex is one source of division of labour in the family and the community. Other sources may be regional, professional, and military (army, navy and air force) within a nation. Others may be cultural and economic within the nation and even among the nations. Another may be capital and labour in the enterprises.

Men are capable of exerting a great concentration on lovemaking and hence on any other activities. Sustained effort characterises the females. Men need refractory period before another lovemaking since they expend a high energy culminating in an orgasm: whereas women don't need refractory period and are capable of having multiple orgasms. Concentration means expenditure of energy, physical or mental, in a short time; sustained effort means that in a prolonged time. Men have more energy than women to start with. The excellence of any human activity is the result of concentration rather than sustained effort. This fact explains why men have shown high achievements in the various cultural activities. For example, the high standard in the sporting events, as for most of the activities, comes about as a result of the practice of concentration. Olympic sports are the displays of concentration. Luckily for women, they don't have to compete with men; majority of women would not make to the Olympic Games if the discrimination on the basis of sex is not enforced.

Some activities do not need high degree of concentration to be proficient. For example, the school learning can be achieved to a high degree of excellence by sustained effort, as has been shown in many researches that the girls on average exceed the boys at school on many subjects.

Aristotle insisted that slavery and subjugation of women were in accordance with the nature of some men and all women. Some men are superior and accorded with the position of rulers, and some men and all women are inferior and accorded with the position of ruled. (Galbraith 1987, p. 11)

Matriarchy means women dominate men. By matrilineality decent is reckoned through mother. The occurrence of matrilineality is in no doubt, but the anthropologists have not found any case in which women dominate men as a social system. (Whitehouse & Wilkins 1986, p. 163)

Since the male and female body appearances are easily recognised to be different, it is expected that their ways of thinking and also their sexual attitudes are not the same. Though men's sexual drive is strong, women and sex are only a part of men's existence; whereas men and love are the whole existence for women. Corresponding to the above observation, men's sexual whimsicality is only a part of men's body; whereas women's sexual physiology dominates the whole of the female body. (Velde 1965, p. 43) It seems that in cohabitation, one partner does not comprehend the other in terms of thinking and sex, which leads to the various conflicts.

Musaeus, an ancient Greek, wrote, 'Of beauty women are ever jealous' (Harbottle 1897, p. 372). Men are ever jealous of the men whose girlfriends or wives are beautiful. A Persian proverb says: All people envy, the strong openly, the weak in secret (Dawood 1974, p. 87). Men don't understand why women can be so jealous of beautiful things. When women look at the photographs of the naked girls, their predominant feeling may be jealousy, thinking that they are not as good as the girls in the pictures. Men say women are emotional and do not understand certain things in the same way the toddlers do not understand certain things, which gives men the urge to strike women and toddlers. Women have been described as illogical, emotional, fickle, fragile, and absorbed with trivial and domestic matters (Davison 1993, p. 304). Philosophically speaking, if they were the same, there might not be attractions between them, and people may not be bothered to cohabit as often as they do today. Generosity and courage in a man appeal to the feminine admiration; modesty and dignity in a woman attract men (Velde 1965, p. 21). Certainly two friends of the same sex live together for mutual company but the bonding seems not so strong as the bonds between the opposite sexes. It seems that men's strength and capabilities are passed only to their sons and not to their daughters in the long course of evolution. Women's sexual attraction and capabilities are passed only to their daughters in the evolutionary terms.

Males are often referred to as stronger sex and females weaker sex. The difference of strength here is probably physical but seems also to be sexual. Fewer females masturbate as presented statistically in the United States: one-half to two-thirds of the females has masturbatory experience compared to nine out of 10 males. Lesbian couples have sex less frequently than heterosexual couples do. Male homosexual couples have sex more often than heterosexual couples do. The conclusion from these observations is that women have a weaker sex drive than men. (Taylor 1996, p. 75)

Male sexual desire is expulsion urge: men feel they must discharge semen. Female sexual desire is absorption urge: women want to absorb penis into their bodies. Expulsion urge is, by nature, stronger than absorption urge as we can infer by comparing urinating and defecating with thirst and hunger. Semen stored in the male body must come out if it takes the natural course in the same logic urine and faeces stored in the body must come out, though there is a difference in that the body can remove dead semen but not urine and faeces. Thirst and hunger are certainly strong feelings but weak compared with urinating and defecating. Besides, women, if they are unmarried and sensible, have to be worried about pregnancy at the time of lovemaking. This pregnancy concern makes females enjoy less the experience of sex intercourse. Some women are afraid they become ugly after each session of sex. These are the reasons why women generally are reluctant to have sex in spite of the urge they have.

Possibly average women think about sex as much as average men do. It is observed that some women are sexually aroused by looking at the sexually explicit pictures, though the incidents of arousal by looking at the dirty pictures are rarer among women than among men. The libido, or sex drive in particular, of the males as well as the females is largely controlled by the male hormone testosterone, one of androgen steroids, of which men have plethora and women have some; men produce 10-20 times more testosterone than women do. In case of women, lubrication of vagina at the time of lovemaking is regulated by the female hormone, mainly oestrogen, with the help of blood vessels and nerves.

The various factors in such a complex fashion determine the level of sexual desire at any time that people are not aware how they work. Good health contributes to raise the sex drive. Fatigue lowers the drive. Anxiety raises the drive: in an effort to escape the anxiety many people have sex. It is established that the strong anxiety gives rise to strong sex drive.

Women are definitely the winners in regard with sexual dealings but are well behind men in the physical or intellectual performances. For men orgasm can be equated with ejaculation of semen but for women orgasm is not easily pinpointed. Most women do not experience orgasm every time they make love. Non-orgasmic sex or sex without orgasm can be highly pleasurable and satisfying for women under certain circumstances (Masters, Johnson & Kolodny 1994, p. 65), in the same way some boys and girls enjoy kissing and petting only. Average women have orgasm only once in four sessions of lovemaking. Some women have even less and some not even once in their life time. (Wright 1977, p. 15) Between 20 and 35 per cent of women do not have any sexual responses in lovemaking. One striking sexual advantage of women over men is the former's adaptability and flexibility. Women can repeat sexual intercourses over a short period if they want to. Many of them have the capacity to make love to orgasm at their will. Also in the other extreme many can live without having sex especially if they do not live with men.

Women in power can pick and enjoy sex with good-looking boys under their supervision if they have an opportunity to do so. This is an example where a minority misuse their power of authority if they have a chance to do. In these cases it is the opportunity to do rather than the inherent will that plays the decisive role. The minority, sexual or racial, will abuse power as much as or even more than the majority if the opportunity presents itself. This fact that the minority is more prone to exploit their privilege is one reason why they have been prevented from holding high office up to recent times even in the so-called developed countries. In the recent development, the advanced countries of the world are trying to suppress sexism and racism, both emotive issues, placing anti-discriminatory regulations at the various levels of the government and also at the various sections of the community.

It is observed in the wild that a dominant mammalian male of many species keeps a harem within the herd. There are a few good reasons that a male rather than a female should lead a herd. Even if a female mammal dominates the mob by the wits, it is hard for her to keep a harem around. To start with, an erection of the male penis initiates the sexual intercourse. The female mammal, as for the human female, could be put at times in an embarrassing situation where she urges an unwilling male to have a go. She cannot force him because of both the position and her physical weakness. Besides, she may become pregnant and may not be able to look after the herd for a considerable period. The reasons why the dominating male keeps the harem are for him to enjoy sex as well as to impregnate the females with his superior seed for the survival of the species. The females have to submit to the strong males for the survival of the species. Hence for these reasons the female head of a herd does not make sense though a few exceptions are observed in the wild.

In the human society, men have the final say by virtue of their penile power whether the couples should have sexual intercourses or not. Men, when sexually excited, are desperate to have sex; however, they want sex as much as they feel like having and no more. In this men clearly reveal a selfish nature, though many men accuse women of selfishness. In an organisation such as a family, a firm and a government department a person who makes important decisions is in authority by definition. Hence, we can say that men are in authority in deciding to have sex or not between the consenting couples. In the above context we have to keep in our mind that sex is an important aspect of human life. I still cannot work out how the woman who is rich enough to acquire a male harem can get the penis of her chosen love for the night erected if he is not in a proper mood. Does the woman use threat, reward, affection or something else to induce him into sexual mode? Similarly, how can a male prostitute repeat the lovemaking process if he wants to earn a good living? Does it help if he tries hard or fantasises a beautiful woman in place of a mature woman or a homosexual man, who are generally their clients.

The sexual attitudes of both men and women are reflections of their respective life styles. The male self-confidence comes from the sense of achievement, whereas the female self-confidence comes from the sense of being appreciated. This difference appears in the respective sexual life. (*Encyclopedia of Love & Sex* 1972, p. 214)

Sexually and in other respects the males are essentially givers and are active and intense, whereas the females are essentially receivers and are passive and mild. Male's sexual organ (penis) is exposed and people can see when men are turned on. Female's sexual organ (vagina) is hidden and it is not easy to see when women are sexually aroused. These observations symbolically signify the sexual characteristics of two sexes. Men have a set pattern of making love. The strong expressions on the part of men during lovemaking assure women that they are needed and loved by their men and happy to take the submissive role. (Velde 1965, p. 110) In bed men normally take the lead and display their sexual mode. Women, as for the other activities, need external stimulation for guidance. Women are receptive and ask men how they want to be treated rather than taking the initiative. When women submit to men, women take off their clothes, lie on their back, and open their legs to let in men's body and penis. Many women testify that they don't forget the men and the sexual act when they lost their virginity. As stimulants to sex activity, men want pornography or erotica which gives expressive body parts and actions. Women want the romance novels which hide direct sexual activities. (Bader 2002, p. 234) Similarly in the sexual fantasies of both males and females, men are doers and dominant, and women are receivers and submissive (p. 235). I cannot make any value judgement if it is possible or beneficial to alter the life style by consciously changing the sex life.

It is generally talked about that women are shy hence they don't make the first move in the sexual politics and wait until men approach them. Men, driven by sexual urge, keep trying to have a break with a number of girls whom they like and have some chance of success, in the similar manner, men, if they want a good job within their reach, have to keep trying until they have a break. Women pick the men whom they think are the best among the suitors and agree to go out. Until this point women are in a better position to take the upper hand. The foregoing is the basic pattern and there is more than shyness to explain this generally observed female reservation.

When the swindlers approach people, they invariably use veneer of goodness to hide their intentions and try to get under people's skin for their ultimate gains. This is a widely observed stratagem not only of the swindlers but of the wicked persons, and Aeschines, an ancient Greek, expressed it in the following verse: He is specially deserving of our hatred, in that being wicked he has all the outward signs of virtue (Harbottle 1897, p. 411). When men approach women, women often use veneer of beauty to hide their true self and try to get under men' skin for their ultimate advantage. The females also hide their nakedness by beautiful clothes such that men are eager to see more. Feminine attitude, as for female clothing, induces men wanting to know more about the women who hide their body and real personality. Women try to delay submitting their bodies to men as long as possible, thinking that once men have enough of them men will lose interest in them. This is the survival technique women have used over the millenniums. These are the female ploys which make them more attractive to men than they really are. Women often betray these pretences to the dismay of men. These betrayals are not important for women, since there are always the other men who want them. Goodness and beauty are rare and very much sought after in life: the swindlers and women cleverly utilise them to their advantage. Demophilus, an ancient Greek, wrote, 'Be sure that no pretence can long remain undetected' (p. 375), thus, the swindlers and women revealing their true identity in no time.

Men on their part learn quickly that it is best to hide that they want only sex from the women when they approach them. They show a veneer of respectability that they want something else which the women have.

Men are in many ways deficient in understanding in regard with the desired women:

- At the first contact men are not capable of distinguishing the smell of the perfume from that of the female body; the clothes from the body of the women; the pretence of the women from their true nature.
- Men are not conscious under the strong sexual desire that women fart and defecate in the hiding; the young and beautiful women become old and ugly in no time; men would become sick of the women after men fully know them.

The females have a secret in that their bodies fully revealed in bed with the males are not as beautiful as the males imagined to be. Hence women try to keep this secret to as few men and as long as possible and behave accordingly. It seems that women are intuitively aware that their bodies are illusions, while men are not until they have naked women in their hands. The prostitutes have the overriding aim of making money hence discard this secret readily.

The core teaching of Buddhism is that everything is an illusion. Women have not learned that their body is an illusion from Buddhism but learned from the experience of the ancestors and themselves. The above concept is detailed in Section 1, Chapter 2, Book Two, and how the idea was imparted to the general public is explained in Section 2, Chapter 5, Book One. Women the world over integrated the concept into their way of life from the survival instinct over the millenniums. It shows up to make up their faces, to dress up and to talk, all to enhance their sexual attractiveness. They also show reluctance to men's advances and submitting their bodies to men.

Women have sat on the toilet several times a day for millenniums and observed their physiological processes. Gas, liquid and solid come out of their vagina and anus. What come out are disgusting, and they can see, smell, hear, touch and taste, that is, stimulating all five senses in the most repulsing way with the exception that they cannot see their anus. Women must have reasoned that it must be an illusion that men are eager to get to these holes which are anything but mysterious. Women try to enhance their bodily appearance by making up their faces, wearing fine clothes and using perfumes. Women hide their bodily secrets and delay submission to men as much as they can. Thus the females have formed their attitudes to the males, consciously and subconsciously, by these schemes. The instinct of self-preservation makes the basis of the above attitude. The pleasure principle may induce women to enjoy sex: pleasure in this context also originates in the instinct of self-preservation. Some women want to have sex under certain circumstances, and some women do by their in-born inclination or acquired habit.

Women think that their bodily attractions are illusions. This is the conclusion the Buddha reached after many years of mortifications though he referred to everything with a few exceptions in the world and life; the female body is only one of the multitudes of illusions which he implied.

What happens if men observe the females' physiological processes every time the females go to toilet. A man pays or persuades or threats a prostitute or a girlfriend or a wife to let him observe what she does in the toilet. Most likely outcome is that the man loses a sexual interest in that woman; however, he still has a sexual desire on the other women. This is an indication that women are illusions but sexual desire is not. The man will be parted with the prostitute or the girlfriend; he will think the loss of sexual interest in her is for good. What happens to his wife with whom he still lives? Will he regain his desire to her after a while even if he keeps observing her physiological process? If he finds suitable sex mates, he may lose sexual interest in his wife for good. But if not, he feels he has to have sex with her now and again, though his sexual interest may be diminished. His sexual desire originates in the instinct of self-preservation as for all men and all women.

Whether men's sexual drive may proceed from the central nervous system (brain) or from the penis, the effect is the same (Velde 1965, p. 81). Whatever way men are sexually excited, from thinking about sex to watching an erotic movie to having an erotic dream, the basic physiologic mechanisms of arousal are the same (Masters, Johnson & Kolodny 1994, p. 53). Men have their sexual sensation concentrated in the head of their penis. The most sensitive part of a man's penis is the helmet at the top and the ridge. (Brewer 1997, p. 62) In lovemaking, they unfailingly shake their organ inside the vagina or on any other part of the female body, after preliminary caress. In masturbation they likewise pull their organ in some fashion or another with the aid of sexual fantasy. In both cases the mode of stimulation on the glans penis is the same; rubbing repeated strokes in the length wise. Sex flush occurs for about 25% of men (Masters, Johnson & Kolodny 1994, p. 55).

Women respond sexually extremely diverse ways. Women have virtually no tactile sensation within the vaginal canal which receives the penis in coitus (Kinsey et al. 1953, pp. 158-9). However, women have so-called G-spot situated on the front wall of vagina a third of the way up and highly sensitive sexually on stimulation. G-spot was named after the German gynaecologist Ernst Grafenberg in the 1970s. G-spot is highly sensitive to pressure and can swell and trigger orgasm. However, some scientists are critical of its existence and function as claimed. Women have erogenous zones all over their bodies. The major erogenous zones are sensitive areas of skin covered with a high density of nerve endings. (Brewer 1997, p. 50) Human touch on the high density area stimulates a large number of the nerve endings, thus the female feels the raised sexual sensation by the accumulation of signals. Any point on the skin is supplied by at least three, sometimes up to 40 where the skin is extremely sensitive, nerve fibres. The sense organs have special sensory neurons called receptors which carry the information to the central nervous system by electrical signals. The receptors are sometimes called nerve endings or nerve fibres or simply neurons. The female's whole body can be said to be virtually a sexual organ. Women's most sexually sensitive regions are clitoris and inner surface of labia minora. The clitoris is an organ of voluptuous sensation, provided with an abundant net-work of sensory nerves. (Velde 1965, p. 43) Mouth and breasts are also sexually sensitive.

It had been thought in the past that there were two kinds of orgasms originating in vagina and clitoris. Sigmund Freud pointed this out in *Three Essays on the Theory of Sexuality*

(1905). However, the subsequent researches by Masters and Johnson demonstrated conclusively that the vaginal orgasm from coitus comes about by indirect clitoris stimulation. They showed that there is only one kind of orgasm from a physiological point of view, irrespective of how the stimulation has been applied. (Wright 1977, p. 252) During coition, the penis stretches and excites the labia minora and vagina. Because these organs are connected to the clitoris through the tissues, the penis stimulates the clitoris through the tissues indirectly. The female obtains orgasm by this stimulation. (Westheimer 1994, p. 75)

Dr Masters and Mrs Johnson concluded that penile size is usually a minor factor in sexual stimulation on the female partner. A fair number (14% of women Kinsey interviewed) of women reported that they experience multiple orgasms. It seems that a lot higher percentage of women is capable of multiple orgasms provided men can keep up with erectile endurance. (Brecher 1967, pp. 83-6)

In sexual coitus between men and women, the head of the male penis rub against the inner surface of the female labia minora, and the female clitoris is left out. Hence it may be advisable to massage the clitoris before intercourse for maximum satisfaction of the female participants, though certainly the clitoris is stimulated indirectly during coitus. While the stimulation of the female clitoris by the partner is important during foreplay, the female must express how, possibly when and how long it should be done. (Masters & Johnson 1966, p. 64) Masters and Johnson found that the direct manipulation of clitoris retards sexual excitement for some women under certain circumstances (*Encyclopedia of Love & Sex* 1972, p. 192). If men stroke repeatedly the same erogenous zone of the female body, eventually dullness sets in for both parties. Women often don't like the rough clitoral stimulation. They want the clitoris rubbed only after they are sexually excited, and only for a while and return to it. (Masters, Johnson & Kolodny 1994, pp. 53, 59)

Anus of both sexes is endowed with dense nerve endings and can be a source of erotic pleasure (Zilbergeld 1992, p. 76). Lips, tongues and fingertips are all sensitive to touch in the general term and sensitive sexually, and can be called erogenous. The neurologic system relays the sensory information into the brain and also relays back into the end-organs in electro-chemical form. (Masters, Johnson & Kolodny 1994, p. 50)

Women masturbate in a variety of ways. When women masturbate, most of them rub clitoris and labia minora with one of their palms in repeated strokes. Female masturbators make minimum use of penetration into the vagina since there are no sense nerves inside the canal except for G-spot, whose existence is a suspect. For this reason virgin hymens may be intact though they may masturbate regularly. Fascinatingly, many females, unlike males, do not have to have sexual fantasy to effect masturbation and can achieve orgasm by physical stimulation only. It is also widely observed that lesbians are not normally dependent on the use of a dildo, a substitute erect penis, to perpetuate their sexual act. (Wright 1977, p. 189)

In almost all women, the stimulation of their breasts, especially nipples and areolae, makes them sexually aroused. The nipples are cylindrical in shape, usually flat and being made up largely of muscle fibres. They are sensitive because of the concentration of nerve endings and easily become erect to the stimulation of touch or cold. (Westheimer 1994, p. 62) About 40% of men experience nipple erection during sexual excitement whether they receive the massage on the breasts or not (Masters, Johnson & Kolodny 1994, p. 54). Masters and Johnson found that three out of 382 females could bring themselves to orgasm simply by manipulating their breasts (*Encyclopedia of Love & Sex* 1972, p. 191).

Masters and Johnson claimed to have proved that women's capacity for orgasm was actually greater than men's.

Masters and Johnson found that women have as great a capacity for sexual response as men and that most women are capable of orgasm if they are properly stimulated and the interpersonal relationship is satisfying to them (p. 125). They also found that frigidity and inorgasmia, lack of orgasmic capacity, are two different things (p. 214). Some females cannot be sexually aroused, and some can be sexually aroused but do not attain orgasm. Only the former merits the label frigid. It has been established that few, if any, females lack the neurophysiology for orgasm, and inorgasmia is psychogenic in origin. We must also note that the inorgasmic females can derive great pleasure and satisfaction out of sex acts.

A woman can totally surrender herself to a man whom she loves and derive her happiness and enjoyment by observing that her man is happy and enjoying her. However, women definitely show greater sexual restraints than men under normal circumstances, especially if women do not cohabit with men. This female self-control may come about among other factors from lesser secretion of testosterone and may manifest among other things in the masturbatory practice. The masturbatory experience by women is about half to two-third of men's as surveyed in the United States for the different age groups. The number of masturbations per week among all the masturbators is also approximately half to two-third for women compared with men as surveyed in the United States for the married as well as single people. (pp. 222-3)

There is another statistical evidence to support the observation that generally women have more sexual control than men. By 15 years of age, 92 per cent of the males have had orgasms, but at the same age less than a quarter of the females have had such experience; and the female population is 29 years old before it includes as high a percentage of experienced individuals as is to be found in the male curve at 15. (Kinsey, Pomeroy & Martin 1948, p. 187)

Stronger male sexual urge makes men pay for the act of lovemaking and wait on women when the male sexual intention is obvious. It seems that women feel power over men and at the same time some cruel satisfaction by making men wait on them. Generally base people get a kick out of making the needy wait.

After the initial experience in ejaculation, practically all males become regular in their sexual activity. They don't or more precisely cannot stop the practice until the old age. Many women, after initiation, can go without any sexual activity for many years. (p. 191)

Beards of men are symbolic of strong sexual drive since male hormone makes the beards grow. Body hairs of apes and monkeys are not beards and have different interpretation from above.

Men normally want one thing from women since women do not have anything else men want, and the male sexual sensitivity is concentrated in the head of their penis: women they want are invariably young and pretty. Whereas women want various things from men; friendship, prestige, protection, money and sex. The female erogenous zones, corresponding to the above variety, are spread out in the various parts of their bodies. Men they want can be handsome, rich, famous or powerful, offering the above-mentioned desirables. Further, corresponding to the above observations, the male penises are similar in shape but the female vaginas are characterised by some observable differences. The female genitalia vary individually in size and shape, especially in regard with the labia minora and the hymen. (Velde 1965, p. 42) Men's obsession for good-looking women is perennial. Women feel that friendship, love and marriage justify their sexual acts.

The hymen, which has no known physiological function and is peculiar to the females, has perforations to allow menstrual flow and vary in shape, size and thickness. A doctor cannot necessarily affirm if a girl is a virgin or not by the physical examination. Some girls are born with a partial hymen or none at all. The hymen can be broken by an exercise or by an accident. Also the hymen may not be broken after the first intercourse. (Masters, Johnson, and Kolodny 1985, p. 33) However, the breakage of the virgin membrane is normally a sure sign that the girl had the first sexual intercourse.

The Bible says: A young woman who is not a virgin at the wedding night shall be stoned to death (Deuteronomy 22:20-1). Because of the medical evidence presented in the last paragraph we cannot practise this teaching. I suspect that some injustice was done through the course of the Jewish and European histories by punishing the innocent girls.

Men often complain that their wives are possessive: the wives think that they own their husbands. Women often complain that their husbands are jealous: the husbands do not tolerate any other man approaching their wives without their permission.

When men say that they want outright sex and women respond saying they don't want it. Both parties are not lying. Both are expressing their inner feelings which are quite hard to understand at times by the opposite sex. Seeing the eagerness of men, women feel they are giving away something important and at the same time they feel they can have sex at any time they choose. Women have more restraining force in regard to sex than men. The sexual urge and restraint are different in two sexes in nature and particularly in intensity.

There are a few good reasons why women are reluctant to have outright sex:

- Women are afraid they may become pregnant.
- Women want to sell sex as dear as possible, at times consciously and at times subconsciously. If women give in easily to the men's sexual advances, they feel that they are giving away something valuable.
- Many women feel they become a bit uglier after each sexual session. We know that the repeated sex makes the lower eye lids discoloured.
- Women feel that their men would lose an interest in them after having sex with them.
- The moral stricture may make women feel that sex is dirty.
- The male partners may disapprove if their women enjoy sex.
- Women sometimes fear pains.
- Women would know their bodies are not really attractive once exposed to men; hence they try to delay the exposure as long as possible. Women may think it is better for them to keep the secret of their bodies, that is, they are beautiful to look at but on close examination they are not, to a limited number of men in order to ensure their mystical status of their bodies.

Women are intuitively aware that their body attractions are illusory, that is to say, once men know their bodies men lose interest in them in no time. Mind Only (or Emptiness), as I explain in Chapter 3 Buddhism, Book Two, says everything is an illusion. Women acquired this knowledge through the experience of the ancestors and themselves, and act on the survival instinct. The virgins know this truth intuitively and non-virgins know from the intuition as well as their experience. Why then do men not have this knowledge? Men's immediate and overwhelming concern is to lay sperm inside female bodies, and have to push away any other notions. Both sexes work on the survival principles regarding sexual activities and know intuitively that female bodies are illusions.

Men have the strongest sexual urge during adolescence and its intensity is apt to decrease as they get older. Women tend to have weaker urge when young and its strength is apt to increase as they get older, until around 50 years of age when their menopause commences and then the sexual drive gradually decreases. (Kinsey et al. 1953, p. 143) After menopause women do not get pregnant hence naturally women attain decreased sex drive. The average

age of last menstruation in American women is 51. The above phenomenon is natural from the viewpoint of supply and demand. Women, if young and pretty, can attract men hence they don't need to have sexual desire. As they get older, fewer men are interested in them hence they have to look for men, driven by the sex drive. Nature shows incredible adaptation of the humans for survival. Men have strong sexual desire for young and pretty women but the interest declines when women start to get old, that is, towards the end of their twenties. Around this age women start feeling sexual drive by which means women become pregnant and preserve the species.

Menopause, or change of life in technical jargon, refers to the time during which women's menstrual cycles cease, normally occurring at the age of 45 to 50. The word 'climacteric' is occasionally used to denote the above state of women but this term is also used to refer to the time in the life of men corresponding to the female menopause, chiefly characterised by diminished sexual activity. Men's sexual capacity declines as they age, but climacteric does not refer to the sudden end of the sexual life: sperm are produced in the testes probably as long as men live. (*Encyclopedia of Love & Sex* 1972, p. 72)

In a sex survey sponsored by Consumers Union in the 1980s, 33% of the women aged 70 and over reported that they currently masturbated, as did 43% of the men (Westheimer 1994, p. 175).

About 90 per cent of the boys experience the first ejaculation between the ages of 11 and 15 (inclusive) and most of them reach the maximum sexual strength in the next few years (Kinsey, Pomeroy & Martin 1948, pp. 183, 186). The girls' sexual maturity is many years behind that of the boys and comes gradually over a long period of time. This female delay of sexual maturity has corresponding delay in the sexual response at lovemaking. Men's sexual response is said to be immediate while women's is delayed. Women tend to have sexual arousal only after the men they approve caress.

Women have delayed mechanism built into them in the sexual term. They take longer to excite on the individual sexual act and also longer to mature sexually than men do. The delayed mechanism can be also expressed that women have greater specific heat built into their body in the sexual term: women take longer to heat and also longer to cool than men do. The sexual arousal for both sexes shows itself as vasocongestion and the build-up of neuromuscular tension and both sexes have muscular spasm at orgasm to release the build-up tension. Women's capacity varies a greater deal than men's. Contrary to the foregoing general statement, some women can be more quickly aroused sexually than men. (Masters, Johnson & Kolodny 1994, p. 52)

The erotic dreams and consequent orgasms are most common during the teens and twenties for males, and during the forties for females (Westheimer 1994, p. 188). Majority of men reported that they had nocturnal emissions, that is, so-called wet dreams, and at least one third of all women reported having experienced erotic dreams leading to orgasm (p. 188). The latter surveys are based only on experience and disregard the ages of the respondents.

Recent research revealed that virtually all women have sexual fantasy of some sort. The young women tend to have romance in their fantasies and fall in love easily and do not have the strong sexual drive. As they get older, the sexual nature replaces the romance in their fantasies since their sex drive increases as they age. This fact indicates to us that women, young and old, are not really sated sexually and have to rely on fantasy to relieve unsatisfied longing. However, to effect masturbation women do not need to have fantasies and any stimulants, their fingers and various objects, serve the purpose. It is well established that women use a surprisingly wide variety of objects as an aid during self-stimulation. Our experiences also show that most women think and enjoy sex as much as men do. I could not believe that a young virgin wanted a sexual intercourse with me after I had caressed her for some time. Some women even have wet dreams, though in less dramatic way than men do. Among hundreds of prostitutes I made love to, there was only one girl who did not respond to my making love: she told me she was a frigid.

Emergence of females as sex subject, that is, they seek and enjoy sex, probably coincides with the trend that women can support themselves financially. Women do not have to be passive any more in sexual and other matters in the economically developed countries. In the past, women did not hold responsible positions and had to rely on men for the various supports and hence the pretence that the females were only sex objects was useful for both sexes. Unless women, particularly if they are pretty, tell lies to the adoring men, they will end up being in bed with them.

The question arises, then, why men have to pay for sex. Is it a gigantic fraud perpetuated by women through the course of human history? Karl Marx pointed out that capitalism was in fact a fraud perpetuated by the capitalists on the workers; however, he did not say that the transfer of money from men to women in conjunction with the sexual union was a fraud. It is quite strange that he did not notice this since the latter is more pronounced than the former under the normal circumstances: The workers spent more money on women than the amount of money being exploited by the capitalists as Marx alleged. Is it ordained by the psychological differences of approach to sex between men and women? Is it because women are slower to respond sexually than men in terms of both an individual sex act and the sexual maturity? Is it because men generally have more money than women and women want money and there is one easy way of getting money from men? Is it a matter of demand and supply? The answer lies, probably, in the mix of these propositions. To give an extreme example, Arthur Schopenhauer strongly advocated that it was the female scam: women plotted to protect their interests by withholding sexual favours from men whenever they deemed advantageous.

Whatever the underlying reasons may be, men, if they want sex from women, have to pay in some way or another. If men do not have money they normally don't get sex.

Many girls prior to marriage take the affectation of feminine attitude, knowing that they would be more attractive to their fiancé. After marriage these women relax or drop altogether this affectation to the disgust of their husbands. Many men on their part while courting give their fiancée presents at every occasion, knowing that she would appreciate the generous men. Once married these men tend not to give presents to their wife. They give out presents only occasionally or not at all, which we hear from their wives.

Which sex would pay for sexual acts if from some reasons or another--biological freak or selective infection of deadly virus--women outnumber men out of proportion?

In an attempt to answer the above question I like to mention a couple of examples from my real life experience.

When I was young, I got to know a rich widow. She was desperately in need of companion and sex; I happened to walk into her life to satisfy these needs. Her need for me was far greater than my need for her on both accounts; hence money could have flowed from her to me. In fact she proposed that I live at her place. Since I did not have a job at that time, she would have paid me some money as well from time to time for my occasional expenses if I had lived with her.

I once worked for a factory where the majority of workers were females by the nature of the works to be done. There was no appreciable difference in the male-female relationship. This factory was in the open community and the female workers could mix with men freely at home. I am sure the setup of different kind, where the females far outnumber the males in a confined community, such as an island or a remote town, will produce the male-female relationship considerably different from what we know.

The foregoing two examples give a clue to our original question. When women vastly outnumber men in the world or even in a confined social setting, I would imagine that a custom would develop such that women make payment to the sexual service of men. In this fanciful instance the payment is based on need, suppressing psychological differences between men and women.

It is generally believed that a woman wants only one man and a man wants a variety of women, as sexual partner. There is some doubt about the accuracy of this statement but the following incident may seem to concur it on the surface.

I knew a woman in Tasmania who had been divorced from her lawful husband. Though she was young and nice-looking, she killed herself sometime after the separation. I heard from the woman close to her that she could take only one man and no other in her life. An incident of this nature is not typical of what happens after a divorce nowadays.

At the time of breakdown of marriage, men as well as women go through traumatic period. That the woman in Tasmania believed that she did not want another man does not mean that she might not have taken a fancy on whom she believed was a good man had she survived the dejection, seeing that humans are remarkably adaptable creatures.

It is beyond dispute that men, under normal circumstances, are physically stronger than women. Where does the muscular superiority of men over women come from? I would surmise that the difference originated in different sexual roles of men and women.

Since the primitive age onwards to the present day, men, in an effort--serious and even desperate--to secure women for sexual gratification, have had to give presents to women, thus men had to work hard and as a consequence built strong bodies together with strong mind. Women when pressed for sex feel that they are giving away something important or a monetary value. To start with men have to show their fine and strong physique to impress women as good lovers and providers. Women on their part want to get pregnant with men who not only have good bodies but are generous and willing to have a go at them. Also in an established sexual intercourse, men have taken an upper position and done all the necessary work, which has given men sturdy physique. Women normally have taken a receptive position in lovemaking and consequently have not needed bodily strength. Repetitions of the sexual exercises by men and non-exercises by women as well as the hard work by men as providers over thousands of millenniums should have made the muscular differences of men and women as we see today. Once the people recognised the strength of men, the community gave men physically strenuous jobs, which had to come about since every community had to struggle for sheer survival. People even today allocate the jobs requiring strength to men in the family and at work. Women did the jobs which required dexterity but were relatively unimportant to carry on the community. Men had to rely on strength and intelligence both to acquire women and to gain community respectability: women on beauty to attract men. Nature designed the female skins to support the high pressure of the pregnancy, though they have little muscles. Though men developed muscles for their survival in the broad sense, men’s skins are too rigid to support the pregnancy and would burst with the internal pressure.

It seems that the love mode like animals was the norm for the humans since the immemorial past and the primitive people still surviving take this position, that is, a woman sits on her fours or in the knee-chest position and a man inserts his penis from her behind. For the primitive people in the jungle, the belly-buttocks mode is natural since the animals around copulate in this fashion. When the missionaries in the modern era went into the jungle to spread Christianity, they introduced the belly-belly mode to the primitive people everywhere. The natives thought it quite odd and called it missionary position. If men insert the penis from the rear into the vagina, the penis is less likely to stimulate the clitoris. The face to face position stimulates the clitoris more effectively hence the female experiences more satisfaction from this consideration alone. (Smith 1968, p. 71) Sometime in the past possibly when people were civilised, people made love with a woman lying on her back, that is, in the supine position and a man inserted his penis from under her belly. It is interesting to note how this transition was made. The belly-buttocks mode is less exhaustive than the belly-belly mode definitely for men; however, the former is less satisfying for both sexes because of lack of communication, two faces not facing each other, apart from the ineffective clitoral stimulation. Men after being civilised and wanting to have more satisfaction out of sex insisted on the belly-belly mode. In both modes men did all the sexual work but men had to develop a lot more muscles with the belly-belly mode.

Until recent times, most women had to use sex as a survival means. In the course of evolution, women have learned to rely on their sexual attraction to get what they wanted. Traditionally it was proper and possibly beneficial for young women to pay attention to their mannerism in order to attract suitable men rather than spending time in training their mind and body. They have been often abused to be good at only one thing and for nothing else. This tongue-lashing is wrong at least in one respect: women surpassed men by a long distance in the written and oral communication skills. Anyway there is nothing wrong in this general approach of women, that is, heavy reliance on sexual attraction. Sex is what women have, hence according to the general rule of a community, they must make the best use of it, otherwise they go down within the community as much as any men must make the best use of what they have to prevent going down in the community. We can liken women in this to clever merchants who deal with only one merchandise which men cannot live without.

It has been an insult for men to be called effeminate. It has not complimented women, either, when they were labelled man-like. Men try to be man-like and women, woman-like. Being otherwise draws criticism. Men want to be stronger and women more beautiful, apart from acquiring the specialised knowledge of each person. Thus over the past millenniums, the physical differences between men and women have been accentuated and the present state of affairs has been established. It was the norm until recently in historical terms that men supported women in exchange for sexual favour. Sex was, and still is in many nations today, a surviving means for women. The children and women cry a lot, hence the culture regards crying as childish and feminine. Men invariably do their utmost not to show childishness and femininity by not crying. The recent female interest in their muscle development is based on the knowledge that it does not interfere with their feminine beauty: if the muscle development makes women ugly no women would strain their bodies. In the foregoing argument, it is assumed that the masculine traits of the parents are passed to the boys and the feminine traits to the girls. This passage of the genes is for the long process of evolution and we normally don't see the changes of the traits from parents to offspring in the short span of one generation. The assumption is hard to beat if we reflect on our everyday experience.

At around the time when the first book of the Bible, Genesis, was narrated, men's superiority over women was firmly established in the Jewish community. Among the various evidence in the text supporting the above proposition, the following is the typical verse, which God uttered after the famous breach of the prohibition concerning the tree of knowledge in the Garden of Eden:

... yet your [sexual] desire shall be for your husband, and he shall rule over you (Genesis 3:16).

Confucius (551-479 BC) said, 'Women and base men are difficult to deal with'. In China Confucius onwards, the general public always considered women inferior (Chan 1963, p. 47). Even today in China which is under one child policy, there is a strong feeling among the population wanting to have a baby boy than a baby girl in the family.

In both of these countries, the subjugated status of women did not come about suddenly as the above passages may infer, but was already prevalent when the above extracts pointed out the fact.

The Chinese always esteemed that Yin and Yang are two basic forces in the universe. Yin is negative, dark and female; Yang is positive, bright and male. The concept stems from *The Book of Changes* (*I Ching*), whose author is traditionally attributed to Wen Wang (fl. 12 century BC), father of the founder of the Zhou dynasty.

Masturbation is acceptable way of releasing sexual tension. About 80 per cent of adolescent girls and 90 per cent of adolescent boys masturbate with frequencies ranging from once a day to once a week. (Westheimer 1994, p. 264)

Pre-puberty boys are incapable of ejaculating semen, though they are capable of having erection and reaching orgasm. The orgasm attained by the pre-puberty boys is not different from that of the grown-up men. (Kinsey, Pomeroy & Martin 1948, p. 176) Their bodies at this stage do not make semen and hence the storage sacs for semen are empty. Interestingly enough, adult females can have orgasms but without ejaculate, though many of them have lubricating liquid oozing in the vagina as a preparation for coitus. Hence the pre-puberty boys and adult females have similar responses to the climax of sexual acts. The similarity does not end here. The physiques of the two groups are similar and we often cannot make distinction of the voices uttered by these people. Women and boys speak an octave higher than men. (Wells 1925, p. 150)

Adolescence is between the middle teens and 20 years of age. We call boys in the early teens pre-adolescent and after 20, adults. Adolescent begins to produce an ejaculate which contains sperm. Possibly the first ejaculate marks the distinction between pre-adolescent and adolescent. (Kinsey, Pomeroy & Martin 1948, p. 182)

Sexual Response Cycles of Men and Women

The physiologic reaction to sexual stimuli may be divided into four separate phases of one sexual cycle, applicable to both men and women. Masters and Johnson made the first systematic study of the following sexual response cycles in 312 men and 382 women during the late 1950s and early 1960s. (Westheimer 1994, p. 254)

- the excitement phase
- the plateau phase
- the orgasmic phase
- the resolution phase

Erection of penis is the first sign that men are sexually excited. The full engorgement reaches in three to five seconds from the sexual excitement. Erection of penis is obviously to effect its penetration into vagina: without hardening of the penis the penetration is not possible. Also the erection of penis by vasocongestion is to raise the sensibility. 'The base of the penis is connected to muscles that allow it to swing upright into an erection and contract during orgasm to propel semen forward.' (Brewer 1997, p. 16) 'Also during orgasm the vas deferens, two narrow muscular tubes, contract to pump secretions up into the penis.' (p. 19) Men and women experience high blood pressure and rapid heartbeats in all the phases.

The first sign of women being turned on is lubrication of their vagina, and not the erection of clitoris as we might expect from the partial homologue of clitoris with penis. The lubrication of vagina is delayed five to 10 seconds further from the rapid erection of penis, from the onset of the effective sexual stimulation. These reactions are neurophysiologically parallel and occur whether the stimulation is physical or psychic. It was thought in the past that the Bartholin's glands in the labia lubricated the vaginal cavity. However, Masters and Johnson reported in 1966 that the seepage of mucous like fluid through the walls of the vagina lubricated the vagina. This is further indication that women are receptive by preparing for coition. As the sexual activity continues, with or without partner, men discharge a small amount of clear but thick liquid through urethra. This mucous substance is secreted by Cowper's glands, also called bulbourethral glands, two small glands near the prostate. The secretion, so-called precoital mucus, works as a flushing agent to clear the passage of semen and also as a lubricant; the latter functions in the same way as the females' vaginal lubricant.

Erection of nipples and swelling of breasts are the further signs that women are sexually excited and clitoris becomes prominent. When the female breasts are fondled with the fingers or the lips, the whole breasts swell with an increased blood supply and tension, and the nipples and the areolae become rigid and protrude. (Velde 1965, p. 35) Both men and women finish the act by orgasm which is similar basically but with some noteworthy differences. Men's orgasm can be equated with ejaculation of semen. Most women feel at orgasm a sudden burst of warmth in the clitoris with 3-15 vaginal contractions. When men reach a point of ejaculatory inevitability, nothing can stop reaching orgasm; however, women are capable of suspending on the brink of orgasm. (Masters, Johnson & Kolodny 1994, p. 67)

The excitement phases of both sexes may be the neurophysiologic parallel and are vasocongestive in character. (Masters & Johnson 1966, p. 68) The messages are carried from the subconscious level of the brain to the internal organs by nerve impulses (electrical signals) in the autonomic nervous system. This activity regulates the smooth muscles and is beyond voluntary control. The orgasms of both males and females produce contraction at the similar rate of 0.8 second intervals, though this happens at the penis for the male and at the vagina for the female. (p. 185)

The clitoris is similar in construction to the penis of the male, and can be stretched and relaxed. It contains muscles and vessels, and inflates with blood. (Graaf 1972, p. 91) The blood is driven constantly through the arteries to the penis and clitoris. At the sexual excitation the veins are closed by the muscles with the direction of the autonomic (involuntary) nerves hence the penis and clitoris are inflated. At completion of orgasm the neuromuscular tension built up is released in several seconds. (p. 53)

At ejaculation the muscle coatings of the epididymis, of the vas deferens, of the seminal vesicles and prostate all contract and a wave of contraction from the muscles around them shoots the semen straight out of the penis (Smith 1968, p. 67). At the time of ejaculation, a sphincter to the bladder has to be closed, to prevent either sperm being shot into the bladder or urine being discharged with the sperm. Urine is spermicidal. (p. 66)

The acme refers to the highest point of sexual pleasure for both men and women, prior to and during the ejaculation of semen for men and the vaginal contractions for women. At ejaculation there are five to seven muscular spasms. Men's orgasm often gives rise to the female orgasm in the sexual climax. The woman receives the signal from the men's acme; his muscular spasms and the impact of seminal fluid. (Velde 1965, p. 121-9)

The penis consists almost entirely of three cylindrical cords of erectile tissue, which are actually vascular spaces. When men are sexually excited, facilitating input from the brain centres triggers the reflex by mechanoreceptors in the penis. Thus the blood runs into the erectile tissue and the emptying veins are passively compressed. The penis becomes engorged. When men have an ejaculation, the brain centres put out the inhibitory signal which reverses the process.

The male and female sexual responses are similar in many ways and characterised by marked vasocongestion and muscular contraction in many parts of the body. The engorgement of the breasts and erection of the nipples result from the contraction of muscle fibres in them. The clitoris is made primarily from the erectile tissue and endowed with sensory nerve endings. At sexual excitement for both sexes, the heart rate and blood pressure increase. (Arthur, Sherman & Luciano 1986, p. 579)

The scrotum and testes respond to sexual stimulation, as do all other male primary and secondary organs of reproduction, with both localised vasocongestion and increased myotonia, that is, muscle rigidity. When a female is sexually excited, her breasts achieve erection; small number of men experience the erection of the breasts under sexual excitement. The females also go through the enlargement of major and minor labia during the sexual excitement phase. The females frequently use voluntary gluteal contractions to elevate sexual tensions during preorgasmic stage, more than the males do. The males' enlargement and elevation of the testes has a physiologic parallel in the females' expansion and extension of the vaginal barrel. Aside from obvious anatomic differences, men and women are homogeneous in their physiologic responses to sexual stimuli. Vasocongestion or venous congestive reaction means that blood runs to the sex organs and stays there to heighten the sexual sensitivity. (Masters & Johnson 1966, p. 204-94) Both vasocongestion and swelling increase the sensitivity of nerve endings in a bumped body region, though sexual sensitivity and smarting of bruised part arise from the different reasons and different ways.

Dr Kinsey reported that some women regularly reach orgasm within 15 to 30 seconds after sexual arousal begins. Within marriage most men reach orgasm in all sexual acts; whereas women reach orgasm only 75% of the time. (*Encyclopedia of Love & Sex* 1972, p. 124)

The sexual feeling after orgasm is termed afterglow. Both men and women enjoy the fore-play before the coitus. Many sex therapists insist the couple should engage in the after-play such that they can share the mutual feelings after the intercourse. This is particularly important for the female who carries over the sexual feelings after the coition, and is emotionally demanding some sort of her partner's assurance of affection. (Westheimer 1994, p. 29)

After orgasm, men and women go into resolution phase. Both sexes experience detumescence of the various organs, with men rapidly and with women slowly, and return to the normal unexcited state.

Men have to go through a considerable period of resolution or recovery before they are capable of having another cycle of sexual act. During the resolution the body returns to the base line, unaroused state. The refractory period is duration for men to be incapable of responding to the stimulation. The refractory period is the initial stage of the resolution for men. Women don't have a refractory period. (Masters, Johnson & Kolodny 1994, p. 69)

Some women do not reach orgasm at all and attain only the plateau phase of enjoyment. Some women have only one orgasm, some a few orgasms in a rapid succession, up to 20 times on rare occasions. (*Encyclopedia of Love & Sex* 1972, p. 9)

'Almost all women have the physical capacity to achieve multiple orgasms, while virtually no men can.' (p. 13) Immediately after orgasm, women can have additional orgasms with continued stimulation, without ever dropping below the plateau level of sexual arousal. For women, after orgasm, the orgasmic platform or sexual arousal disappears rapidly unless the further stimulation is added. (Masters, Johnson & Kolodny 1994, p. 68-70)

Women are more prone to achieve multiple orgasms when masturbating than when making love to men (*Encyclopedia of Love & Sex* 1972, p. 14).

Women who experience multi-orgasms report invariably that the later orgasm is more pleasure inducing. Men, though incapable of experiencing multi-orgasms, report that the first orgasm is most enjoyable in a love session.

Kinsey found that only about 2 per cent of women were genuinely incapable of experiencing sexual arousal or orgasm. He also found that masturbation was more certain way of achieving orgasm for women. 'Only 4 per cent of men were exclusively homosexual and never aroused by women; a full 37 per cent had at least one homosexual experience between adolescence and old age.' (Wright 1977, p. 247)

Section 15 Sex as Basis of Civilisation

In the Rig Veda, Indra is the most popular god. Indra is supposed to have a thousand testicles and a source of energy, both constructive and destructive. (Eliade 1978, p. 205)

Lust means strong sexual desire. In Old English it meant pleasure and delight. Lusty does not mean lustful, that is, sexually strong, but means full of vigour in the general sense. Wanderlust is a noun meaning a great desire to travel; people in the general conversation use 'have itchy feet' for this sense.

Sex is the source of all civilisations in the literal sense: Without sexual activities, there is no procreation and hence no humans on earth to talk about culture. In this section we do not go so far as to regard sex in the above sense but we explore how important roles sex played in forming the so-called civilisations, in other words, how vital sex was in shaping the course of human development.

Sigmund Freud originated the concept of libido to signify the instinctual, psychological or psychic energy associated with sexual urges, and in his later writings, with all constructive human activity. Carl Jung used the term in line with Freud's latter idea, and libido is a psychological term for life drive, particularly in the form of instinctive needs for everything that is essential for living. Both libidinous and libidinal mean of excessive sexual desire as well as of excessive life energy.

According to Freud, sexual urge is an energy source for all human activities after basic human needs are met. Intense sexual drive can be translated into intense drive for knowledge and activities. Shame, disgust and morality mostly organically determined by heredity rather than education impede the expression of the sexual drive to be sublimated to the other spheres. (Freud 1962, pp. 43-4) In the late nineteenth and early twentieth centuries, when Freud put forward his psychological theories centring on sex, sex was still a taboo subject in Europe. He saw sex everywhere as the cause of human behaviours in the similar fashion the Christians saw God everywhere as the cause of all human experiences. He even wrote that the majority of images in the dreams are sexual symbols. (Mercer 1996, p. 916) His view certainly satisfies some of the observations:

The sexually strong men naturally have strong motivations hence they have energy to do the works if they are properly directed.

I remember one psychoanalyst's conviction that an able man has a tendency to go through a high degree of sexual abnormality at puberty. This theory is an extension and at the same time a reinforcement of Freud's proposition. Sexual abnormality here is used to mean the mental state of an adolescent boy who cannot adjust himself at onset of sexual awakening. Though the feeling of inadequacy on sexual urges and indulgences is universal, it leads to serious psychological disturbances for about 10% of the boys.

There is another theory as to the cause of high libido. Anxiety puts men on high alert, making them both repeat sexual acts and carry out the various activities.

My sexual conducts at puberty was bad to the extreme and I am still ashamed of what I did at the time under the strongest sex drive. However, I console myself by the notion that sex is energy and I have done many things I set my mind on and even at the onset of old age, I still enjoy learning something new at every opportunity.

Humans have stronger sexual desire than the rest of the mammals and the former manifests various cultural activities which are beyond sheer physical survival. The other mammals exhibit rudimentary cultural activities corresponding to their seasonal sex drive: They play, collect some items of interest, carry out some rituals and at times tease their predators.

Men's sexual urge is generally more aggressive than women's. Men have dominated all the communities of the world as a rule and have played a major role in forming the so-called history--up to the present.

Civilised peoples, men and women, generally have a higher degree of libido than uncivilised peoples, as the various researches indicate.

With extreme malnutrition, sperm creation for men and menstruation for women may stop, which indicates that procreation must come from the excess nutrition and spare energy of the body.

However, the aforementioned proposition still does not explain why a high civilisation visited a group of people on a particular site at a certain time of history, and after a while departed leaving some marks on the people and the site. Is it conceivable that high libido corresponded with high culture of the people at a certain era and also that high culture was characterised by the people with strong libido? The historians normally give emphasis on political, economic or religious climates; however, is it possible that the favourable environments gave the people confidence and higher libido to have large families and intense social activities?

Malthus, in the process of formulating the population theory, assumed that the passion of sexes, though strong, was constant through human development.

The proposal that sex is energy has some difficulties. The other primates other than humans, such as apes and chimpanzees, are observed to have oversexed life style; however, they don't participate in the cultural activities as humans do. They certainly exhibit crude form of mores which are disproportionately small in comparison with their sexual activities. Also the proposition does not seem to be compatible with Compulsive Sexual Behaviours of humans which is said to be caused by the persons' need to reduce anxiety. Hypersexuality is more often referred to as Compulsive Sexual Behaviours. The extreme cases of CSB manifest as paraphilia which is unusual sexual obsessions, such as satyriasis, nymphomania, erotomania, paedophilia, fetishism, zoophilia, voyeurism, sadomasochism or exhibitionism. (Westheimer 1994, p. 145)

Paraphilia is not a physiologic dysfunction but is characterised by abnormally strong sexual desire, focusing on a specific sexual interest with its compulsive urgency (Masters, Johnson & Kolodny 1994, pp. 211, 214). The severe paraphilia has the overwhelming constant sense of anxiety or depression. In less severe cases, the paraphiliac urge is triggered by a specific stressful condition such as having a conflict or being slighted. The paraphiliacs are not normally aroused by the normal sexual theme, and the exposed acts have more to do with reducing the anxiety rather than having sexual satisfaction. (p. 213)

Antiandrogens, drugs that lower circulatory testosterone levels, sometimes have dramatic effect in treating paraphilia. This drug reduces a man’s sex drive significantly.

Sex is energy. At the same time anxiety makes men have repeated sex. What is the relationship between sex energy and anxiety? Do they have the same origin? Are sexual energy and anxiety of men one and the same thing? Is sex energy inherent or does it come from the nervous tension? Do both of the sources contribute to the activity energy?

It is widely understood today that unmanageable sexual and aggressive impulses are neurotic symptoms (Guntrip 1964, p. 12). It is established that the heroes are of nervous type.

Sex energy may be in biological discipline as for food. Food gives us the energy to live and to do the various activities. Heat, work, light, electricity, chemical bonds, coal, petrol, uranium and even mass are energies which are all interchangeable according to the strict rules of physical discipline. At first sight the energies of these two spheres seem that they have no connections conceptually and in their interchangeability. However, according to the proposition under investigation, men of high libido tend to work hard and do their duties in the community, thus promoting the welfare and culture; they may also indulge in drunken orgies or fights with zest. A few of them with exceptionally high libido may do remarkable feats, creating something new--a machine, an idea, a law governing humans and so on--uniting a nation for a cause and setting out for an adventure; they may also indulge in criminal activities. We cannot tell beforehand what the people with high libido do are for good or evil of the world. Hence upon reflecting in these lights, two sets of energies may not be entirely separate entities. Plotinus wrote: All life, even in its lowest form, is energy (Harbottle 1897, p. 475).

Simultaneously, by simply working up the separate physical results already arrived at, Grove--not a natural scientist but an English lawyer by profession--proved in his book *On the Correlation of the Physical Forces* (1846) that all so-called physical energy, mechanical energy, heat, light, electricity, magnetism, indeed even so-called chemical energy become transformed into one another under definite conditions without loss of energy occurring, and so proved subsequently, along physical lines, Descartes' principle that the quantity of motion present in the world is constant.

The physical, mechanical, chemical etc. energies aforementioned can be used for the good cause or the bad cause of the mankind. Similarly the sex energy can be used constructively or destructively and the inherent nature of sex does not tell which way it is directed. The inclination of the biological instincts of sex may be channelled to the aggressive drive for socially approved and culturally valuable ends. (Guntrip 1964, p. 28) Some people with high libido may engage in criminal activities.

If sex is energy, men who have a strong sexual drive do not have anything to be ashamed of. In fact they should be proud of the fact that they have a large reservoir of energy. However, the source of sex energy may be anxiety of the person; an indication that the person is emotionally unstable and desperately trying to escape from the anxiety.

Sexual activity expends energy in a short run; however, men with adequate sexual habit have more energy for the other activities as well, in the same way after the adequate sporting activity men feel tired but are eventually recharged with more vitality. Sex and sports are not mere sink of energy but the source of zip if they are properly controlled. Sex energy is not a finite quantity like fossil resources are but is renewable like water and the sunlight, and possibly unlimited in the realistic sense for the people who know how to use them.

Jean Baptise Lamarck (1744-1829), a French naturalist, asserted that body organs are improved with repeated use and weakened by disuse. He further said that the above changes are passed to the offspring and disused organs can even disappear in the end. (Mercer 1996, p. 727) It is unthinkable that the body organ in focus in this book, that is, penis as a sexual tool, cease to be used; however, the repeated sex makes the organ suitable for repeated sex and if rarely used it is conditioned for decay.

The concept that sex is energy of fixed quantity led to the traditional ethics which states men should minimise the sexual activity such that they can dispense that energy on something more useful for them and the community. This teaching is right or wrong, depending on the degree of sexual activities and the assumptions made.

Strong sexual desire and high level of energy may not be in cause and effect relationship. There may be an inherent energy within the body, which manifests itself as sexual desire or activity energy. Only if men can sublimate libido, men can use that extra energy for cultural activities. If men with a large libido engage in constant sexual activities, they do not have any spare energy.

Libido manifests as the urge to have sex for men and further:

- Men are active and eager to learn. Intense sexual desire which can manifest itself as the drive to see naked women, to touch the beautiful women, to have intercourses with the desired women and to own beautiful women can transform into intense urge to learn or act. If men don't have intense feeling in the sexual matters, we do not expect that men have any intense urge at all for any other matter.
- Men start thinking as humans.
- Men choose the good or the evil consciously.

Libido is literally strong at the youth of an individual; and also strong, figuratively, and even literally as I am proposing here, at the youth of a nation.

We may be able to formulate the libido theory on causes of civilisation in the following way:

increased libido-->increased population-->increased economic activity to support a large population-->progress of civilisation
Also, increased libido-->drive for higher mode of life such as adventures, arts, philosophy or conquering the neighbouring nations-->progress of civilisation

decreased libido-->decreased population-->decreased economic activity-->stagnation of civilisation
Also, decreased libido-->spent force and apathy-->stagnation of society and decline of civilisation

For example, people in the several parts of the world abandoned the easy-going hunting and gathering mode of life and took up toiling farming as their way of life, soon after the end of the ice age. This was postulated as emanating from the population pressure since the farming can support a far more number of people than hunting and gathering for the same acreage, though the farming took up much more human labour. However, the above argument does not satisfy totally our logical thinking. It does not answer the following rather intriguing questions:

- Why didn't the rest of the world take up the farming?
- Why are some primitive peoples today such as the Aboriginal people of Australia not engaged in farming?
- Where did they acquire the knowledge of farming?

Is it conceivable that the above peoples in the several parts of the world acquired the higher degree of libido by some chance, which led to the desire to support more population resulting from the incessant sexual activities? Did these peoples with high libido observe the nature closely and discover the secret of farming?

Heightened libido may give rise to the relentless sexual acts. However, the increased libido may not result in the increased population if the social environments are not suitable. People may abort pregnancies or kill the born babies if people do not want to support the extra babies. We can argue in the reverse cause and effect that the population increase may be the results of such social phenomena as the introduction of agriculture after the end of the glacial period or the mechanised industry since the middle of the 18th century. The Industrial Revolution is the other social event of the two which triggered the enormous increase of population. Here again we can argue that these social changes were made because of the raised libido.

It is a historical fact that the Caucasians migrated out of the Caucasus area centuries and after centuries. I offer the possible explanations in Section 1, Chapter 1, Book One. Anybody can conjecture that the emigration resulted from the overpopulation in the Caucasus. Is it a satisfactory answer that the Caucasians got higher libido from some reason, and the constant sex resulted in the higher population density, which forced out the surplus people over the centuries?

The Roman Empire, the Renaissance and the British Empire all have the common cause in that the peoples responsible for these historical designations engaged in the successful trades and accumulated wealth at the beginning. Even we assume that these peoples had raised libido without any documentary evidence, we also have to explain why the Romans and the British engaged in the empire building and the Italians in the diverse cultural activities such as science, political theory and various arts.

Various reasons are put forward to try to explain the fundamental cause for rise and decline of civilisations but none of them are totally satisfactory. The following are suggested to be the causes of the civilisations:

- race
- environments (human, geography and weather)

However, none of them independently or even the combination of them satisfy the various investigations. Any one single cause is not satisfactory and only the combination seems to give adequate solution in one particular situation; however, we still have to explain why one satisfactory combination is not satisfactory for another situation and we have to devise a different set of combination. The divine intervention may be the causes of all civilisations, which may be satisfactory to the religious. God said, 'Let there be light' and light was there. God said, 'Let there be the Mongol Empire' and the empire came forward. The proposition that everything is a will of God is hard to beat.

As far as I know nobody has ever proposed the libido theory. The problem here is that we cannot prove the proposition with the absence of documentations. Hence the theory is only a speculation, though the theory adequately explains the cause of cultures in all cases to my satisfaction.

At youth of an individual or a nation, people tend to take high risks in selection and prosecution of the tasks. The high risk is likely to result in big gain if successful, and big loss if unsuccessful. We know that the young people tend to be radical; however, these same people tend to become conservative as they get old. At an old age, people tend to take low risks in selection and prosecution of the tasks. This may result from the fact that as people get older, they have less libido and hence they have to adjust their methods of activities. I have found much the same principle, that is, high gain to high risk and low gain to low risk if successful, apply in gambling and making money which are practically no different.

In the youth of a nation, the society is unstable, which leads to the anxiety of people. These worried people tend to have more sex and at the same time try to discover a new way of thinking and life. As the result the society makes a progress. Here again as for individuals, the relationship of inherent sex urge and sex urge coming from anxiety is not clear.

Religion and communism have tried to dominate societies ever since they were established as systematic creeds. Did sex drive try to dominate societies in the similar logic? Is there any ideology emanating from sexual desire, comparable to Christian theology, Buddhist doctrine, Confucianism, Marxist dogma? Did sexual drive become the governing policy of the ruling body in the past in the sense that Christianity was the governing teaching of the medieval Europe; Buddhism governed the minds of many East Asians for millenniums; Confucianism was the central idealism of the Chinese celestial empires; Marxism was the governing doctrine of Communist Russia; racism was the governing idea of Nazi Germany and South Africa during apartheid? All the empires that have existed in the human history had the cohesive and central bonds based on religion, communism, capitalism, sex in the sense of men and women, race, family, class, or most likely the combined form of a few of these disciplines. Sexism was the dominant idea of families and societies the world over until the recent years. What sort of empire can we expect if its driving force is sexual? Did the Mongol Empire have the sexual motive behind the conquering urge?

Sex plays its direct role in marriage, friendship and favours of various kinds. History teachers taught us that the cause of wars was basically economic and such wars as the crusades or the American Civil War had the economic root in spite of ostentatious intentions. I swallowed this piece of proposition like pills prescribed by a doctor, not questioning if it was true or not: after all both came from authorities. However, it is beyond question that the primary purpose of some wars in the past was to obtain women for sexual purpose. I am not referring to just the raids of the barbarians in the jungles to the neighbouring tribes for plunder but to the full scale wars with discernible economic and political consequences. The Mongol Empire seems to me a typical example of wars whose purpose was to acquire women and I present it as an example in the subsequent pages. I esteem sex as a general base of civilisation up to now in this section, and in the rest of the section am to probe what sex played in the few events and persons in the human history.

Certainly a few presentations of the sexual phenomena do not give us the overall assessment of human sexuality. Rather they may reveal only the nature of sex. The sex life of people shows what sort of people they are because the sex life and the personality are inseparably linked. We know that sexism played a dominant role in education and professional appointment as well as in the family life in the past. We also know well that sex continues to play an important role in our daily life.

What I am going to present in this section is not a law. We cannot predict what sort of sexual and political life these people would lead beforehand. They were all constrained by the changing environment they were in. These people (individually and as a group) made most use of the circumstances.

The following case studies may give some clues how sex played a part in forming the history and civilisation. The average people on the street in the past and today would have done and would do what these powerful people, some are popularly thought to be good and some, bad, did regarding sex, though the ordinary people may be far short of achieving what the historically eminent people did in non-sexual context. The difference between the former and the latter is the opportunity in the sexual encounter and also possibly the latter had a lot higher libido than the former.

Moses, David and Solomon

In the biblical tradition, Moses is associated with laws; David, with Psalms; Solomon, with wisdom. It is hard for us to imagine that the book now called the Bible could have survived all these millenniums without these three characters; however, all three had a weakness in the sexual matter. Moses took a Cushite woman as his wife, though he had been married and had two sons. Even if his first wife could have been dead by the time of his second marriage, the problem was that his second wife was not a Jew but an Arab. Because of this his second marriage nearly triggered a rebellion. (Numbers 12:1) It seems that the dispute was the power challenge from Miriam (Moses' sister) and Aaron (Moses' brother) against Moses. Moses prevailed over his siblings. Earlier Moses committed a sin not circumcising his two sons (Exodus 4:24) from his first wife Zipporah. She was from the Midianites who were distant blood relatives of Israel (Genesis 25:2). Moses also sinned against God at the waters of Kadesh in the Desert of Zin (Numbers 20:1-13); Moses did not put a trust in God against the people's rebellion about the lack of water.

King David slept with another man's wife and got Uriah, her husband, killed, and as a consequence God punished him. King Solomon married foreign women and neglected his duties. He had seven hundred wives of royal births and three hundred concubines. Many of these women were from the nations about which the Lord prohibited intermarriage. (1 Kings 11:2)

What they did in regard with women was against the biblical teaching beyond any doubt. They were virtually perfect men except in the sexual matter. These characters were no different from the ordinary people as far as their sex drive was concerned, though they all had extraordinary personalities and led remarkable lives.

We can draw another inference from the sexual impropriety of the above three. The authors were anxious to give the accurate account of what really happened rather than to give the false pictures of the adored characters. They wrote the bad as well as good aspects of the leaders. It is sometimes cited that Moses himself wrote the Pentateuch, the first five books of the Old Testament; however, in view of the reference to Moses' marital impropriety, that may not be the case. We expect that Moses would have omitted the reference. That is to say, judging from these narrations, we can say with a good reason that the Bible is accurate in the other respects too. We have to take into account that there is ample evidence that the Old Testament was revised many times hence what is in the Old Testament today does not necessarily reflect what was in the Old Testament in the past. These biblical authors, unlike the surrounding nations in the Levant, were free to express whatever they believed true, not fearing any retributions from the authority. However, against the above general statement, a few prophets in the Old Testament, notably Jeremiah, and Jesus Christ himself in the New Testament, received persecutions for what they prophesied.

Rape of Half-Sister by Crown Prince Ammon (Taken from chapters 13-18, 2 Samuel, the Bible)

King David had a number of wives and concubines, which in itself was against the biblical teaching. He took over the royal wives as well as the house of Israel when King Saul died in a battle.

The Bible further narrates that because King David committed a grievous sin to unblemished and loyal Uriah, Absalom (David's son) revolted and took over in turn the royal crown and the harem for a while. Uriah was a Hittite of the Indo-European family. From the David's union with Bathsheba, Uriah's wife, Solomon was born.

The biblical ordinance prohibits a Jew's marrying a non-Jew, a Hittite in the above story, yet the Bible does not condemn the fact that Solomon's mother was a Hittite. Also Ruth, the great-grand mother of David and an ancestress of Jesus Christ, was a Moabite, yet her blood maintained the royal blood of the Jewish people: the Bible seems to take pride in the fact that Ruth was not a Jew. The Moabites are Semitic people, traditionally descended from Lot; however, the Bible treats them as foreigners.

The book of Samuel narrates the story of Ammon, King David's eldest son, and Tamar, his half-sister. Tamar is David's daughter by Maacah and Absalom's full sister. Ammon fell desperately in love with beautiful Tamar, and executed a trickery to force her to sleep with him. As soon as he made love to her, he loathed her intensely and got her thrown out of his bed chamber. My Bible has the annotation which says that the reversal of Ammon's feeling towards Tamar demonstrates that his initial 'love' was nothing but sexual desire.

Two years later Absalom, full brother of Tamar, invited all the king's sons to the festivities of sheep shearing, and had Ammon killed for the stated reason of raping his sister. His true intent could have been to get rid of Ammon who was the most senior in the succession line: Absalom was the next in line to the throne. After the murder of Ammon, King David forgave Absalom, though not totally to allow his smooth accession to the throne. Absalom subsequently revolted against the king and died in the battlefield. The reason for the revolt was conjectured that Absalom thought, judging from the prevailing state of affairs, that he would not be appointed as king when David died. As a consequence of deaths of his two eldest sons, the king anointed Solomon as the heir and subsequently Solomon became king, though he was by birth far down in the line of succession. King David favoured Solomon most likely because Solomon was the most intelligent among his remaining but substantial number of his sons.

Even Ammon had not raped his half-sister, Absalom could have wanted to kill Ammon, believing that by removing him he could have become king himself. However, the rape gave a moral justification for the murder. David eventually forgave Absalom for the crime, though he probably did not think that Absalom should succeed him, which led to the revolt. All in all, it is a fair comment that without the rape, King David could have punished severely Absalom for the crime, and hence Absalom would not have carried out the murder even he had secretly wanted.

It is hard to predict what might have happened convincingly if Ammon had not raped Tamar. It is most probable that Absalom would not have had Ammon killed and the latter would have succeeded David as king of the Jews. If this causal relationship is correct, Ammon lost his life simply because he forced sex on his half-sister. To understand what happened and what might have happened in relation to the rape incident, we may have to resort to psychological analyses on Ammon.

Primogeniture was the standard practice among the Israelis at the time as the Bible indicates. The Bible explains this point by saying that the first born from a woman and the first crops of the season are sanctified by God. Hence Ammon must have been confident that he would be appointed king after King David in due course, being the eldest son among the David's scores of offspring. People around him must have believed in the same way and paid due respects to him. We can reinforce this observation from the fact that when Ammon raped Tamar, King David did not punish him. When he wanted Tamar, he could have proposed marriage in the hope David would approve, though marrying his half-sister was prohibited in Israel. But he wanted her immediately since he was accustomed to get what he wanted without delay. He did not even weigh the feeling of Tamar: he must have thought he did not have to. We naturally think he should have proposed marriage if he loved her at all.

Another problem is that he did not seem to know anything about the laws concerning sex. The Bible says Tamar was a virgin prior to the incident. It does not say anything about the sexual habits, if any, of Ammon. Was he a virgin before the rape? Did he have girls he could go to bed with? Did he visit the brothels now and again? Did he masturbate regularly? We don't know the answers to these questions which may give some clues about the state of Ammon's mind as to force sex on his half-sister.

We do know that he so desperately wanted Tamar that he did not and could not wait till he obtained her favour. As soon as he forced her to make love to him, he lost all interest in her. If he had mastered some of the sexual laws as described in this book, he might have taken another course of action instead of such a rash act as to lose his senses. One sexual observation--this is stated as a law in the next chapter--asserts that the female bodies as imagined by men as sex objects are nothing but illusions and have no substance. This knowledge and possibly paying a visit to a brothel in the absence of available women could have prevented his deep disappointment after knowing Tamar's body. Another law states that masturbation can be as good as or even better than making love to a good-looking woman.

With this knowledge, he could have opted to masturbate. Thus he might not have raped his half-sister, and saved his life and the crown.

Interestingly there is a further twist to the above story. According to the Bible, Solomon is an ancestor of Jesus Christ (Matthew 1:6-16). It is probable that unless Solomon became king of the Jews Christ might not have been born, thus the history of the world could have been entirely different, though his son Rehoboam who succeeded Solomon as king was born shortly before Solomon became king. If we stretch our imagination to the limit, Jesus Christ was born to this world as a consequence of the rape of Tamar by Ammon.

Julius Caesar

Julius Caesar (100-44 BC) was well known to be an ardent womaniser in his contemporary society. He was learned, a superb campaigner, a good administrator, and he became a king or an emperor except by name. It is amazing that after all these activities he had energy to spare to go after females as his bed mates and was keen to hide his baldness. It is said that Caesar, with all his sexual debauchery, gave away promptly when it collided with his other ambitions in his life (Montaigne 1965, p. 551). In these senses his womanising zeal should be a credit to him rather than a blot to his character.

In spite of his will to subordinate his sexual exploits to his political ambition, at times his sexual adventures overstepped the obvious boundaries, indicating his enormous sexual promiscuity:

- Caesar had homosexual relationships through his life though not proved, and also heterosexual relationships with married women.
- He had an affair with Pompey's wife, thus risking his entente with Pompey, which he carefully nurtured. It was rumoured that Caesar was having an affair with Mucia, Pompey's third wife. Pompey divorced her for infidelity in 62 BC. It was alleged that Claudius, a young patrician, slept with Pompeia, Caesar's second wife, during the religious festival. He was prosecuted for sacrilege but acquitted since Caesar did not give any evidence. Nevertheless, Caesar divorced Pompeia, Pompey's cousin, saying, 'My wife ought not even to be under suspicion'. In 61 BC, Pompey, Caesar and Crassus formed the First Triumvirate. In 59 BC, Pompey married Julia, Caesar's daughter. However, Julia died in 54 BC, and Pompey and Caesar became bitter enemies in their ambition to dominate Rome.
- He had a liaison with Cleopatra, which antagonised many people in Rome. Knowing this, the plotters assassinated him while Cleopatra was in Rome.

Caesar's energy, physical and intellectual, was out of ordinary and matched by his sexual exploits, though he had several epileptic seizures in his advanced years. He was a masterly public speaker. He showed a genius in his writings too. Though written for propaganda purpose, his accounts of the Gallic War and the civil war have survived though both are incomplete and supplemented by other hands.

Plutarch compares Caesar with Alexander the Great, a Macedonian--a strain of the Greeks, in his book *Parallel Lives* (c. 100) whose thrust of presentations is the comparisons of the eminent Greeks and the eminent Romans. Alexander was cold towards women though he indulged in excessive drinking.

Muhammad

Muhammad (Mohammad) was born in Mecca c. 570. Unlike Christ he never claimed his divinity and he had many wives, though he tactically chose his wives to enhance him as a prophet and ruler. He claimed to be the last and greatest prophet in the line of Judaism and Christianity.

Muhammad married a rich widow, Khadijah, in about 595; he was about 25 and she was about 40. In fact this marriage was the turning point of his life. His wife gave an encouragement and support when he received the first revelations from the angel Gabriel. He did not take any other wife until Khadijah died in 619. They had two sons, who died young, and four daughters. In all these decisions concerning his marriage, that is, he married a rich widow and did not take any other wife until she died and secured offspring and wealth, we can see his shrewd judgements which characterised his ruling policies in his later life. He took over the capital (substantial) from his dead wife and engaged in mercantile activity.

After her death, he married nine women (Eliade 1985, p. 63). Some followers said that he obtained them in consideration of uniting various tribes rather than enjoyment of flesh. Some followers said that Muhammad wedded at his old age to save women from widowhood. (Sheowring & Thies 1982, p. 256) He did not marry indiscriminately but did so only to enhance his social standing. Muhammad taught his followers as he expressed in the Koran that they can marry up to four wives if they could treat all their wives with equal justice and equal love.

He began to teach in Mecca in 610 but the persecution forced him to flee with his followers to Medina in 622. The house built for him in Medina had apartments grouped around a central courtyard for each of his wives.

In the wake of the victory at Badr against the Meccans in 624, he was able to contrive the marriage alliances. Of his daughters, Fatimah was married to Ali (the fourth Caliph in the later years), and Umm Kulthum to Uthman (the third Caliph in the later years). Muhammad himself married Aishah, daughter of Abu Bakr (the first Caliph in the later years), and also Hafsah, daughter of Umar (the second Caliph in the later years).

Muhammad concluded the treaty of al-Hudaybiyah in 628. Hostilities were to cease and the Muslims were allowed to make pilgrimage to Mecca. Muhammad entered Mecca with his army in 629, virtually with no resistance and the Meccans submitted. Shortly after the treaty, Muhammad married Umm Habibah, a daughter of Abu Sufyan, a leading Meccan. He also reconciled with another uncle, al-Abbas and married his uncle's sister-in-law Maymunah.

The Mongol Empire

For the expansion of the Mongol Empire see B Mongol Empire, Section 4, Chapter 2, Book One *Idealism and Materialism*.

In studying the Mongol Empire, it struck me more or less suddenly that the empire may not have come into existence in the first place without the Mongol warriors' desire for women. Genghis Khan initiated the Mongol Empire in the 13th century and the succeeding khans held sway over a vast area of the Eurasian continent for a few centuries.

Before I come to disclose how the sexual desire of its soldiers kept the empire going, I like to draw the readers' attention to two interesting theories. They are only possible propositions, nevertheless they show that the Mongol invasion into Russia, eastern Europe and China had far reaching effect in the history of the world in spite of the underlying reasons such as the desires for tributes and possibly women as I am proposing here. Some scholars conjectured that the Mongol (or Tartar) armies brought in the Black Death that erupted in Europe since the fourteenth century. Also, according to some scholars these same armies brought technological expertise to the Europeans, which eventually led to the Industrial Revolution in the eighteenth century. Book One *Idealism and Materialism* stresses that the East was very much on higher level of material knowledge than the West at the time.

The Black Death in the fourteenth century was not the first outbreak of this form of bubonic plague in Europe. The Black Death struck Rome at the time Gregory I was elected pope in 590. The plague was probably brought to western Asia by traders from China bearing furs infected by plague-carrying fleas.

For 300 years, from the 1300s to the 1600s, the plague was one of the scourges of Europe together with war and famine (Davison 1993, p. 98). The plague also affected Europe in the 18th century. There was a great epidemic in China in 1890s, during which a French scientist Alexander Yersin identified the plague bacterium. (p. 101)

The Mongols were acutely aware that their customs and laws were not adequate to be introduced into the subjugated people. Therefore they ruled the conquered territories through the local aristocrats and did not interfere into the local governance except in China and later in India as Book One discloses.

The Tartar warriors gathered wives as well as loots and tributes (tax) from the subjugated territories, the latter two are often cited as the major motivation of their conquering zeal. Apart from the loots and tributes, acquisition of territories must have given them both sense of the dominance and satisfaction of the ownership, and further they made huge profits from the trade through controlling the trade routes. (Polo 1959, pp. 85-6)

Each warrior had a considerable number of wives (normally 10-15) and contrary to our expectation, these women with children engaged in some trade or business with the help of servants brought considerable financial benefits to their husbands. When a warrior died in a battle or from a natural cause, his wives and children were bequeathed to the member of his kin according to the set rule. Knowing the above system, we can see why the Tartars were ever eager to go to wars. First of all, the warriors wanted more territories and more tributes, and more beautiful women as their wives. They were free to go to battles, leaving their households to their wives who were capable of supporting themselves and their children. Should the warriors have been incapacitated, their families would have looked after them for life. Should they have died, their families were looked after by the relatives whom the families knew well and possibly were fond of. Hence, we can imagine that both the fighting men and their families were not overly worried about the injuries or death of these men at the battle fields. A goodly number of wives with sound financial backing naturally produced a large number of children from single households. The boys grew up quickly to be anxious warriors in the military environment and were more than sufficient in number and valour to replenish the dead, crippled and aged warriors. These young warriors wanted territories with tributes and young women to their credits, thus voting for wars on every opportunity. They did not know any other way of life, whether they were right or wrong.

I deliberately chose the term ‘wives’ rather than ‘harem’ to describe women collected by the Mongol fighters. The harem as I define in Section 7 is the sink of wealth; however, the Mongol wives produced wealth and children apart from giving sexual pleasure to their masters.

This cycle, originating in the desires for tributes and women to conquests to surplus children to more conquests and empire building, must also be explained how and why it came about in the first place and ceased to exist eventually. This is a lot harder than simply to note the phenomenon. The above cycle is only a postulate rather than an indisputable fact. However, if we can prove the proposition, we must conclude that the world history would have been entirely different without unquenchable money and sex drives of the Tartars. The desires for money and women are the driving force of men the world over for millenniums, not restricted to the Mongol warriors, not confined to a particular age and region. The Mongols’ urge to acquire wealth and women was raised and they saw the opportunity to conquer and plunder. This is where the libido theory comes in. The libido of the Mongol warriors became heightened from some reason, possibly from angst originating in the overpopulation. Apart from the yoke people in the conquered lands had to carry for 250 years, the Black Death and technological spreads in Europe played major roles in shaping the course of European history and hence the world history. Admittedly there are too many assumptions in the above reasonings.

Without acquiring wives, would the Mongols have carried out the campaign of conquest? This is as hard as answering the question if men cannot get sex from their wives men would still marry. There are certainly more than acquiring women in the Mongol conquest in the similar logic there are certainly more than sex in marriage. The question would eventually reduce to the statistical presentations, though again we don't know what the overall answer might be:

- Some Mongols would not have joined the campaign without an opportunity to obtain women. Some would have joined in any case.
- Some men would not marry unless they can have sex in marriage. Some would marry regardless.

Kublai Khan (?1216-1294), grandson of Genghis Khan, was a patron of scholarship and the arts, and was well aware that commerce could bring as much profit as pillage (Mercer 1996, p. 331). However, the easy victories the Mongols experienced would have contributed to the war decisions rather than engaging in commerce: the Mongol warriors simply dispersed when they met strong resistance. Besides, the commercial gains would have increased if they held large territories for easy transport and communication.

The proposition that the Mongol soldiers might have started the wars of conquest primarily to secure tributes and women may sound strange to us, modern people, who are conditioned to think in logic and common sense. However, the peculiarity is not so pronounced if we learn that there have been many causes of wars through the history: some were quite bizarre. For example, in Western society in the first half of the eighteenth century, the kings and emperors looked at their states as their private possessions as we look at our houses as belonging to us. They sought to expand their territories by marriage of themselves or their offspring. Only when they could not secure good marriage, they resorted to wars to try to increase their estates. (Toynbee 1962, p. 286)

Another illustration may be English wars for acquisition of markets both for imports of material and for exports of the products after the Industrial Revolution, and these wars can be called the sport of the merchants (p. 287). Some readers may think that the reasons for this kind of wars were economic and hence legitimate; however their intentions were not much different from those of the Mongol hordes. There is another striking instance from the ancient world. Helen, a daughter of the Spartan king, was seduced and carried away, and the Greeks laid siege to Troy to recover her for 10 years as I narrate in Section 9 Three Ultimate Beauties in History.

Some men rape a woman and take a risk of being sentenced to jail as long as several years in the Western world at present. If we think some men have a single sexual intercourse risking so many years in prison, what the Mongols did, that is, risk their lives to secure a large number of women is not hard to swallow.

Henry the Eighth and Church of England

I took the articles on Henry and Elizabeth to follow mainly from *The Tudors* (1979) by Josephine Ross.

Henry VII (Henry Tudor), of Welsh descent, won the battle of Bosworth over the numerically superior forces of Richard III (last Yorkist king of England) in 1485 and started 118 years of Tudor rule in England (Ross 1979, p. 17). In 1486, King Henry VII of the House of Lancaster married Elizabeth of York, and the warring red (Lancaster) and white (York) roses for the control of the English throne were united at last (p. 19). England became stable under the rule of Henry VII and he encouraged the learning within the realm. England entered the period of the Renaissance under his rule, leaving behind the wanton Middle Ages. (p. 27)

> Henry placed great importance on scholarship, and encouraged the spread of learning within the realm. The stability of Henry VII's reign allowed Europe's flowering Renaissance to enter England. (p. 28)

Henry VII succeeded to the throne of England when the crown was weak and insolvent and the realm was disarray. When he died, he left a stable government, an efficient legal system with a peaceful and prospering people. (p. 37)

He put all his efforts to avoid expensive and disruptive foreign wars. By treaties and marriages he secured delicate balance for peace, which was thought to be one of his major achievements. (p. 44) Particularly the marriage between Princess Margaret Tudor, daughter of Henry VII, and King of Scotland in 1503 seemed to secure peace on all fronts (p. 44).

Arthur, Prince of Wales, Henry VII's eldest son and heir to the throne, married in 1501 Catherine of Aragon, a daughter of Ferdinand and Isabella. This Spanish-Tudor alliance was to enhance greatly England's power and prestige. However, Arthur became sick after wedding and died from consumption in the following year. Catherine insisted that marriage was not consummated. (p. 30)

When Henry VII died in 1509, Henry VIII, at 17 years of age, came to the throne of England. One of his first acts as king was to marry his brother's widow, Catherine of Aragon. (p. 31)

Catherine bore him six children, but only one daughter survived and she would later reign as Mary I, known as *Bloody Mary*: She would desperately want to uphold England under Catholicism. Henry VIII eagerly wanted a male heir and at the same time he grew aversion to Catherine and turned his attention to a maid of honour at court, Anne Boleyn. (p. 31)

Henry VIII was perfectly suited to promote and progress the Renaissance that had been already under way in England (p. 43). Henry also paid the papacy almost a slavish respect. He wrote a book in 1521, in which he attacked Luther and expressed a profound devotion to the papacy. He was awarded the title of Defender of Faith.

During Henry VIII's reign, England became a power to be reckoned with, if not the equal of mighty France and Spain (p. 52).

In 1530, Anne Boleyn was virtually a queen of King Henry VIII, but he could not get the divorce of Catherine of Aragon from the pope. Thomas Cromwell, Henry's new councillor, suggested to deny the pope's authority and Henry VIII himself become head of the church in England. (p. 62) Henry VIII took the above course of action. The notion that he would become the supreme authority, both spiritual and temporal, within the realm and he could get hold of the enormous church wealth was extremely attractive to him. (p. 65)

In 1532, Anne Boleyn became pregnant and the king married her in secrete in the following year. Unfortunately the baby was a girl, later Elizabeth I, and the king's passion for her, once sated, began to cool quickly. She failed to secure a baby boy.

He soon got tired of Anne and had her executed for alleged adultery in 1536. Catherine of Aragon, rejected but unbowed, had died a little earlier.

Henry immediately married Jane Seymour, who bore him a son, later Edward VI, in 1537 but died in the childbirth. After three years, he married Anne, sister of the Duke of Cleves, but he rejected her outright and got a divorce.

By 1540, Thomas Cromwell completed the task of closing down the religious houses, seizing the church properties and lands. The operation was known as the Dissolution of Monasteries, which started in 1536. (p. 70)

The pope excommunicated Henry VIII in 1538 after the birth of Elizabeth, and England was dangerously isolated and vulnerable for attack (p. 71). By cutting the tie with the Roman pope and becoming the head of the English Church, Henry VIII was in effect encouraging the Protestant Reformation. In fear of the invasion from the two great powers of France and Spain, both were Catholic states, Henry VIII formed a powerful naval force. He was fond of ships and justifiably carried a title of 'Father of Navy'. (p. 72)

Henry VIII regarded himself as a devout Catholic even after cutting ties with the pope, and he despised Luther (p. 74).

He married young Catherine Howard in 1540. Catherine, Henry's fifth wife, committed adultery incredibly boldly, though she knew that Anne Boleyn and her lovers had been all executed. Catherine and her lovers were all executed. (pp. 77-9)

Henry married once more to find a measure of peace with the calm and obedient Catherine Parr.

> It was well known that the English were by nature suspicious of foreigners, and in the years that had passed since Henry VIII isolated the kingdom by breaking with Rome and ending the century-old spiritual unity with Europe those suspicions hardened into dislike (p. 119).

Elizabeth I and Catherine the Great were the most famous female rulers in the modern history. Their lives offer us good and interesting contrasts not only politically but sexually. The next paragraphs describe the open sexual life of these characters. Nobody knows what really happened in their innermost mind sexually and often even politically.

Queen Elizabeth I of England

The queen inherited an impoverished, disunited England in 1558 and left a great nation when she died in 1603 (Ross 1979, p. 178).

The queen herself was virtually responsible for the great flowering of the theatre by her active interest in plays and players (p. 163). Elizabeth was a great patron of the theatre, actively supporting it against criticism by the disapproving Puritans (p. 164). She herself had a keen sense of drama and spectacle (p. 170).

Under King Edward VI and Queen Mary I the disputes took place whether the Church of England was primarily Protestant or Roman Catholic. Queen Elizabeth established a compromise between the two positions.

Elizabeth was by no means a beauty in a feminine sense like Mary Stuart was but she naturally enjoyed the company of men. She enjoyed being courted in the European nations. England was an increasingly powerful nation at that time and many envoys vied with each other to tempt the queen into a favourable marriage alliance. (p. 138) It seems she came to believe that the interest of England was best served she being unmarried. Besides, her husband, being a king, would have considerable dominance over her, which she would have detested. (p. 135)

There was a rumour of romance before, but Elizabeth passionately fell in love in 1559 when she was 26 with an unpopular, ambitious, married man, Robert Dudley. He was the fifth son of John Dudley, duke of Northumberland, virtual ruler of England during the late part of the reign of Edward VI. All the evidence suggests that they were lovers of the ordinary sense. In 1560 Robert's wife was found dead, suspiciously looking like a murder. Though Dudley wanted to marry the queen, by the spring of 1561 their tempestuous relationship was over. However, they remained warm and intimate for many years, in fact till Dudley died. (p. 137)

There were rather incredible stories concerning Elizabeth and Robert Dudley. In October 1562, she desperately became ill from small pox and for several days she lay hovering between life and death. As soon as she was able to communicate, she asked that Lord Robert Dudley should be made Protector of the realm in the event of her death. In 1564, Elizabeth made a startling proposal that Robert Dudley marry Mary, Queen of Scots, whose husband died and who was looking out for a second husband. Nobody took the proposal seriously but it seems that she was quite keen and pressed for the marriage for months. (p. 141)

Elizabeth at last fulfilled her old intention of making Robert Dudley Earl of Leicester in 1564. She must have thought that this will help her marriage arrangement with Queen Mary. (p. 142)

In 1578, when Elizabeth was 41, the most serious marriage proposal began to unfold. Francois, Duke of Anjou in France, came near to marrying the queen. On hearing this arrangement Leicester (Robert Dudley) secretly married another woman. Elizabeth was really furious on hearing about the marriage and wanted to punish him but was eventually persuaded against the confinement in the Tower. (p. 156)

Elizabeth bitterly lamented the death of Leicester in 1588, which came after the defeat of Spanish Armada (p. 171). Leicester's stepson, Robert Devereux Essex, was to hold the first place in her heart after the death of Leicester through closing phase of her life. The queen put up his importunate ambition for years and he finally revolted against her and was executed. (p. 172)

There were a few other favourites of the Queen Elizabeth I.

Sir Christopher Hatton became one of the queen's bodyguards in 1564. He, being handsome and accomplished, impressed the queen. He was gradually promoted and became Lord Chancellor in 1587. There is no evidence that they were lovers.

Sir Walter Raleigh fought against the Irish rebels in 1580 and his criticism of English policies in Ireland brought him to the attention of the queen. By 1582, he became the queen's favourite and began acquiring lucrative monopolies, properties and influential positions. He married in secret to the jealous queen possibly in 1588. The birth of a son in 1592 betrayed the marriage, and both he and his wife were imprisoned. Though he secured his release from prison, he never regained confidence of the queen.

Though the queen's hold on power was slipping away in her late years, she remained queen until she died in 1603. Thence the Tudor dynasty was terminated, she being childless.

<u>Catherine the Great of Russia</u>

I took in the main the story under the above sub-heading from *Elizabeth and Catherine* (1974) by Robert Coughlan.

The future Empress of Russia, Catherine, was born a German princess and married Peter, a future sovereign of Russia, in 1744. She successfully carried out a coup in 1762 assisted by her lover, Grigory Orlov, which brought deposition and death to her husband and made herself Empress Catherine II. (Riasanovsky 1977, p. 283)

'As Russian historians like to put it, Peter the Great had solved one of the three fundamental problems of Russian foreign relations: the Swedish. Catherine the Great settled the other two: the Turkish and the Polish.' (p. 292)

During Catherine's reign, serfdom and the gentry privileges developed and Westernisation progressed (p. 302). Catherine, contrary to her view of Enlightenment, brought zenith of serfdom in Russia (p. 301).

Catherine was notorious for her love affairs. It has been asserted that her son and successor, Paul, was born out of the wedlock. The empress had 21 known lovers, and the last after she turned 60. From 1776 to 1789 her favourites succeeded one another almost every year. Some of her lovers played politically influential roles. (p. 284) For example, she had one of her ex-lovers, Stanislaw Poniatowski, elected King of Poland while Russian troops stood by.

The story of Catherine is so interesting as a woman in regard with sex that I am to give the detailed treatments in conjunction with the pieces of relevant Russian history in the following paragraphs.

Kievan Russia, so called after its capital Kiev, owed its wealth as an aggressive trading state, being placed at an advantageous trading position. Kiev thrived and expanded until the eleventh century and it ruled a vast territory stretching from the Black Sea to the Baltic and from the Carpathians to the Volga. (Coughlan 1974, p. 25)

However, civil wars and changes in the natures and patterns of the trade brought the downfall of Kiev's economic and political primacy in little more than a century. It was still an important city until the Tartars destroyed the city in 1240 and only barely two hundred houses were left standing. The Tartars devastated many other cities and won control of the entire country and withdrew to the southern steppe, which they kept for themselves, as the domain of the Golden Horde. They established their capital in the lower Volga town of Sarai, later known as Volgograd. From this capital they held the rest of Russia as their fiefdom; and the Russian princes and dukes sent their annual tributes there. (p. 26)

Tsar Ivan III, better known as Ivan the Great, defied the Tartars withholding the tribute in 1480 and threw away the yoke, though the Tartar rule in the south, particularly in the Crimea, remained (p. 27).

Kievan Russia had access to both the Black Sea and the Baltic Sea. When Peter was born in 1672, the accesses to both of the seas were blocked though Russia was the largest nation on earth. Either the Swedes or the Germans or the Poles held all the eastern perimeter of the Baltic. The northern shores and hinterland of the Black Sea were held by the Tartar Khanate of Crimea. The Ottoman Turks conquered Byzantium in the sixteenth century and the Tartars accepted the suzerainty and protection of the Ottoman Turks. (p. 27)

Peter the Great, failing to form an anti-Turkish coalition, made peace with the Turks and gave up the ambition to have the ports into the Black Sea. Thereafter he concentrated his efforts to have a port access to the Baltic Sea. (p. 38)

Peter the Great, by defeating the invincible Charles and his Swedish army at the Battle of Poltava in 1709, projected Russia into the European civilisation: Russia became a part of Europe (pp. 40-1).

The war with Sweden continued intermittently. But the hostilities were brought to an end on August 30, 1721 on the Russian terms after consistent Russian victories and shrewd diplomacy. This was also an end of 21 years of physical and emotional ordeal for Peter, and for Russia this was the end of the quest of centuries to secure an outlet to the Baltic and to Europe. (p. 48)

Peter the Great was the founder of the Russian navy, and St Petersburg which he founded from the swamped area not only was made the national capital in 1721 but grew into the naval base and seaport (p. 32).

Catherine, wife of Peter the Great, bore eight daughters, but only two, Anna and Elizabeth, lived to adulthood. Anna was affianced to the Duke of Holstein-Gottorp, the nephew of Sweden's late King Charles XII, Peter's old adversary. (p. 50)

After the death of Peter the Great in 1725, the throne of Russia passed to Catherine I (wife of Peter the Great) to Peter II to Anne (daughter of Peter the Great) to Ivan VI. These tsars and tsarinas were all Romanov as was Elizabeth (daughter of Peter the Great) to follow. The Romanov dynasty started at the crowning of Michael in 1613 and ended at the abdication of Nicholas II in 1917.

Elizabeth overthrew the infant Ivan VI (1740-1741) and the regent in 1741 and became Empress of Russia. Ivan VI came down from Ivan V, half-brother of Peter the Great. (p. 50)

Peter (later Peter III) was born in Kiel, Holstein-Gottorp in 1728. His mother was Anna, daughter of Peter the Great and his father was Charles Frederick, the Duke of Holstein-Gottorp aforementioned. The young duke was brought to Russia by his aunt Elizabeth shortly after she became Empress of Russia. Empress Elizabeth was childless and she had selected and brought her nephew the duke as the heir to the throne, when he was 14 years of age. The duke was known to be feeble-minded and also extremely pro-Prussian.

The daughter of a poor German princeling, Catherine, came to Russia at the age of 15 in 1744 to be the bride of the heir presumptive Peter. 'Catherine, shy and uncertain fourteen years old, was not pretty and had an insignificant title and no money.' (p. 204) As a matter of fact, Sophia, the maiden name of Catherine the Great, was excessively ugly and she herself was convinced that she was plain from the opinions of the other people and from looking at her in the mirror and the portraits. Because of her plainness she resolved to acquire wits and other merits. (p. 67) Empress Elizabeth earlier married Prince Karl Augustus of Holstein-Gottorp--a cousin of Charles Frederick--her first love but Karl died. Prince Karl Augustus had a sister who married a Prussian army officer and their first child was Catherine. Hence the empress was emotionally attached to Catherine, and for this reason selected her as the future bride of Peter.

Peter and Catherine married on August 21, 1745. Peter was extremely unhappy in his role as the heir apparent and indulged in the numerous infatuations with the females, though possibly he was impotent. It also seems that he told every female adventure to Catherine. This unhappiness also goaded him into excessive admiration for all things German, especially Prussian. (pp. 79-89)

Peter was also nearly alcoholic. Catherine, after getting married to the heir apparent, was humiliated and bored hence she devoted her time to extensive reading, preparing herself unwittingly as long as 17 years as a future competent empress. One subject she spent so much time was Russian history (p. 284), which contributed greatly to her role as the Russian ruler. Possibly without this knowledge she would not have devised and executed successfully the Greek Project in the late years of her reign. She was extraordinarily energetic in both sexual terms and non-sexual terms, that is, she had a very high libido. During her husband's life time, she had at least three lovers. She hinted that none of her three children, not even the heir apparent Paul, was fathered by her husband.

Catherine started a love affair with Serge Saltikov during the summer of 1752. She became deeply and passionately in love with him. In all the large number of love affairs she had in her life, Serge Saltikov was probably the only man she loved for love's sake. In conjunction with this love affair, she became entangled with politics and showed her talent in this field together with the ambitions to match. (p. 104)

Catherine had two miscarriages but she gave birth to a son, Paul, in 1754. His blood was possibly not of Romanov but of Saltikov. (p. 106)

Peter, Catherine's husband, was unconcerned with her infidelity and the birth of the son (p. 107). In this matter we have to keep in mind that Catherine was extremely ugly and Peter was distressed about his marriage and the role of the heir apparent.

Peter had a simple operation at the age of almost 27 and was initiated into full manhood. Thereafter he had numerous affairs and a succession of mistresses. However, it seems that he remained sterile. He continued to share Catherine's bed for a while at least. (pp. 107, 110)

Just before and after the birth of the heir, Serge Saltikov stopped visiting Catherine. She was still very much in love with him as for the past two years. His ardour for her could have cooled or Empress Elizabeth put the pressure on him to leave Catherine since he was no longer wanted after the birth of the heir. (p. 115)

Serge Saltikov had many frivolous affairs with women, using his charm and personal history. Catherine herself was hurt and withdrew from the public appearance for many years. (p. 115)

Peter and Catherine lived separate lives, coming together only when there were duties to be performed together. Both pursued their own love affairs, not fearing any objections from the other. (p. 115)

Towards the end of the summer of 1755, Catherine and Poniatowski were in a glow of new love (p. 131).

Count Stanislaw Poniatowski, a Pole, was 25, two years younger than Catherine and touted to be 'one of the best looking men of his time'. He was the scion of a great family in Poland, though the family's fortune and power were at low ebb at the time. (p. 125)

In 1757, Catherine gave birth to a daughter, and the father was probably Poniatowski (p. 141).

Within a few weeks of Poniatowski's departure from Petersburg in 1758, a worthy successor arrived to meet Catherine (p. 169).

Lieutenant Grigory Orlov was a handsome daredevil whose bravery and zeal at the battle of Zorndorf against the Prussian army made him a notable war hero. He led his troops in furious assaults even after he had been wounded three times. (p. 169)

At some point of 1759, Catherine and Orlov met and for both it was a passion at first sight. Their love affair lasted 14 years and it was the direct avenue for the throne for Catherine. Catherine was nearly 30 when her love affair with Orlov started. (p. 169)

When Empress Elizabeth died in 1762, Grand Duke Peter, Catherine's husband, became Tsar Peter III. He ordered the cessation of all hostilities against Prussia. (p. 180)

This war was a part of Seven Years' War (1756-63) which resulted from the desire of Maria Theresa, ruler of Austria, to recover Silesia from Frederick the Great, King of Prussia. The cessation of the war engagement ordered by Peter saved Prussia from the almost certain defeat. By the terms of the peace in early 1763, Prussia was to keep most of the province of Silesia.

Peter III, being an utter Lutheran in heart, next attacked the Orthodox Church. He became the official head of the Church and ordered the priests to change the Church on the Prussian model. (p. 183)

Peter III made clear his intention at the great feast on June 12, 1762 that he wanted to divorce Catherine and marry Elizabeth Worontsov (p. 187).

Catherine, sensing that the divorce was imminent, was forced to carry out the plot on 28 June. Catherine had Empress Elizabeth as a model: the latter had usurped the throne though under the different circumstances. The ring leader of the plot was Alexis Orlov, a brother of Grigory Orlov. The coup succeeded easily because Peter III was silly and unpopular and at the same time Catherine was intelligent and acted with the spirit of the Enlightenment. On July 5, 1762 Peter was murdered, most likely by Alexis Orlov. (pp. 188, 196)

Catherine thus initiated her reign with the spirit of the Enlightenment, admiring French culture especially the rationalist elements represented by Voltaire and Diderot (p. 226). As the Grand Duchess she had corresponded with Voltaire, the most influential figure in the Enlightenment. The great French Encyclopaedia was compiled under the direction of Diderot, and notably Voltaire and Jean Jacques Rousseau made contributions to it. 'The Encyclopaedia was to the Enlightenment much what Aristotle had been to the Middle Ages and Plato to the Renaissance.' (p. 206) Her reign was to last 34 years. However, she could not practise the conformance of speech and conduct in her rule. Towards the end of her reign the spirit of the Enlightenment disappeared from her policies. (p. 200)

She eventually became a despot. She spread the serfdom to bind the nobles and gentry class to her. In this she did the opposite of her cherished idea of the Enlightenment. (p. 201)

Peter the Great was her idol and she tried to follow his path of the advancement of knowledge in science, humanities and arts (p. 202).

Catherine's love affair with Grigory Orlov was settling into a relationship of quasi-marriage (p. 211). After a few years since the coup, Catherine had two sons by Orlov (p. 216). Though Catherine loved Orlov who reciprocated his love towards her, she thought that the marriage was out of question because of the imperial legitimacy; Orlov was only a common soldier (p. 218).

Catherine gave Orlov everything but marriage; money, jewels, honour, a sumptuous apartment and palaces. She did the same to the brothers of Orlov. Catherine, as a tsarina, was the richest and most powerful woman in the world. (p. 225) Orlov was even made a prince. Still Orlov was unhappy and showed his frustrations whenever he could. From 1764 on he was unfaithful to her and made no effort to hide his philandering. (pp. 220-1)

Though Count Stanislaw Poniatowski was forced to leave Russia in 1758 in the aftermath of the Apraxin scandal, Catherine and Poniatowski continued correspondence regularly in the years between his departure and the coup (p. 228). Apraxin of the distinguished Russian family was charged with treason while he was the field marshal in the campaign against the Prussians, and he was recalled and died during the investigation. After the successful coup and death of Peter III, Poniatowski desperately wanted to join Catherine but she insisted that was not a good idea, and offered a Polish crown after the death of the present monarch, Augustus III (p. 229). Poniatowski had a weak personality but entirely devoted to Catherine. Catherine was ambitious and spent her energy to try to satisfy her intellectual curiosity, desiring to create and control.

Augustus III died in September 1763, a year after the first alarm of death. In September 1764, Poniatowski was elected King of Poland; Catherine had bribed the electors and made an alliance with Frederick of Prussia and in addition she had posted 80 000 Russian troops across the Polish border to make Russian interest in the outcome quite clear. (p. 230)

After only a little more than two years, Catherine and Frederick demanded religious toleration for the Orthodox and the Protestants in Poland. Poland was a stiff-necked Catholic country at the time. Catherine and Frederick both sent the troops to suppress the Roman Catholic revolutionary movement. The Russian troops pursued the revolutionary troops into the Turkish territory, and as a consequence the Muslim Turks declared war on Russia. (p. 230)

Within two years after the Turkish declaration of war, a Russian fleet commanded by Alexis Orlov destroyed the main Turkish fleet in the Mediterranean. Another newly built Russian fleet defeated and largely destroyed the Turkey's Black Sea forces. (p. 234)

Austria, Prussia and Russia undertook the First Partition of Poland in 1772. It was widely suspected that Catherine took the initiative on the idea and took the biggest piece. On the next year the partitioning was ratified by the Polish Diet and King Stanislaw II, the same Poniatowski and still the admirer of Catherine. Poland lost a third of its territory and half of its population. (p. 236)

Pugachov's rebellion, making use of the Russian engagement with Turkey, developed into a massive revolution--the largest uprising ever seen in Russia by that time. Pugachov's army was at one time only 120 miles of Moscow and occupied one third of Russia. Alarmed by the rebellion, Catherine sued for peace with Turkey in 1774. Subsequently the rebellion was crushed by the Russian army released from the Turkish conflict. (p. 248)

Catherine's energy was nothing less than remarkable. 'Rising every day at dawn, fortified at breakfast by five cups of strong black coffee and through the day by large quantities of snuff, she attended to her vast correspondence and all important matters of state.' (p. 251) It is truly amazing that she was alert and remained insatiable in her political ambitions as in her appetites for life, art, love and laughter well into her sixties (p. 321).

With all her intelligence and the energy, Catherine realised that the statecraft in reality was so different from the arguments of the Enlightenment that she could not put them into practice (p. 252).

Catherine showed her abnormal energy for life in the capacity to be curious in many matters among other traits. One was shown to be the art lover and another, to collect useful people for her various projects. Her two most essential needs were power and love. (p. 268)

In 1771 Catherine gave birth to her third baby boy by Orlov (p. 269).

Grigory Orlov, apart from philandering, made a major affront to Catherine during the peace treaty mission with the Turks in 1772. Thence Catherine organised to replace Orlov as a lover with a young guards man, Alexander Vasilchikov. (p. 270)

It is strange that after paying attention to another lover, Catherine kept giving gifts of various kinds, estates, cash, annual allowance, etc., to the Orlovs (p. 271).

After two years, Catherine made Vasilchikov retire with large rewards for his services (p. 272).

As soon as Vasilchikov retired, Grigory Potemkin entered the scene (p. 273). Catherine thought that his mind, judgement and general capacities were equal to her own and she honoured and respected him. He effectively became the co-ruler for many years, and the executor of the Greek Project, which established Russian security in the Crimea. (p. 274) They were perfectly matched and devoted with each other. They both had had the great vision of the Greek Project. (p. 283)

The Greek Project as Catherine and Potemkin dreamed entails the following steps:

- Recovery of the entire northern Black Sea coast and all the lands along and above it, from the Caucasus to the mouth of the Danube. These territories once belonged to Kievan Russia. The Tartars nominally held these regions. Hence the recovery meant the subjection or expulsion of the Tartars.
- Expulsion of the Turks from the Black Sea regions and the re-establishment of the Byzantine Empire. Russia acquired Christian culture through the Byzantine Empire, which was more Greek than Roman in substance. (p. 283)

In 1774, Catherine and Potemkin almost certainly married secretly in Petersburg (p. 280).

Potemkin, at the first appearance in an arena of international politics, concluded as a Catherine's personal representative a peace treaty with Turkey, spectacularly favourable to Russia in 1774 (p. 281).

Since the autumn of 1774, Potemkin's special role would be that of viceroy of New Russia--the southern lands extending to the lower Ukraine and all the territories newly reclaimed from the Turks (p. 284).

Early in 1776, Potemkin went south to take up his active vice royalty of New Russia. It was organised that Catherine was to acquire adjutants to satisfy her longing for love while Potemkin was away. Peter Zavadovsky was appointed first. Then Simon Zorich took over, then Ivan Rimsky-Korsakov did in 1777. Then Alexander Lanskoy until his death four years later. The successor was Ermolov. He behaved foolishly and was sacked at once to be replaced by Alexander Dmitriev-Mamanov. (p. 286)

With these changes of the guards or lovers, Catherine's reputation went down, even unsettling her hardiest admires. Rumour had it that her ladies-in-waiting acted as testers of these young men's virility before Catherine accepted them. (p. 287) As she grew older, her adjutant, generally stayed young: their average age at appointment was 23. Catherine became the scandal of Europe as an archetype of licentiousness. All these years, Potemkin, with numerous liaisons on his part, and Catherine devoted to each other. (p. 288)

By mid-1782 the plans for the Greek Project, Potemkin carefully nurtured, was far advanced: it was almost time to occupy the Crimea, securing the neutrality of such country as England (pp. 289-90).

Dmitriev-Mamanov, her handsome adjutant, fell in love with her pretty young lady-in-waiting and wanted to marry her. Catherine was 60 years old and she was for the first time in her life to be deserted by her lover. It happened that Platon Zubov, a good-looking 22 year old man, was waiting for a chance to become an adjutant. Catherine, after months of agonising, appointed Zubov as her adjutant. (pp. 310-11)

Potemkin demanded Catherine to discard Zubov and she refused for the first time his demand of this nature. He was very much depressed and on the trip to Jassy, he died. (p. 312) Catherine herself had only a few more years to live.

Catherine and Joseph signed a treaty that Russia and Austria would fight the Turks and divide their empire. The Turks did not wait to be attacked. The Sultan sent an ultimatum demanding among other things that Russia vacate the Crimea. When she refused the Turks declared war and attacked. (p. 305)

In 1792, Russia and Turkey concluded the peace treaty. Turkey acknowledged Russia's sovereignty over Crimea-Taurus and ceded the remainder of the northwest coast of the Black Sea all the way to the Dniester River. Thus Catherine fulfilled the dream of Peter the Great. (p. 316)

In the spring of 1792, Russian troops occupied Warsaw and the Second Partition of Poland occurred in 1793. Prussia was bought off with a substantial chunk of territory. Catherine took the great swath: most of White Russia and most of the Western Ukraine. At her command, King Stanislaw revoked the new constitution. What remained of Poland was attached by treaty to Russia as a satellite with its foreign relations under direct Russian control. (p. 319)

Little more than a year afterward there was a national uprising in Poland and Stanislaw abdicated. The remnant of Poland disappeared in the Third Partition by Austria, Prussia and Russia. (p. 319)

Catherine was a really remarkable woman with an extraordinarily high libido. She was unusually ambitious politically and promiscuous sexually; both were well matched. Though she was born daughter of a poor German princeling and carried German accents until her death, she did a great deal for Russia and the Russian people recognised it. Her string of lovers satisfied her sexual longing, and more remarkably her quasi-husbands among them except perhaps Serge Saltikov were perfectly suited to achieve her political ambitions. Her political events were inseparable from her love affairs. She could have adjusted her political projects to suit her lovers or vice versa. Whichever way she did, there is no other way to describe her but a genius.

Rasputin

Even 'Holy Man' Rasputin used to mutter, when drunk, that he wanted a pretty girl. Considering he was a debaucher in the Russian court in his height of public life, surprisingly he was no different from ordinary men in his sexual preference. He had unusually strong sex drive, and without doubt some psychic power. I surmised that the latter came from the former. His influence within the Russian ruling family (Romanov) came from the fact that Alexandra (Tsarina) believed in his psychic ability to save the life of her haemophiliac son Alexis. She became emotionally dependent on Rasputin. Queen Vitoria was the carrier of haemophilia and passed the disease to her granddaughter Alexandra, who in turn passed it to her son,

In 1915 during World War One Nicolas II, Russian Tzar, left Moscow to command his forces in the fields, and Alexandra, whom Nicolas nominated in supreme power in his absence, dismissed capable ministers to be replaced by the non-entities which Rasputin favoured. These gross misrules, that is, the misguided dismissals and nominations, greatly contributed to the collapse of the imperial Russia.

In studying the Russian history, it occurred to me that if Alexis (Tsarevitch) had not suffered from haemophilia, the chains of events might have been entirely different and the Russian Revolution might not have happened. I am sure that this view would offend the remaining communists who believe in the historical inevitability of the communist revolution and scoff at the notion that one boy's disease can affect the course of human history.

There is another twist in the Russian history at that time. It is only my conjecture that Rasputin's mystic power rested on his strong sex drive, though not all sexually strong men have psychic ability. However, it is well established that sex is a kind of energy, though we do not know in what form the energy can come about nor how it can be used, for good or for evil. Rasputin must have turned the sex energy to his mind power. If this logic is to be upheld, the Communist Revolution in Russia might not have eventuated if Rasputin had not been endowed with extremely powerful sex urge.

Adolf Hitler

Hitler loved women and feminine beauty as the majority of men would do. He started having a love affair with Eva Braun in 1931. She came from the humble background as Hitler did. Hitler thought it advantageous to keep his mistress, Eva Braun, from public scrutiny, and the German public did not know Hitler had a mistress until after the war. I spoke with an elderly German woman at work and she did not know he had a mistress until the war ended, hardly concealing she still admired him. The fact he needed a mistress to solve his sex problem did not sound right for the political standing of his style. The persons close to Hitler testified after the war that he, during the chancellorship, had many sexual exploits apart from Eva Braun. He was also a multi-billionaire of today's standard. He so cleverly concealed the latter fact that the researchers got to know about it only in the year 2002.

Chairman Mao

For the development of the communist revolution in China refer to Section 3 Communism in China, Chapter 1, Book Three *Communism.*

I took the information for this article from the book *The Private Life of Chairman Mao* (1994) by Dr Zhisui Li. He studied medicine at the West Union University Medical School in Sichuan Province during World War Two. He also has the record that he emigrated to the United States, and received training in Australia. The above book was banned in the People's Republic of China. I added a few supplementary remarks from the other sources. The author was Chairman Mao's personal physician from 1954 to 1976, the year Mao died, and privy to Mao's most intimate thoughts and secrets, and a witness to his passing away. In recent years, the personal life of Mao Zedong (Tse-tung) (1893-1976) has come to light, which is in sharp contrast with the approved version. Many of the un-flattering life style of Mao, as described in this article, matches with the other reports of the various origins. For example, the book *The Unknown Story* by Jung Chang and Jon Halliday (her husband) exposes Mao as he really was, after 11 years of painstaking on-site researches. The authors cast critical eyes on Mao's personality and many of his noted, generally accepted, achievements. Also according to the newspaper reports after his death, Chairman Mao acquired women for his sexual exploits. One report gave an account that he was particularly fond of young girls--in their early teens, and the orgies went on till he was well advanced in age, and most girls, many of whom were virgins, cooperated with the great leader they admired.

This is an example of sexual debauchery where a perpetrator was regarded in high esteem by the general public: he was a fine communist theoretician as well as a strategic, military and political genius and besides he had charismatic common touch with people. Yet what he did in the sexual term was no different from what the ordinary men desired in their secret thought except Mao's sexual drive far outstripped those of the common people.

Mao was an actor and put up an elaborate make-up on stage, that is, in public, but was an entirely different person off stage (Li 1994, p. xix). He was far different from Mao portrayed by the mass media and authorised memoirs. He cleverly used psychology to control people around him, manipulating his anger and contempt with frightening effect, humiliating his subordinates and rivals. He was fond of Chinese history and it seems that he learned his strategy in military and personal conflicts from history and was an expert in waiting, feinting, withdrawing, and how to attack obliquely. (pp. viii-ix)

Officially he promoted puritanism; however, in his private life he engaged in an extravagant life style especially in eating and recruited young and beautiful women for his sexual service. He set aside a special room in the Great Hall of People to engage in the sexual frolic even while high-level party meetings and ball room dancing were going on in his name. (p. ix)

Though Mao was modest in drinking alcohol, he was addicted to barbiturates, took a lot of sleeping pills, and heavily smoked tobacco (p. x).

Whatever the natures of the upheavals such as the Great Leap Forward and the Cultural Revolution, their aim was only one as far as Mao was concerned: he wanted the total power (p. xx). The Cultural Revolution was his attempt to sustain the momentum in the face of the failed Great Leap Forward (p. x).

Mao led an appalling private life, which he kept secret even from his high-ranking officers. In public he was composed and dignified as well as friendly and personable. Especially in the matter of women he was a dedicated philanderer and as he grew older his sexual adventures became worse, involving an uncountable number of young women. (p. xx) Many of the high-ranking officers who helped to procure young women for him did so to show submission to him. They had to know that he wanted young and innocent girls. In some occasions he did not like the women provided because they were not young enough.

Jiang Qing was Mao's third wife and they married in 1939, though Li claims that she was his fourth wife. I could ascertain only three of Mao's wives with certainty. After becoming Chairman, Mao, possibly being afraid of the adverse publicity, did not divorce her. She became politically active since the Cultural Revolution when she was appointed a member of the politburo. (p. 7) It seems that Jiang Qing believed when Mao was near death in 1976 that once he died she would be appointed a new leader taking all the political control (p. 11).

Mao led an isolated life, seldom saw his wife and had no friends. He was interested in Chinese history and philosophy. (p. 85)

Mao wrote two essays; *On Practice* and *On Contradiction.* The two articles summarise his experience of the revolution, integrating the theory of Marxism with the reality of China. He expounded in *On Practice* that the real knowledge comes from doing rather than reading about how to do, and *On Contradiction* that the solution to any problem requires locating the major contradiction--going to the root and looking at the causes rather than the symptoms. They are superb essays and major contributions to the philosophical aspect of Marxism-Leninism. (p. 70)

Mao was a great military strategist and learned the strategies from *Art of War* by Sun Zi, *Romance of the Three Kingdoms,* and the various historical books. It seems that he also learned the strategy by playing mah-jongg, though he mostly played the games with pretty young girls, frolicking with them during the games. (p. 83)

Only Peng Dehuai, vice-Chairman of the Military Affairs Commission, had the honesty and bravery in criticising Mao's sexual infidelity once in 1953 and again in 1957 in conjunction with the Cultural Work Troupe. He also criticised Mao's Great Leap Forward in 1959 and was purged and imprisoned in 1966 and died in prison in 1974. (p. 94)

China is a multi-ethnic nation, but the dominant race, some 93% of the population, is the Han--the group most people associate with the Chinese (p. 101).

Mao became infertile in mid-life: the laboratory test confirmed in 1955 on his semen extracted. He had fathered several children by his three wives before he became infertile. He still had his sexual desire. (p. 103) He married Yang Kai-hui in 1920, but the Chinese Nationalist officials executed her in 1930. He remarried He Zizhen in the same year. He did not officially divorce her but married Jiang Qing in 1939. He had two daughters surviving: Lin Min, his daughter by He Zizhen, and Li Na, his daughter by Jiang Qing. Mao and Jiang Qing did not show any interest in their daughters and met them only a few times a year, though they looked after the two daughters financially. (p. 79)

In around 1955, when he was 62 years of age, Mao experienced bouts of sexual impotency (p. 104). It seems that his sexual impotency was more psychological than physiological, that is, imagined rather than real. He did not have any idea about Western medicine. (p. 105)

At the height of the Cultural Revolution, that is, in the late 1960s, he and Jiang Qing were sexually estranged; however, Mao had no problems with the young women he brought to his bed--their number increasing and their average age declining as he attempted to add years to his life according to the imperial formula. (p. 105)

Mao frequently accused others of fomenting conspiracies but he was the greatest manipulator of all (p. 106).

Mao was a man of tremendous energy (p. 106). His overall obsession was the power over the other people. He always feared that his officers were not loyal to him; he had few within the party he could trust. (p. 110)

Mao wanted to transform China quickly. The rural land reform was carried out in the early 1950s, just after the establishment of the People's Republic; lands and farm tools were seized from the rich and distributed to the poor. Private ownership still prevailed. Mao wanted socialism and that meant agricultural collectives. China was too poor to mechanise the agricultural sector. (p. 110)

After the revolution, the Chinese party leaders destroyed Buddhist temples all over China (p. 113).

Mao had very little emotional ties with his family. The Guomindang (Kuo-min Tang) executed his first wife, Yang Kai-hui, and his two brothers. A few children had been lost during the Long March in the mid-1930s. His eldest son was killed in the Korean War. He did not express any emotions over these losses. (p. 121) His last surviving son Anqing by Yang Kai-hui died in 2007. The Great Helmsman had wanted to appoint him as his heir but Anqing developed mental problem and the plan fell through. Though there were rumours that Mao had more children, none has been identified. These last three statements contradict Dr Li's statements earlier referred.

Mao did not see any morality in history. He admired the Shang dynasty tyrant Emperor Zhou (Chou), who reigned during the eleventh century BC. 'The Chinese people have always regarded Emperor Zhou with revulsion, horrified by his cruelty. The lives of his subjects meant nothing to him, and he was in a habit of displaying the mutilated bodies of his victims as a warning to potential rebels.' (p. 122)

Just after the establishment of the Republic of China, Mao with his wife Jiang Qing and his high-ranking officers moved into Zhongnanhai in the centre of the old imperial city and lived like an emperor. It is on history that the imperial city surrounded the Forbidden City which was the emperors' residence. Zhongnanhai is located just west of the Forbidden City. He thought himself like an emperor (p. 480). Mao took most of his meals alone in his bed room. He and Jiang Qing lived separate lives. (p. 80) Mao was careful to hide his philandering from his wife initially anyway. She sometimes caught him with another woman and was with tears being hurt. She also knew there was nothing she could do about it. He could have divorced her without any problem. (p. 144) Jiang Qing was once an actress (p. 153), and because of her vulnerability she always supported him in any matter (p. 166).

Mao had genital herpes, which was in fact contagious through sexual contact. He ignored the warnings and did not think the problem was serious. (p. 490)

Mao was preoccupied with sex and freely discussed about it though he did not understand anything about the human reproductive system. His wife also spoke freely about sex and was proud to tell people that Mao and she made love the night before. (p. 150)

Mao was deeply suspicious of China's intellectuals. Thought Reform of educated Chinese began immediately after the liberation. (p. 198)

In the anti-rightist campaign of 1957 led by Mao, hundreds of thousands of scientists and intellectuals were fired, demoted, or sent to do labour reform (p. 388).

Mao was convinced that the labouring class--workers and peasants, not scientists and intellectuals--made history, and also the peasant rebellions were the driving force of Chinese history (p. 389).

Mao attended the fortieth anniversary of the founding of the Soviet Union in November 1957. On his return he geared up to launch an all-out drive to increase production. This is the so-called Great Leap Forward, a name given to China's Second Five Year Plan launched in 1958. It was based on the Mao's belief that human willpower and effort could overcome all the obstacles such as China's lack of capital and modern technology. He had to get the support of the Communist Party first. (p. 226)

Mao wanted to catch up with Britain in 15 years and criticised the Communist Party leaders at the meeting held from March 8 to 26, 1958 for their low economic targets in China (p. 234).

The communist leaders, pressed by Mao, agreed to higher targets though they knew fully well that these figures were impossible to achieve. They claimed they reached the targets even when they had fallen short. The leaders lied to Mao to make him happy and it seemed he enjoyed those lies. (p. 236)

The weather in China in 1958 and 1959 was good for sowing and harvesting the grains. Agricultural production figures in the fall of 1958 were the highest in China's history. The figures were inflated in the first place. Much of the grains that were sent to the states as taxes were exported. A large portion of the huge harvest lay uncollected in the fields. A huge number of men had been transferred from the fields to work in the backyard steel furnaces or water conservation projects. Mao's 10 great construction projects in line for the tenth anniversary were on, and a new form of corvèe labour at the behest of China's twentieth century emperor was enforced. (p. 299) What came out of the backyard steel furnaces was useless for anything for lack of engineering expertise. Food became scarce for everyone during the winter of 1958-9. The food supply became worse every month. (pp. 282-3)

Mao visited Manchuria, the largest coal and steel producing region in China, in 1959 (p. 290). He learned that high-quality steel could be produced only in modern factories using reliable fuel like coal. But he gave no order to halt the backyard steel furnaces. (p. 291)

The Great Leap Forward shattered China's economy. From 1959 to 1961, China experienced a series of economic difficulties, manifested as a decline in industrial and agricultural outputs and food shortages.

In the course of 1959 Mao realised that the Great Leap Forward was not working as it should have. Despite the worst famine in the world history from 1958 to 1963 when over 30 million Chinese starved to death, Mao was not aware of the problem in the mid-1959. He wanted to believe in the success of the Great Leap Forward and many high-ranking officials made false reports which made him happy. (p. 31) There were too many false reports and inflated statistics, and Mao blamed the party leadership for the dislocation (p. 295).

The harvest of 1959 was worse than one year before (p. 330). As the food crisis worsened in the early 1960s, corruption within the party grew worse and Chinese leaders deluded themselves by formulating unworkable economic plans. At night they played and were entertained by acrobats and music and dance troupes recruited from all over the country. (p. 332)

In the wake of the Great Leap Forward, millions of Chinese died of starvation. Mao kept aloof from the problem and showed every sign that he did not care about the problem. (p. 125)

Since around this time, Mao no longer attempted to hide his affairs from his wife. His female lovers made no secrets with their love affairs from Jiang Qing. (p. 333)

In early 1960 Mao got to know the severity of famine in China; reports were coming in from all over the country. He got depressed and resorted to his usual tactic, that is, took to bed. (p. 339) He blamed in part the party officials and in part counterrevolutionaries for the famine he could no longer ignore (p. 343).

Mao genuinely wanted the Great Leap Forward to succeed and bring China into the modern world. However, he did not have any modern education and did not have any idea how to bring about the economically prosperous China into being. (p. 351)

At 67 Mao's complaint of sexual impotence stopped altogether. He became the adherent of Daoist sexual practices. He alleged that the sex with young women add his longevity and strength. He was happiest when he shared his bed with several young women. His appetite for sex extended even to young good-looking men. It was observed that Mao wanted to make love to young men to try to satisfy his unquenchable sex drive. (p. 358)

Mao made himself clear that his bedmates should bring their sisters and relatives to him. It did not matter if Mao's servile lovers were married or not: usually their husbands felt honoured their wives served in his bed and at the same time felt it was a stepping stone to a promotion. Very rare occasions his sexual advances were knocked back but most young women were proud to serve their great leader sexually. (p. 362)

Most of Mao's women were innocent young girls when they first came to him. They became corrupt through the association with him. They behaved arrogantly and were abusive of the power they had through him. It seems that they even looked down him as a human being: he was no different from the ordinary men as far as the sexual exploit was concerned. It is often heard that they quarrelled with him.

When the famine became severe in the early 1960s, Zeng Xisheng suggested the household contract production. When agricultural production went up according to this policy, the support for him grew. However, this policy was in essence the private farming. Mao wanted socialism and allowed the private farming only in way of alleviating the shortage of food. He was well aware that the Chinese people acutely wanted to own the land. However, he insisted on collective farming and communes. (p. 377)

In 1961 and in 1962, the party sent 10 million city residents on each occasion to the farms, to cultivate crops and ease the food shortage (p. 378).

Some people, notably Chen Yun, insisted the abolition of the communes through the transfer of the urban residents to the rural areas. Mao made revisions on his 60 point draft of the communes, which were kept going. (p. 378)

Mao felt a deep disgrace when the Great Leap Forward failed miserably and the people starved. He avoided the public limelight and sought solace in the adoring females around him. (p. 381)

In 1962, the famine still under way, Liu Shaoqi challenged Mao in his speech in the 7000 cadres' conference. He argued that natural disasters hit only one region of the country but the man-made disasters strike the whole country. Nobody in the conference attacked Mao but he criticised the policies of the Great Leap Forward. Everyone knew that those policies were Mao's. Mao had to retreat as a political strategy. (p. 384)

Mao could not purge the leaders he did not want; he did not have the power. By citing the Marxist morality, he could mobilise the masses against the leaders he wanted to purge. (p. 394) In the autumn of 1962 Mao started the purges of the leaders who advocated liberation and the household contract production, culminating in the Cultural Revolution of 1966 (p. 396).

Jiang Qing made her first public appearance on September 29, 1962: she met the wife of Indonesia's president Sukarno. This was the start of her active political role, and Chinese culture and art were the stage for which she was to play the prominent role. (p. 401)

Just after the public appearance of Jiang Qing, Zhang Yufeng appeared to the scene as the close female companion to Mao. As his trust in her grew she yielded a considerable influence over people as a secretary to him until his death. (p. 407) Zhang Yufeng was said to be shameless, ill-tempered, fond of alcohol and rude to Mao (p. 417). On the seventy-second birthday of Mao, he and Zhang Yufeng had a bitter fight. She had been having an affair with one of Mao's staffs. (p. 438)

Mao was not monogamous. Several women surrounded him whenever Jiang Qing was not around. He normally did not stay with one woman more than a few days at a time. (p. 407)

During the Cultural Revolution, Mao did not go through the cumbersome bureaucracy of the party and state, and went straight to the masses and he considered the young his most reliable allies (p. 469).

The ultimate targets of the Cultural Revolution were Liu Shaoqi and Deng Xiaoping: Mao wanted to destroy these characters (p. 470). A group of youngsters at Qinghua University had formed a rebel organisation called the Red Guards. Mao encouraged them in August 1965 to rebel against the authority. (p. 471) When Mao launched the Cultural Revolution--calling the youths to rise up in criticism against their professors and the Communist Party, he had been thinking about it years before (p. 235). The words became the rallying cry of young people everywhere in China. Backed by Mao, the rebel students took to the streets, and the house searches of those suspected of 'bourgeois' tendencies began. (p. 473)

> Even when the Cultural Revolution was at its height, Tiananmen Square in an uproar and the streets outside in turmoil, Mao continued to savour the imperial life, playing with his young women inside the Great Hall of the People and within the walls of Zhongnanhai (p. 479).

By January 1967, the country was in chaos. Party and government offices were paralysed. Factory production was plummeting. Lin Biao and Jiang Qing were leading the rebels. The conservatives and rightists were still holding out. Mao took the side of the rebels or leftists. (p. 482)

Mao's adventurism resulted in two serious problems among others. The Great Leap Forward resulted in the worst famine in the human history. The Cultural Revolution plunged the country into chaos, destroying lives, families, friendships, and the whole fabric of Chinese society. (p. 507)

At the Ninth Party Congress in April 1969, the resolution of anti-Mao stance of the Eighth Party Congress was reversed. Lin Biao came out as the winner and was designated as Mao's successor. (p. 512) Under the influence of Lin Biao, the army took control of government offices and work units at every level of Chinese society (p. 513). However, Mao became dissatisfied with Lin Biao after the Ninth Congress. In September 1971, he was killed in the plane crash after allegedly plotting a coup against Mao. (p. 516)

As Mao aged, he spent most of the time with Zhang Yufeng, even having dinner with her. She controlled the access to Mao. By the end of 1972 she became pregnant, though Mao was infertile by that time. (p. 570)

Mao said in front of his wife in early 1972 that he intended to hand over all the powers to Zhou Enlai. She was very upset, having thought that she would take over the power, and tried to overthrow Zhou Enlai. In March 1973, Mao rehabilitated Deng Xiaoping to restore the balance. (p. 576) Zhou was premier from 1949 to 1976, and sought to restore Deng and other moderate former leaders. Zhou died in January 1976 and Mao died in September the same year.

After the deaths of Zhou Enlai and Mao in 1976, the power struggles ensued between moderates led by Hua Guofeng and radicals led by Jiang Qing. Hua Guofeng won and became both Premier and Chairman of the Communist Party. Jiang Qing lost all political powers and nobody listened to her. (p. 629) The Gang of Four, one of whom was Jiang Qing, were arrested and put into isolation ward (p. 635). By 1980 Deng Xiaoping, a moderate, became the most powerful man in China, and Hua lost out and subsequently resigned from the political posts.

Chapter 2 Sexual Laws

I have written this book primarily to assist single men who have sexual problem. In the course of discussing sex, the particular reasons why we should study sex cropped up occasionally. The summary of them may be in order here before enlisting the sexual laws. The following are the listed reasons for writing this book; however, the readers may not find the straight answers for each query in the text. Some queries are hard to give answers by their nature.

- Single men may be able to cope better sexually by learning the laws governing their sexual drive.
- Men's sexual habit is not arbitrary but rooted in the deep psychological process. Hence by studying sexual behaviours, we should be able to understand human behaviours.
- Most men, though agonised through millenniums in cohabiting with women, have not learned to live without women. There must be good reasons for this fact.
- Men cannot stop having sex and criminals cannot stop committing crimes. On both activities they cannot stop because of the pleasures they derive. I like to know the basic mechanism.
- If the enthusiasm men spend in acquiring women can be tapped for study and work, the society must be a lot better place to live in. Also all men do their best in lovemaking, which men can use for the other activities. In other words, men are at their best acquiring women and making love, and they may be able to direct this energy to the other channels for the good of themselves and the society. The idea is that men should direct their best performance of sexual activity to something else.
- Men expend enormous amount of money and time in an effort to quench their sexual thirst. In this sense men have to study sex from the economic (of both finance and time) viewpoint.
- Men often use unethical means to try to sleep with women. In this sense men have to learn about sex from the moral viewpoint.
- However hard I tried I could not suppress the lewd feeling, though I stopped having sex for some months. The willpower developed during the sex suppression seems to work in controlling any other activities such as learning, drinking and gambling. I want to know the underlying mechanisms for the above observations.
- The question why the heterosexual men universally and unquestionably want to make love to young and pretty women may hold the key to explaining not only the male sexual behavior but the human existence.
- None of the causes of civilisation proposed by scholars on its own and even their combination is satisfactory, except saying that everything is done by divine intervention. Is it possible that the rise of the cultures can be attributable to raised libido of the bulk of men in one region from unknown reasons?

Sexual Laws

Sexual cycle for men starts in semen secretion (biological process) and ends in semen discharge (physiological process). A healthy man produces in his testes about 50 000 sperm every minute after puberty well into an old age. Possibly a man keeps producing sperm until he dies. However, the urge to have sex is very much psychological and is a sign of good health. Average men, after puberty, have always sexual thought in their minds and feel they must eject the stored semen from their bodies in some way or another. Whatever views men put forward for the reasons of the sexual activities for the intellectual satisfaction, men must have sex. However, the sexual preferences are very much psychological. For a very small number of men, the ejaculation does not have to take place and the un-ejaculated semen die after a while and are removed from the bodies in accordance with the biological process. However, the number of these men is insignificant as for the men who rape, and consequently both of these extreme cases are not treated in this book which seeks the laws of average men.

The hormone testosterone largely controls the sperm secretion and sexual drive of men. Corresponding to the amount of testosterone, the sexual drive of men reaches the highest level at about the age of 19 and gradually declines for the rest of their life. Women's sexual drive also mostly depends on the lesser amount of testosterone secreted. Women have weaker urge when young and tend to have increased sexual drive as they age until around 50 years of age when their menopause commences. However, the general statements about women are harder to make than those about men because of greater female individual differences. It is generally talked about, backed by the lower secretion of testosterone, that the female sexual drive is weaker than the male's; however, the research indicates that the females have potentially greater sex drive than the males, though this research result contradicts the earlier statement that the sexual drive depends on the secreted amount of testosterone. This observation matches with my experience and women are just as eager to have sex when they are in a certain mood or in a certain relation such as in marriage or friendship with men.

The average men cannot stop having sex because semen generated in the body must come out of the body if it takes the natural course. This is the physiological need and this book treats it as the reality. Another reason may be there are five senses involved in lovemaking. Seeing, hearing, touching, smelling and tasting play their roles in sexual activities and men derive pleasures in the process.

Men and women have to pay for the pleasures of the various kinds in some way or another; sexual pleasure is one of them. Men and women reap the benefits out of the various sufferings, provided they don't corrupt themselves from the hardship. These are the universal or cosmic laws they cannot escape whether they believe in religion or not.

Sex is dualism, that is, it needs the cooperation of mind and body (matter) for its fulfilment. Some ideologists insist on dualism, or monism of either mind or matter, for such disciplines as of history, evolution, and forming of human characters.

Sex is fundamental to men's need and the other basic human requirements are to eat, drink, and keep themselves warm. Sex is dependent on eating, drinking and being warm, that is, men want sex only after hunger, thirst and warmth are satisfied. However, happiness and sexual drive operate in different spheres and are independent of each other. Hence, men want to have sex even if it is shown to them that having sex in a particular situation will result in unhappiness. Wealth acquisition is often cited as the worldly desire together with sex and is also probably independent of sex.

The inferiority of women is the result of the evolution through which they relied on sexual usefulness for survival and is the other side of coin of strong male sex drive. Most men believe that women are evil yet they dream of possessing a harem.

Sex is a dichotomy as for the various aspects of life. Men do their best to persuade beautiful women to come to bed with them yet men have the final say if they have sex or not, that is, the onus is on men who must have a penile erection to proceed. Men want happiness and wealth yet they have to sacrifice a large part of both so as to acquire and live with women.

Sex lies within men, and is not the joining of two bodies as is generally thought. Men choose sexual object to derive maximum pleasure. This choosing process is psychological and men may prefer fantasy (masturbatory), a female, a male, an animal or an inanimate object.

Heterosexual men, if normal, always desire a female who satisfies three requirements: young, beautiful and compatible. When men acquire the desired woman, men invariably lose interest in her after repeated (undefined) sex and fancy other women as they did before. Since the sexually desirable women are scarce, men experience a strong competition to try to get the women who go through on their part a deep division to attract the desirable men.

Possessing a harem has been the dream of all heterosexual men, though only a tiny number of men have enjoyed this dream in the real life; for its establishment a huge expenditure of wealth is required. There is no way for men to sleep with every girl they want. Hence they may be helped by nurturing an outlook by which they imagine the prostitutes to be their harem: when the sexual desire grips them, they go out and pick a hooker to whom they take a fancy, in the similar way a powerful ruler did with a large number of women in his harem.

Average men can derive sexual gratification by masturbating as much as or even more than they would do from their preferred sexual object, whatever sexual preference they may have. Since this notion is contrary to common belief, men may have to go through fundamental change on their sexual outlook before they accept it. There are many assertions to support the above proposition on masturbation. For instance, the women the masturbators dream in their sexual fantasy are better than any which the experts in drawings or sculpturing or photographing can create.

Women's sexuality, in terms of desire and fulfilment, would be similar to men's, provided cultural inhibitions and economic restraints are removed. In the matter of sex rather incredibly women's physiological responses are similar to men's, and also the females' adaptability, flexibility and even capability exceed those of males. However, there are still physical and emotional differences between the two sexes.

Sexual taboos are not inherent to humans and can be removed from the human culture without serious problems, excepting one taboo concerning sex among blood related relatives: it has a high probability of producing inferior or even defective babies.

Some sexual laws support the institution of marriage and some go against. However, the overall result, whether it supports marriage or not, is not consequential to the institution since the urge to marry--sex comes with marriage--is more psychological and is independent of another urge to be happy. That is to say, people will marry whether they are happy or not. Another basic desire of men apart from sex may be acquisition of wealth. Men have to sacrifice a large part of their wealth in marriage. They marry regardless of the loss of wealth. It is true that a small number of men are not capable of obtaining wives, and some are not interested in marriage, some don't marry because of wealth consideration, and some refrain from marriage because of their way of life, religious or otherwise.

The sexual laws are in fact the reflections of our life and tell us what we are, and the similar laws can be built for the other human desires such as happiness, wealth, honour, fame and power.

Moderate sex, as for moderate drinking and exercise, promotes physical health and reduces irritability, though men still have the hassles in acquiring or cohabiting with women. This conclusion about moderate sex seems to go against my conviction that every pleasure is met by some suffering in the future of which men are not certain as to when and how.

The strong sex drive comes from the fundamental human need, that is, survival of the individual and species. Men's preferences for the desirable women, that is, beauty, youth, compatibility and need to change are also essentially the survival instinct, though the decisions are made subconsciously and men are not aware of the reasons why they reject or accept a woman for sexual purpose. However, the deviates, that is, homosexuals and men who want immature girls or old women as their sexual objects, do not have the survival as their selection criteria. This book proceeds on the premise that sex is the reality but the sexual objects are the illusions. This premise can explain the sexual deviates; however, I cannot answer why they deviate from the survival mode of the heterosexual men.

Sex has played an important role in forming what we call culture or civilisation. Our individual life style has a remarkable correspondence with our sexual life. The high culture in the course of history may be attributable to high libido of the people in that community: high libido corresponds to high culture. The historical personalities and events presented may suggest the above correspondence: however, I feel they are insufficient in number and logic to prove the postulate. Libido may be inherent in persons or may come from the anxiety. Either way the substance of argument does not change.

The considerations of happiness and wealth are not sufficient reasons for the average men not to get married against the overwhelming sexual drive. Men need the concept of the Third Prophecy to keep away from women in the domestic context.

When I was 58 years of age, that is, in the year 2002, I made another effort to stop having sex of any form. Since my death was approaching, I wanted to die a better man. This time it worked with a little determination. The suppression came naturally, that is, the undue will was not necessary to attain the status. I was getting older and had diabetes. My feeling is that age, diabetes and my willpower had equal shares in discontinuing all the sexual activities. The willpower probably had to suppress only a portion of the willpower with the suppression adventure of 42 years of age which I mention in the text. I still have sexual drive but I am not sure if I can have an ejaculation, which is really a strange feeling. I used to equate the sexual drive with the semen ejaculation. I am on an entirely new phase which I did not expect, and I wrote this book on a different premise.

What happens to the sexual laws of Book Five. I have written this book on the premise, among others, that I cannot suppress the sexual orgasm from social or solitary sex. The observations and conclusions were true at the time of writing. Some premises no longer hold true and this book has only a small value to me at this time. It may interest and have a value to some people. It certainly helped me both coping with the sexual problem and on the way to the present sexual abstention. I do not feel like scrapping the publication of this book for which I spent so many years compiling.

I started masturbating at the age of 14 and stopped having sex at 58; I kept having sex for 44 years with some abstinence periods. Possibly I had sex, including masturbations, lovemaking to women and wet dreams, four times a week. That means I had about 9200 orgasms totally. At the age of 58, I finally reached the ideal of sexual abstention preached by religion; religion is one fundamental concept in my life. The ideal state is also in conformity with the Third Prophecy whose presentation is the reason why I wrote this series of books in the first place.

I still think about women and sex. When I look at a good-looking woman in a picture, in a movie or in the real life, I feel my desire stir up. I sometimes dream about them in my sleep but it has not eventuated as a wet dream so far. Strangely the urge to have sex in a dream sometimes appears as the desire to masturbate. Next stage may be to stop thinking about women and eliminate all sexual longing: the ultimate stage to be perfect in the religious sense. I am not sure if I can attain that stage. I know that my body will produce sperm till I die hence the sexual desire may be with me for the rest of my life.

There is a further development. The statements in the last two paragraphs were true and lasted for some years. Thence I had further sexual activities--though occasionally—and indulged in looking at pornographies, paying to touch prostitutes and having solitary sex. As I age I have a less interest in the sexual matters, and I try not to think about sex and women.

Reference List with Text Citations Marked

Arthur, J Vander; Sherman, James H & Luciano, Dorothy S 1986, *Human Physiology: The Mechanisms of Body Function,* 4th edn, McGraw-Hill Book Co, New York.
18 (18) (19) 19 26 49 49 113 128

Bader, Michael J 2002, *Arousal: The Secret Logic of Sexual Fantasies,* Thomas Dunne Books, New York.
5 62 100 (100) (100) (100) (100) (100) (100) (100) 104 (105) 112 116 (116)

Benedict, Ruth 1974, *The Chrysanthemum and the Sword,* Charles E Tuttle Company, Vermont.
88 (88) (88) (88) (88) (88)

Brecher, Ruth and Edward, (eds) 1967, *An Analysis of Human Sexual Response,* Andre Deutsch, London.
6 109 (109) (109) 119

Brewer, Sarah MD 1997, *Better Sex,* Allen & Unwin, St Leonards, NSW.
28 48 101 113 118 118 126 (127)

Buck, Pearl S 1953, *The Good Earth,* 26th edn, Eyre Methuen, London.
67 (67)

Burguiere, A; Klapisch-Zuber, C; Segalen, M & Zonabend, F (eds) 1996, *A History of the Family,* vol. 1, Polity Press, Cambridge.
84 (84) (84) (84) (84) (84) (84) 86 (86)

Burnett, Dr Rosalie 1990, *Human Behavior,* The Marshall Cavendish Encyclopedia of Personal Relationships, vol. 7, Marshall Cavendish, New York.
55 (55)

Carter, John Ross & Palihawadana, Mahinda (trans) 1987, *The Dhammapada,* Oxford University Press, Oxford.
45 (45)

Chan, Wing-Tsit (trans. and comp.) 1963, *A Source Book in Chinese Philosophy,* Princeton University Press, Princeton.
126

Chien, Szuma 1979, *Selections from Records of the Historian,* trans Yang Hsien-yi and Gladys Yang, Foreign Languages Press, Peking.
26

Clayton, Peter A 1994, *Chronicle of the Pharaohs,* Thames and Hudson Ltd, London.
70

Cotterell, Arthur (ed.) 1993, *The Penguin Encyclopedia of Classical Civilizations,* Penguin Group, Hong Kong.
71

Cotterell, Arthur & Morgan, David 1975, *China: An Integrated Study,* Harrap, London.
87

Coughlan, Robert 1974, *Elizabeth and Catherine,* Macdonald and Jane's, London.

145 (145) (145) (145) (145) (145) (145) (145) (145) (146) (146) (146) (146) (146) (146) (146) (146) (146) (147) (147) (147) (147) (147) (147) (147) (147) (147) (147) (147) (147) (147) (147) (147) (147) (148) (148) (148) (148) (148) (148) (148) (148) (148) (148) (148) (148) (148) (148) (149) (149) (149) (149) (149) (149) (149) (149) (149) (149) (149) (149) (149) (149) (149) (149) (149) (150) (150) (150) (150) (150) (150) (150) (150)

Davison, Michael Worth (ed.) 1993, *When, Where, Why and How It Happened,* Reader's Digest, London.
69 (69) 114 140 (140)

Dawood, NJ (trans.) 1974, *Tales from the Thousand and One nights,* Allen Lane, London.
114

Dulbecco, Renato 1987, *The Design of Life,* Yale University Press, New Haven.
18 (18) 19 (19) 24 102

Ebrey, Patricia Buckley 1996, *The Cambridge Illustrated History of China,* Calmann & King Ltd, London.
78 87

The editors of Time-Life Books 1988, *The March of Islam: Time-Life History of the World AD 600-800,* Time-Life Books, Amsterdam.
79

Eliade, Mircea 1978, *From the Stone Age to the Eleusinian Mysteries,* A History of Religious Ideas, vol. 1, trans. Willard R Trask, University of Chicago Press, Chicago.
130

-----1982, *From Gautama Buddha to the Triumph of Christianity,* A History of Religious Ideas, vol. 2, trans. Willard R Trask, University of Chicago Press, Chicago.
87

-----1985, *From Muhammad to the Age of Reforms,* A History of Religious Ideas, vol. 3, trans Alf Hiltebeitel and Diane Aostolos-Cappadona, University of Chicago Press, Chicago.
139

Encyclopedia of Love & Sex 1972, Marshall Cavendish Ltd, London.
20 53 (53) 81 100 116 119 119 (120) (120) (120) 122 128 128 (128) 128

Fenwick, Elizabeth & Walker, Richard 1994, *How Sex Works,* Reader's Digest (Australia), Surry Hills, NSW.
18 20 26 (26)

Fisher, Helen E 1992, *Anatomy of Love: A Natural History of Adultery, Monogamy & Divorce,* Simon & Schuster Ltd, London.
30 90 (90) (90) (90) (90) (90) (90)

Freeman, Charles 1996, *Egypt, Greece and Rome: Civilizations of the Ancient Mediterranean,* Oxford University Press, New York.
56 75 84 88

Freud, Sigmund 1960, *Totem and Taboo,* trans. James Strachey, Routledge & Kegan Paul, London.
82

-----1961, *Beyond the Pleasure Principle,* trans. and ed. James Strachey, WW Norton & Company, New York.
105

-----1962, *Three Essays on the Theory of Sexuality,* trans. and ed. James Strachey, Basic Books Publishers, New York.
95 107 130

-----1982, *The Interpretation of Dreams,* trans. and ed. James Strachey, George Allen & Unwin Ltd, London.
100 (100) (100) (100) (100) (101) (101) 105 (105)

-----1989, *The Future of an Illusion,* trans. and ed. James Strachey, WW Norton & Company, New York.
105 107

Galbraith, John Kenneth 1987, *A History of Economics: The Past as the Present,* Hamish Hamilton, London.
66 113

Graaf, Regnier de 1972, *Regnier de Graaf on the Human Reproductive Organs,* trans HD Jocelyn and BP Setchell, Blackwell Scientific Publications, Oxford.
127 (127)

Guntrip, Harry 1964, *Healing the Sick Mind,* George Allen & Unwin Ltd, London.
41 131 132

Guthrie, WKC 1969, *A History of Greek Philosophy,* vol. 3, Cambridge University Press, Cambridge.
43

-----1975, *A History of Greek Philosophy,* vol. 4, Cambridge University Press, Cambridge.
43

Gwinn, RP 1990, *Plutarch: The Lives of the Noble Grecians and Romans,* 2nd edn, Encyclopaedia Britannica INC, Chicago.
76

Harbottle, Thomas Benfield 1897, *Dictionary of Quotations (Classical) or Classical Quotations, Swan* Sonnenschein & Co Ltd, London.
14 32 (32) (32) (32) (32) (32) (32) 34 (34) (34) (34) (34) (34) (34) (34) (34) (34) (34) (34) (34) (34) (34) (34) (34) (34) (34) (35) (35) (35) (35) (35) (35) (35) 49 60 (60) 72 114 117 (117) 132

Harris, Nathaniel 1999, *Hamlyn History of Imperial China,* Octopus Publishing Group Limited, London.
72 (72)

Janaway, Christopher 1994, *Schopenhauer,* Oxford University Press, Oxford.
5 56 (56)

Janus, Samuel S & Janus, Cynthia L 1994, *The Janus Report on Sexual Behavior,* John Wiley & Sons Inc, New York.
101

Kenez, Peter 2006, *A History of the Soviet Union from the Beginning to the End,* 2nd edn,

Cambridge University Press, New York.
11

Kennedy, Paul 1987, *The Rise and Fall of the Great Powers,* Random House, New York.
8

Kinsey, AC; Pomeroy, WB & Martin, CE 1948, *Sexual Behavior in the Human Male,* WB Saunders Co Ltd, Philadelphia.
28 81 87 108 120 (120) 122 126 126

Kinsey, AC; Pomeroy, WB; Martin, CE & Gebhard, PH 1953, *Sexual Behavior in the Human Female,* WB Saunders Co, Philadelphia.
118 121

Kung, Hans; Ess, Josef van; Stietencron, Heinrich von & Bechert, Heinz 1986, *Christianity and the World Religions,* trans. Peter Heinegg, Doubleday & Co Inc, New York.
103

Li, Dr Zhisui 1994, *The Private Life of Chairman Mao,* trans. Professor Tai Hung-chao, Chatto & Windus, London.
152 (152) (152) (152) (152) (152) (152) (152) (152) (152) (152) (153) (153) (153) (153) (153) (153) (153) (153) (153) (153) (153) (153) (153) (153) (153) (154) (154) (154) (154) (154) (154) (154) (154) (154) (154) (154) (154) (154) (154) (154) (154) (154) (155) (155) (155) (155) (155) (155) (155) (155) (155) (155) (155) (155) (156) (156) (156) (156) (156) (156) (156) (156) (156) (156) (156) (156) (156) (156) (156) (156) (156) (157) (157) (157) (157) (157) (157) (157) (157)

Lloyd, Charles W (ed.) 1964, *Human Reproduction and Sexual Behavior,* Lea & Febiger, Philadelphia.
40 41 112 112 (112)

McTaggart, Douglas; Findley, Christopher & Parkin, Michael 1992, *Economics,* Addison-Wesley Publishing Co, Sydney.
2

Marx, Karl 1971, *Theories of Surplus Value,* part III, (Capital, vol. IV), trans Jack Cohen and SW Ryazanskaya and eds SW Ryazanskaya and Richard Dixon, Progress Publishers, Moscow.
10

Marx, Karl & Engels, Frederick 1970, *Selected Works,* vol. 3, Progress Publishers, Moscow.
30

Masters, WH & Johnson, VE 1966, *Human Sexual Response,* Little, Brown and co, Boston.
6 113 119 127 (127) 128

Masters, William H; Johnson, Virginia E & Kolodny, Robert C 1985, *Masters and Johnson on Sex and Human Loving,* Little, Brown and Co, New York.
19 81 103 (103) (103) (103) (103) (103) (103) (103) (103) (104) (104) 106 (106) (106) (106) 120

-----1994, *Heterosexuality,* Harper Collins Publishers, New York.
25 115 118 118 119 119 119 122 127 128 128 131 (131)

Mathers, Powys (trans.) 1953, *The Thousand Nights and One Night,* vol. II, Routledge & Kegan Paul Ltd, London.

35

Mercer, Derrik (editor-in-chief) 1996, *Chronicle of the World,* Dorling Kindersley, London.
12 13 14 32 53 88 106 130 132 141

Milston, Gwendda 1978, *A Short History of China,* Cassell Australia, Stanmore, NSW.
72 79

Montaigne, Michel de 1965, *The Complete Essays of Montaigne,* trans. DM Frame, Stanford University Press, California.
5 13 (14) 28 35 (35) 44 60 60 64 76 82 138

Murowchick, Robert E (ed.) 1994, *China: Ancient Culture, Modern Land,* Cradles of Civilization Series, Weldon Russell Pty Ltd, North Sydney.
72 86

Polo, Marco 1959, *The Travels of Marco Polo,* Andre Deutsch Ltd, London.
140

Reader's Digest 1983, *Vanished Civilisation,* Reader's Digest, Sydney.
76

Remarque, Erich Maria 1988, *Arch of Triumph,* trans Walter Sorell and Denver Lindley, Pan Books Ltd, London.
97

Riasanovsky, Nicholas V 1977, *A History of Russia,* 3rd edn, Oxford University Press, New York.
144 (144) (144) (144) (144)

Rico, Gabriele Lusser 1983, *Writing the Natural Way,* GP Putnam's Sons, New York.
14 (14) (14) 105 (105) (105)

Robbins, Lionel 1998, *A History of Economic Thought,* Princeton University Press, Princeton.
7 32 78

Roll, Eric 1961, *A History of Economic Thought,* Faber and Faber Ltd, London.
7 33

Ross, Josephine 1979, *The Tudors,* Artus Books, London.
141 (142) (142) (142) (142) (142) (142) (142) (142) (142) (142) (142) (142) (142) (142) (143) (143) (143) (143) (143) 143 (143) (143) (143) (143) (143) (143) (144) (144) (144) (144) (144)

Rowland-Entwistle, Theodore 1988, *Thomas Edison,* Cherry Tree Books, Bath, England.
14

Sadock, Benjamin J; Kaplan, Harold I & Freedman, Alfred M (eds) 1976, *The Sexual Experience, Williams* & Wilkins Co, Baltimore.
7 83 85

St Augustine 1907, *The Confessions of St Augustine,* trans. EB Pusey, JM Dent & Sons Ltd, London.
41 (41) (42)

Shakespeare, William 1985, *Hamlet, Prince of Denmark,* ed. Philip Edwards, Cambridge University Press, Cambridge.

46

Sheowring, William & Thies, Conrad W 1982, *Religious Systems of the World,* Ajay Book Service, New Delhi.
139

Smith, Anthony 1968, *The Body,* Unwin Brothers Ltd, London.
19 (19) (19) (19) 20 (21) 49 83 84 90 125 127 (127)

Spielvogel, Jackson J 1991, *Western Civilization,* West Publishing Co, St Paul.
41

Swanson, Harold D 1974, *Human Reproduction: Biology and Social Change,* Oxford University Press, New York.
26

Taylor, Timothy 1996, *The Prehistory of Sex: Four Million Years of Human Sexual Culture,* Fourth Estate, London.
32 52 52 53 84 (84) (84) (85) (85) (85) (85) (85) (85) 86 110 114

Thomas a Kempis 1980, *Imitation of Christ,* ed. Paul M Bechtel, Moody Press, Chicago.
44 (44) (44) (44) 93

Toynbee, AJ 1962, *A Study of History,* abridged by DC Somervell, Oxford University Press, London.
43 141 (141)

Velde, Van de 1965, *Ideal Marriage,* 2nd edn, Greenwood Press, Westport, Connecticut.
18 109 112 114 114 116 118 118 120 127 127

Wells, HG 1925, *The Outline of History,* revised edn, 2 vols, Cassell and Co Ltd, London.
75 75 76 126

Westheimer, Dr Ruth 1994, *Encyclopaedia of Sex,* Element Books, Brisbane, Queensland.
4 (5) 6 17 (18) 20 (20) 48 52 52 83 92 101 108 109 (109) (109) 110 (110) (110) (110) (110) 119 119 122 122 (122) 126 126 128 131

Whitehouse, Ruth & Wilkins, John 1986, *The Making of Civilization: History Discovered through Archaeology,* Collins, London.
114

Williams, Trevar I 1987, *The History of Invention: from Stone Axes to Silicon Chips,* Macdonald & Co Ltd, London.
12 (12)

Wood, Clive 1974, *Vasectomy & Sterilization,* Temple Smith Ltd, London.
26

Wright, Nicolas (ed.) 1977, *Undestanding Sex,* Paul Hamlyn Pty Ltd, Dee Why West, NSW.
6 6 20 21 32 (32) (32) 48 100 115 119 119 129

Zilbergeld, Bernie PhD 1992, *The New Male Sexuality,* Bantam Books, New York.
93 110 119

Zubin, Joseph & Money, John (eds) 1973, *Contemporary Sexual Behavior: Critical Issues*

in the 1970s, John Hopkins University Press, Baltimore.
81 83

Index

www.ingramcontent.com/pod-product-compliance
Lightning Source LLC
LaVergne TN
LVHW081149110826
845149LV00008B/1609